INFINITE MIND

INFINITE MIND

Science of the Human Vibrations
of Consciousness

Valerie V. Hunt

Malibu Publishing Co.
Malibu, California 90265

Publisher's Cataloging in Publication

Hunt, Valerie V.
    Infinite mind: the science of human vibrations of
consciousness / Valerie V. Hunt.—2nd ed.—2nd printing.
    p. cm.
    Includes bibliographical references.
    ISBN 0-9643988-1-8

    1. Consciousness —Research. 2. Aura—Research. I. Title.
BF311.H86 1996   153
                                QB196-20406

Published by:
Malibu Publishing Co.
P.O. Box 4234
Malibu, California 90265
(310) 457-4694 - FAX (310) 457-2717
www.malibupublishing.com

ACKNOWLEDGEMENTS

I acknowledge that I have been blessed by the brilliance and consciousness of the many people who appeared to work with me.

Emilie Conrad and Rosalyn Bruyere were the first to introduce me to esoteric concepts, strange ideas and new ways of thinking about our world and us humans—all ideas that shook my linear, scientific mind. Wisely, they encouraged me to believe that if I didn't know how, I would somehow find the way to scientifically validate ancient wisdoms. I cherish the joys we shared when our research broke barriers. For these, my first and foremost teachers, my gratitude abounds.

I offer much thanks to the numerous, excellent engineers, mathematicians, and physicists who assisted in my Energy Fields Laboratory at UCLA. During the early years, they questioned my ideas as revolutionary. They challenged the data as unreal. Then they helped design new instruments and in the end, they enthusiastically accepted the direction of the research and the purity of the data we obtained. I thank them also for not making discoveries too easy for me.

My deep gratitude goes to the Board Members of the Bioenergy Fields Foundation, my non-profit educational organization, for their abiding personal and professional support: Iris Schirmer, Robert Quaid, Emilie Conrad Däoud, Darrel Felkner, and Christopher Hegarty, all busy professional persons with magnificent backgrounds in contemporary and ancient thoughts about energy fields. Each read *Infinite Mind*. They gave me their excited approval for a rapid publication. Then, a warm appreciation goes to my two roving angels, Peg Van Pelt and

Eleanor McCulley, who were always available to make things happen, facilitate the impossible, and spread the word to their extensive following.

Todd Chandler of Chandler Design, an award-winning graphic artist, had all the answers for my difficult display and jacket designs. He created this beautiful, sensitive cover that highlights the content and flavor of my book. With only a short discussion, Todd transferred my ideas into this charming communication design. I thank you, Todd, for your interest and your talent.

My special thanks go to two dedicated and loving people, Carol and Joe Cavella, who handled all the technical parts of word processing and book formatting of my manuscript to its present clear, attractive form. They patiently led me through the maze of details necessary for direct printing.

My deep appreciation goes to my editor, Casaundra Franker, for her labor of love. Her background as editor of medical, psychological books and her own spiritual publishing house, The Purple Iris Press, gave her the expertise to polish my words. But she did even more. She clarified the order and articulated facts without changing my thinking or the general flow of my prose. To me, her skill is a true art.

I believe that no teacher can completely appreciate or adequately acknowledge the role her students have had in her growth and evolution. The facts that my students listened attentively, discussed excitedly, and challenged not only the information but the wisdom it carried, left me always open and thinking. I thank each of you deeply for pushing me to develop comprehensive models from all new evidence in order to keep thoughts in perspective. You must know that in the classroom and conferences with you, you allowed me to reach the most creative and satisfying times of my professional life.

—Valerie V. Hunt

CONTENTS

CHAPTER I

A MIND'S JOURNEY

Have you ever become lost in an enthrallingly beautiful daydream or imagery so frightening that you crashed back to ordinary attention, needing time for things to straighten out so that you could separate yourself from the dream? Perhaps you never did. Such experiences fade rapidly from memory so that you can't even remember what the dream is about. It is easy to pass off these happenings as your imagination having "play time" or to attribute them to fatigue. But deep down is a nagging thought that the dream portrayed a vital part of you that was attempting to surface. Such experiences are common to us humans.

Have you ever thought of a friend—wondered what he was up to, when to your surprise, he called? Much more disarming are the times when you sensed the illness, even death, of a loved one, immediately denying its truth until the sad news came.

Have you ever answered a friend's query only to hear—"I never asked you that question, I only thought it." Close friends regularly do this.

In your travels, have you ever found yourself in a strange place, come into a new country with unusual sounds, smells, buildings, and people who dressed and looked different from those back home, when suddenly your wonderment changed into deep attunement, a *deja vu* experience? Somehow, you knew about this new land and what to expect.

Have you ever entered a building, a historical or sacred place, and believed that you heard words, saw people, smelled odors, and sensed things you "knew" didn't exist there, yet your experience insisted that this was real? If we allow it, this happens often.

Perhaps more usual, have you ever heard music or sounds so ephemeral that you soared to some magical place? Or was it an art object, perhaps of a sunset or a peaceful wide valley, that lifted your thoughts beyond the scene on the canvas, away from the shapes and space to a deeper meaning? Sometimes when we are in a place dedicated to the divine, we feel spiritual vibrations all over our bodies. It can seem strange that certain sights trigger moods that don't seem directly related to what we are seeing.

Not long ago, these experiences remained tightly closeted memories. Occasionally, we would find a creative person to share with, or a book to explain our "fantasies." I did, but if you are like me, the "out there" answers didn't ring true. I wanted explanations that I could understand and own. I pondered why it was that scientists refused to investigate those things. They even relegated thought to philosophers, saying that it was too intangible to be explored by scientific methods. Of course, I remembered that we scientists are supposed to stick to the facts; we are to perform experiments that produce verifiable data and can be duplicated in other laboratories. My quandaries were not occasional; they were constant, shaking many of what I had come to believe were irrefutable physiological facts. Accounts that Einstein, Newton, Fuller, and Pythagoras had discovered their deep wisdoms in some other realm was little consolation. At the other end of the spectrum, psychics seemed fuzzy in their thinking; my queries were met with streams of "psychobabble."

In the early 1970s, I was teaching a graduate seminar on the neuromuscular aspects of behavior. In addition to discussing research discoveries, I questioned the vast array of common human experiences that seemed to defy rational understanding, or to lie beyond the scope of scientific inquiry. I suggested that these experiences must have some deep, hidden reality because they contained such sensory, motor, cognitive and emotional stimuli. Certainly the label "imagined" didn't fit. Though my comments were casual, at times it was as if I had lit the fuses of stored fireworks. The class enlivened. Some of the students shared their own strange experiences, while others elaborated on my own doubts.

Often after this class I wondered why mystical experiences generated so much emotional excitement. Was repressed information surfacing or was it because these issues were being discussed at a university twenty-five years ago? In fact, news trickled back to me that small student groups carried on the discussion after class far into the night, not about the course's physiological material, but about unusual consciousness happenings.

My daily restlessness about such matters led me to seek counsel with an older, very wise woman, the Senior Warden of my church. She listened understandingly, but gave no advice until I reasoned that it was probably all right to pose mystical questions as long as I didn't commit answers. Even then, I knew to be cautious because I cherished my position as a tenured faculty member at a major university at a time when there were few women professors.

At the next class meeting, winter quarter in the late afternoon when attention wandered, I acknowledged students' interest in strange happenings, made a few comments, and announced that we would continue with the scheduled course content. I intuited, even hoped, that my statement was sufficient to quiet their curiosity about the parapsychological. Was I ever misinformed! The entire graduate class of thirty-some students awakened. They insisted that this was the class where they should study consciousness, even the ancient literature, and they added a punch by reminding me that the true function of a university is to expand the frontier of knowledge. While I agreed with such a lofty ideal,

I rebutted that I had not found in-depth parapsychological research appropriate for this research class. They were undaunted; what better, they said, than to critique the existing research, question the phenomenological premises, and design a new direction. I was flooded with mixed feelings—what dreamers these students, and yet, aren't students supposed to push professors from their comfortable positions?

Though I did not change the course, I offered to stay an extra half-hour for those who wanted to talk about psychic and esoteric experiences, about chakras, entities, past lives, for fun and just to understand what much of the world believed. This compromise was satisfactory for the students, but I remembered feeling unusually depressed and lonesome, as though I had turned a corner on an unknown path.

My professor friends were not to know of my shift for several years. My former enjoyment of university social events was now shadowed by restlessness. When my colleagues asked what I was up to or what I was thinking about, their questions were met with a hasty "same old thing." This new, compelling interest didn't seem to be leading anywhere except into confusion.

When I attended a few meetings of the more conventional psychics, I came away wanting the pin-pointing clarity of a trained scientific mind to speak to me. I couldn't follow the psychics' channeling process when they called in one of the "Great Ones," a crossed-over soul, to answer their questions. I realized that the questions asked and the answers given had to do with material predictions concerning money, friends, lovers, and solutions to life's situations. Most "channeled" information was so general that it could be interpreted in as many ways as their astrological forecasts. I even sought out five popular psychic readers with my specific questions. They all knew that I had doubts by the nature of my questions, but their metaphysical answers did not ring true to me. Needless to say, I gave up this approach.

Next, I reasoned that I needed a teacher, a guide, but not one locked into a highly structured belief system or religion. Indeed, I was cautious because I was repulsed by many so-called laws of karma, or explanations bordering on black magic, the dark night of the soul, or entity possessions beyond our control. I rejected the idea of dependency on gurus who were becoming plentiful imports from India. With some effort, I found three potential teachers, a Kabbala priest, a physician, and a chiropractor, all with scientific backgrounds and touted to be spiritually high beings who took only a few students.

To each, I told my story. This time I owned my experiences, not just my questions. This time I added what I had not shared with students, situations of my life that now emerged to clarify my confusion. I had been in a coma at age three. During a successful psychotherapy to soften my compulsive work habits in my early adulthood, I had recovered information about my childhood near-death experience. Then I catapulted into a cosmic coma from shock. Equally as suddenly as I entered the coma, I spontaneously recovered, rediscovered the sensory world, and was a deeply mystical child. I knew things that ordinary children didn't know, according to my mother, a trained early childhood teacher. My father, a college-educated engineer, seemed as perplexed as I. He was excited to see me responding to life, but I watched him shake his head in disbelief at my change.

Before this episode I was an outgoing, exuberant child, which probably helped me to adjust better to my new talents and my parents' disbelief, though not to being rejected by my little friends, who didn't want me to play with them anymore. They said I complicated things by making rules too hard. Still, I could escape by composing poetry (or perhaps just rhymes), drawing, singing, and thoroughly indulging in my mystical world.

One day, quite by surprise, my parents took away my paints, my paper, my crayons, and my books. No one wanted to hear about the fun things my mind created. My frustration mounted daily—my world had rejected what I found exciting. I mumbled to myself angrily with little satisfaction. My parents didn't listen. Finally, I started "multiplying words" with God, for real. I flashed back to my months in a coma when I experienced being with God in a beautiful land of flowers, sweetness, and love—quiet serenity. I wanted to stay forever, but I recalled that God had said I would go back to the world to bring it beauty. I complained because I did not like the world, and besides I had no talents for beauty. I was just a very little girl who sensed beauty but didn't know how to create it. I remembered God assuring me that I would be given ample talents to do my "beauty work." It was then that I became aware of people, the room, and things I had known about before. I had returned from my distant journey.

At first, adults praised my pictures and writings, expecting I would grow to be an artist. But also I sensed that despite my new gifts, the world wanted me the old way— a little, ordinary girl, doing what normal little girls my age did. It was then that I hid in a deep, dark hall closet hung with layers of winter clothes, the floor full of scattered, heavy boots. I found my way to the back where I sat feeling quite protected, so that I could argue with God. I knew it was all God's fault. He had pushed me out of Heaven, given me skills that no one would let me use. In spite of my anger, God was kind and understanding with a new solution—if I couldn't bring beauty, I could bring knowledge.

To this frightened, angry little girl in a dark closet, the answer seemed strange, although also sustaining. But could I use my creativity to bring knowledge? All in all, the solution was safe for my parents. I wouldn't bother them anymore if I had a new course and for me, although I had been enthralled at my post-coma skills, there was also a haunting suddenness to my change that was scary, particularly when adults said that it was not "real."

All three of the potential esoteric teachers turned me down, and each with the same reasoning: "You are divinely guided—you need no human teacher." What should have been a compliment I took as rejection, for I desperately needed a great teacher.

One day after several years of exploring these questions with my students, the Dean of Science called me in and asked, "What is this I hear you are studying in your lab and introducing to your students?" It was then that I remembered my students' ardent beliefs that the function of the University is to be on the cutting edge of knowledge. I convinced him that I had paid my dues for 20 years as an orthodox and popular professor, and now that I had seen a new light I wanted him to protect me from unknowing criticism. I promised to keep him posted. Apparently, my non-defensive approach worked. We talked often and he was interested and encouraging. He must have confided with the Chancellor, because I found many strange and mystical people with unusual requests referred to me from the Chancellor's office. Whether he accepted my direction or just "got them off his back" I never knew.

Many unusual things happened as I openly taught classes based upon my frequency recordings of healers, mystics, and meditators. Professors I had never met in such a large university, from departments of engineering, physics, art, philosophy, and medicine called for appointments to talk about what they had read, their patients, or their own research. Invariably as we talked I realized their deeper agenda was to find answers to their own troublesome mystical experiences. Yes, I helped them by confirming with my own experiences, as they helped me to realize the universality of human consciousness; and I shed the loneliness that I had attributed to the cloistered nature of a university.

I have said enough about my journey, for this book is not autobiographic in a time-space sense; it is rather an account of my doubts, deliberations, learnings and tentative answers that have led me to reach deeply into other levels of consciousness. My academic background led me to over 25 years of experimental studies using high frequency instruments to measure human vibrations, while all the time I was also clinically investigating the mystical level of emotional states. When I retired early from UCLA, I had time to collect my own and my students' beginning experiences to rework my accumulated frequency data, and I took on older, more advanced students in private classes.

With this as an introduction, come with me on a journey of

discovery. If it eases you into a deeper understanding of your humanness, I am pleased. If it causes you to challenge some of our culture's most cherished beliefs—even if you don't find complete answers—this book will have served its purpose. You will have discovered a new way of thinking about the questions. If some of the thoughts presented weaken your doubts about this side of humanness, I praise you. And if it strikes one pure note in those of you scientists who never dared to contemplate such "soft science" except as entertaining science fiction, I am thrilled.

CHAPTER II

THE HUMAN AURA:
Living Vibrations
Brought To Light

"The basic texture of research consists of dreams into which threads of reasoning, measurement and calculation are woven."
—*Albert Szent Györgyi*

Too often we scientists get lost in our data, forgetting that the essence of science is careful observation, deep thought, and wise deductions from both reasoning AND the exercise of mystical and dreamlike states. Rarely do we realize that our research springs from our level of awareness and our evolutionary needs. I attest to the fact that the scientist's research is deeply personal.

This chapter is written for lay readers with limited scientific knowledge who often feel confused by scientific explanations. Come with me on a journey of discovery into the research of the vibrant human aura that you can follow and understand. For scientists, my reasoning, although broad and penetrating—and sometimes mystical—is based upon scientific facts and clinical observations.

Margaret Mead, when she was president of the Association of

the Advancement of Science in 1969, spearheaded the acceptance of a new section of parapsychology. She questioned "... whether we can find ways of studying these phenomena which will make them as acceptable as the stars and the chromosomes." She cautioned that "to believe without questioning or to dismiss without investigation is to comport oneself unscientifically." Such beliefs fostered the rapid expansion of sound human energy field research by classical scientists in major institutes and universities.

My background in neurophysiology and psychology neither prepared me to understand nor to be interested in parapsychological happenings. So my introduction to energy field phenomena had to be serendipitous. I had taught at Columbia University, the University of Iowa, and UCLA, where I researched skilled and pathological muscular activity, the movement behavior of individuals, and the neuromuscular patterns of emotions.

To my surprise, data showed relationships between neuromuscular behavior and personality. The individual's movements shadowed his unique personal characteristics. But other strange information emerged that did not fit with accepted physiology.

One day a graduate dance therapy student asked me to record what happened when she entered an altered state of consciousness. At that time, an altered state seemed unreal to me, for there were no guidelines as to how to record consciousness and no agreement even as to what it was. Although I was intrigued, I filed her request deep in my memory with no further intent.

Some weeks later I had a glimmer of how to record her experience. Possibly the neurological level of muscle stimulation held a clue to consciousness levels. Timidly, I placed the electromyographic (EMG) recording electrodes on her lower arm, her upper arm, and her back muscles, each area primarily stimulated by a different level of the spinal cord and brain. Intuitively, in a playful mood, I placed one electrode on top of her head, although I knew nothing about chakras, the vortices of energy described by ancient Eastern literature. When the electrodes were secured, she started her dance routine. At the beginning, nothing unusual happened, in fact she commented on her apprehension about being recorded. Yet, in five minutes the recordings remarkably changed. The muscular signal from her lower arm stopped. The baseline activity characteristic of all living tissue was absent on the scopes. Next, the upper arm recording dropped out. The engineer believed there was no equipment failure, although there was no ordinary energy in the arms. Soon she sat down in a "tailor position" which required back muscle activity to balance her body. Again the spinal muscles showed no recording, no energy expended. We have known as long as there is life, skeletal muscles give off signals. Next, electromagnetic energy poured from the top of her head with intensity beyond what our equipment could handle. This state lasted for seven minutes, followed by a reverse sequence of reactivating the spine, upper arm, and lower arm muscles. In my years of neuromuscular research I had never witnessed any similar situation, nor had any been described in the literature. I was at a total loss to explain, but I could not forget these happenings.

During a student dance concert at UCLA, I noticed several performers whom I had watched many times before. Now, they danced better than ever. They were no longer just good college dancers; they moved like polished professionals. Later, when I congratulated them on their superb performances, they attributed their improvement to Structural Integration, or Rolfing, a manipulative technique where during ten sessions a technician manually stretches and moves various kinds of connective tissue, fascia, tendons and ligaments which make up the body's support system. With ordinary physical and emotional stress, this connective tissue constricts, becoming inelastic, causing muscle imbalance. Generally, people choose to be Rolfed to eliminate pain and to improve posture and health, or it is prescribed to lessen neuromuscular and orthopedic disabilities. These dancers, however, chose Rolfing to increase their flexibility. Additionally, they discovered that they moved better, felt freer, were more alert, and experienced higher states of consciousness. As an experienced physical therapist, I knew about most manipulation regimes, but Rolfing somehow seemed different.

Today there are numerous manipulative and exercise programs like Rolfing which loosen and relax the connective tissues of the body. Now we know that connective tissue has piezoelectric capacities, which can act like an electrical system, where stretching enhances the electrical capacity. Therefore, we conjectured that connective tissue was more than a tissue scaffolding. It seemed to dictate the flow of electromagnetic energy throughout the body at the finest level.

With curiosity I conducted studies and discovered that after Rolfing, muscles did contract more smoothly and with less effort. People moved more efficiently. (Hunt, 1972) But at that time there was no known objective method to evaluate their subjective feelings of health, vitality and consciousness.

Several weeks later another unusual event occurred. At the suggestion of one of my graduate students, Emilie Conrad, a shaman healer, came to my office requesting explanations for her healing techniques. This occurred 25 years ago when shamanic healing was relatively unknown in this country. Emilie is an American dancer who had discovered mystical happenings while she lived and danced in Haiti. At our first meeting, she spoke in esoteric words full of ritualistic sensory metaphors that confused me. Hers was like a foreign language that I could not decode. And yet, for some unknown reason, I sensed that she had something very important to teach me.

Unable to understand her words, I asked her to communicate by movement—to let me watch her "do her thing." Spontaneously, I checked her heart rate and blood pressure before she started. She then danced strenuously, even acrobatically, for 30 minutes with a perfection and repertoire superior to any I had seen in a single dancer. Her movements took in all directions, large and small, were fast and slow, with complicated neuromuscular rhythms flowing through various parts of her body. She demonstrated amazing flexibility and strength as she effortlessly glided about. Beyond her technical elegance, I sensed that she communicated powerful feelings and ideas.

I was not prepared, however, for the shock that came when I realized that my long study of superior athletes, the handicapped, and native ritualistic movements from all over the world did not help me to understand what I observed with Emilie. Furthermore, my training as a movement observer and neuromuscular physiologist didn't help. I was vaguely aware that the results of Rolfing on dancers somehow connected with what I did not understand about Emilie's dancing. I rechecked her heart rate and blood pressure, hoping that her physiological changes would clear up the issue. But to my surprise, neither the heart rate nor the blood pressure had elevated; in fact both had dropped slightly. To make things worse, she was not perspiring nor was she breathing heavily. With total disbelief, I asked for her explanation, not anticipating her simple answer.

She said, "I create a field of energy and ride it." Now it is easy to understand riding the outside force of a wave or wind, or skiing downhill by gravity, but what was this energy that created movement without a physical force or physiological happenings? She seemed to be trying to tell me that there are other ways to move that are beyond the classical neuromuscular contraction that we physiologists accept.

A few months later Emilie returned to tell me that she was going to restore paralyzed muscles of a post-polio victim of 23 years. She asked me to record and explain the healing process. I agreed to measure the polio victim's muscle loss before and after Emilie's treatment, but I did not know how to evaluate a shamanic treatment.

I thought I understood the muscular paralysis of polio. At Columbia University before World War II, I was trained in physical therapy. During the great polio epidemic in the late 1940's, I supervised polio treatments using the Sister Kenny methods at a major New York hospital which handled the most acute polio cases in the state. When I saw this polio victim, I was aghast that Emilie thought she could restore muscle. The young woman wore a long leg brace and walked with great difficulty. Although she had had excellent and lengthy Kenny treatments when the polio occurred in infancy, her condition had not changed since then.

Electromyographic tests showed her leg muscles were extremely weak or degenerated to bands of connective tissue that did not contract. For a long time we have "known" that when a muscle loses its neural connection, it atrophies, disintegrates, and will never recover. Such was the young woman's condition. Although I was curious about shamanic healing techniques, I was convinced that nothing would happen. However, as I watched Emilie moving her hands above the patient's legs, I observed a rippling motion not ordinarily seen with normal muscle contraction and never present in paralyzed muscle.

During the several years of Emilie's regular treatment, this subject recovered almost all of her lost movement. Electro-myographic recordings confirmed the neuromuscular regeneration. She was able to energetically walk without crutches and braces, and muscle contour returned where there was none before. Again, I could verify the changes, but I could not explain them.

Within the same year, Emilie asked me to record another shamanic treatment of a congenitally brain-disturbed young man. He had been evaluated at UCLA's Neuropsychiatric Institute as having abnormal brain waves which physicians believed caused his asocial, disorganized, and immature behavior. They reported that following Emilie's treatment his brain waves were normal and his behavior improved.

At the appointed day, Emilie brought an aura reader, Rosalyn Bruyere, to read the energy field during treatment. Again, having witnessed many shamanic rituals in Africa, Haiti and the South Pacific did not prime me to understand or record healing without physical contact. Emilie described her ritual and the aura reader disclosed that she would read colors and the action of the field and the chakras. They both explained the nature of chakras and located them on the body for me.

The idea of chakras stems from Eastern philosophy and yogic doctrine. These describe wheel-like vortices of energy over nerve plexes and endocrine centers of the body, as well as the third eye and the crown of the head, with small vortices at each joint. They are functional rather than anatomical structures that are connected to the meridians and acupuncture points. Numerous researchers have shown elevated electronic recordings from these locations, particularly with persons in higher states of consciousness or with extrasensory abilities.

I decided to use ordinary bipolar surface sensors on the skin over the chakras, as though these areas were like muscles, just to see if any electrical activity occurred. On the same data-tape we simultaneously recorded Emilie's shamanic chanting, Rosalyn's aura descriptions, and my narrations of the healer's movements. The subject lay passively on the floor while Emilie performed esoteric movements around his body and shouted into his kneecaps. She shook rattles and bells, and waved crystals around his body, but she never touched him.

Somehow, I wanted skilled witnesses, so I had invited professors from the Nursing Department, School of Medicine, and Thelma Moss's parapsychology lab at the Neuropsychiatric Institute. They all attended.

Throughout the experiment, I monitored the oscilloscope and graph data, which looked like elaborate but meaningless random vibrations. Yet at the end of the three-hour session, I noted that the patient's brain waves had stabilized into an alpha-theta pattern.

The experiment went on for many hours with so many reams of graphs and tapes that I postponed even trying to analyze the data until the semester closed. Then, when I carefully compared the electronic information with all the other data, there appeared only one firm relationship. There was no apparent correlation between Emilie's vocal sounds, the bells, or the crystal placement with the electronic data. Likewise, there was no obvious relationship between my running commentary of the quality and pattern of her movement and the electronic recordings. But there was a very close correlation between what the aura reader said and the gross happenings in the electrical activity of the man's auric field. For example, when Rosalyn reported energy entering his arm, the amplitude of the recordings increased. She described that energy had entered his feet and progressed up his legs, "shooting the Kundalini," and "getting balled up in the heart chakra."

These unscientific descriptions were nonetheless synchronized with the electronic data showing sudden energy flowing up both legs with an increased amplitude in the lower abdomen, or Kundalini, and stopping in the heart chakra. The heart showed a two-fold increase in the amplitude of contraction with no change in the rate.

Rosalyn's next description convinced me that some unknown energy was flowing when she described that Emilie had released the energy from the heart which spurted out the crown chakra on top of the head in bursts of white light. The spurts were in sync with the sudden energy bursts which came from the crown electrodes, and the frequencies of these data were the highest recorded during that session. Again, I didn't understand, but I sensed that this data contained within it information about the human organism hitherto undiscovered.

During that same year I attended the First International Acupuncture Conference at Stanford University. This was following President Richard Nixon's trip to China during which two American physicians first witnessed acupuncture anesthesia and treatment. I was thrilled with a new emerging physiological model, the basis of Oriental medicine, which seemed to encompass my experiences with Rolfing, Emilie's movement, her shamanic treatment of polio and brain disturbances, and the observations of an aura reader.

The following semester I took a sabbatical leave to explore

these energy field concepts in Southeast Asia. I observed and worked in the clinics using acupuncture to treat disease and drug addiction in Japan, Taiwan, Hong Kong and Singapore. In Bali I participated in trance dancing and watched native ritual healings in the Indonesian islands and Thailand. On the streets of Kowloon I observed young children copying the older ones in the insertion of acupuncture needles.

In Kyoto, Japan, at the famous Pain Control Clinic, I watched acupuncture and moxibustion treatments, the latter using a small herbal cone placed on acupuncture points and lighted like incense. With arthritics, moxibustion gave faster pain relief than our conventional therapeutic techniques.

One day, an ambulance brought a woman to the pain clinic with second degree steam burns on both arms. She screamed with the pain. The common procedure in America was to first inject narcotics to ease the pain, followed by tissue cooling and ointment. Instead, the Pain Control Clinic therapists wrapped both arms in household aluminum foil, to which they attached a clothespin clamp with a lead wire ending in an acupuncture needle. The needle was inserted into the acupuncture point just below the kneecap on the opposite leg. This constituted the entire treatment.

In a few minutes the burn victim quieted; her face relaxed. In 20 minutes she was totally free of pain. The swollen, turgid, red-blue tissue looked pink and near normal. After three or four more daily treatments, her skin was normal without ulceration, peeling, or scars. The attending physician explained that the steam had created cellular metabolic disturbances affecting the energy field, which caused energy from other areas of the body to rush to the arms to heal them. This excess energy pressed on nerves and blood vessels, causing swelling and pain. He stated that the aluminum foil, wire, and acupuncture needles drained the excess energy from the burned arms back into the legs—a simple, yet profound, explanation.

Armed with my own fresh, mystical awakenings balanced by

the extended reality of the cultures I had witnessed, I returned to the university motivated to critically explore and to find out for myself if claims of subtle energies were valid.

The first equipment we used to measure this energy was a telemetry instrument built especially for us by an engineer who had developed the telemetry systems which NASA used to send back to earth the astronauts' vital physiological recordings of muscle and heart activity during the first manned space trips. Simply stated, telemetry is a radio broadcasting system capable of intercepting and projecting the body's electrical activity. The electrical signal is picked up from the body's surface by surface sensors which lead to a miniature, battery-operated radio transmitter and amplifier attached to the subject by a belt. The instrument broadcasts the electrical body signal by FM radio frequency carrier. The airborne signal then is picked up in the laboratory by a radio receiver and recorded on tape or disk for future analysis.

I believed the wireless nature of this new instrument would free subjects from the cumbersome wires of ordinary sensory devices, allowing them to act more naturally (Exhibit 1.) Actually, it did more than that; it allowed a small, continuous millivoltage (one thousandth of a volt) signal from the body surface, the auric field, to be recorded.

Like all investigations into uncharted areas, we did not set out to prove anything; our aim was to study the effects of shamanic healing; the process of energy transfer; consciousness; the auric field; and elucidate a possible energy field phenomenon, as well as to understand the neuromuscular effects of Rolfing.

Let me relate simply our current understanding of body electricity and how this is measured. Brain nerve cells, when stimulated, create electrical energy which activates nerves. This is recorded as brain waves by an electroencephalogram (EEG.) The nerve activities cause muscles to shorten and move the body, and to stimulate the heart, lungs, blood vessels, intestines, and glands. When a muscle shortens, an electrical current is generated which can be recorded by an electromyogram (EMG.) The electrical heart activity is picked up by an electrocardiogram (EKG.)

These three kinds of recordings can differ, one from another, by frequency patterns and strengths. Brain waves under normal conditions create a characteristic slow wave form from zero to 20 cycles per second. The heart creates a larger and faster wave up to about 225 cycles per second. The muscles, on the other hand, have a wide range from zero to 250 cycles per second; two to three cycles per second in the anal sphincter muscle, and 250 cycles per second in the small, fast-moving eye muscles. Most skeletal muscles during normal movement operate between 40 and 120 cycles per second, each with a built-in physiological frequency signature or speed of operation, some faster and some slower, based on their location, their structure, and their movement function. Each of these separate recordings is an important function of local tissue, but none of them is a measure of general health in the body.

Although we cannot explain life, we do know that electrical activity is essential for life. Most medical and biological research has tried to explain life in terms of gross measures such as heart, muscle, and nerve electricity, or it has unsuccessfully sought a source in the biochemistry of cells and fluids. But with recent discoveries that all cells, even subatomic particles, contain tiny electrical elements, there is a growing belief that life is electromagnetic and cannot be explained by mechanical or biochemical means.

Physics, the scientific source of all natural information about the universe, holds that all matter which exists in space is composed of atoms. Atoms are all the same whether they comprise inert or living matter. In each atom, electrons spin around a nucleus, throwing off some electrons, leaving an unstable state. Other electrons in the environment rush in to fill the space. Some of these free electrons come from living things, others from man-made objects or the natural physical environment.

In the physical body there are two primary electrical systems.

One is the well-known alternating electric current of the nervous system, the brain, neurons, and the nerves, which causes muscle contraction, nerve transmission, glandular secretion, and sensation. The other is a newly discovered electromagnetic system probably emanating from atoms and cells. This energy has been called an aura, though I prefer to describe it as an energy field.

We discovered that this energy field is unique. It is continuous, while all the other body electric recordings of heart, brain, and muscle are off-and-on signals: a muscle contraction is followed by muscle relaxation; a heartbeat is followed by a quiet rest period; and a brain wave is followed by lesser action.

The pool of electromagnetic energy around an object or a person allows energy exchange. This corona, invisible to most people, is seen at times as a halo or light-colored mist around a living body. Although composed of the same electrons as inert substances, the human field absorbs and throws off energy dynamically. It interacts with and influences matter, whereas fields associated with inert matter react passively. Again, there have been many names associated with this human energy: *chi*, life force, *prana*, odic force, and aura.

The electromagnetic components of the human energy field can be detected with special electronic instruments, although probably this field is more complex, possibly like the little understood scaler wave, or it may be composed of undiscovered energy as illusive as ether. If the recording sensor or probe is a needle inserted into a nerve or muscle, only the very local electricity or small units are intercepted. If the electrodes are adhered to the skin surface, there is a larger signal of electrical activity, or a composite of the underlying muscles or cells (Exhibit 1.)

Throughout our recordings, we placed surface sensors over the chakra where the baseline electricity was strongest, although we could obtain a similar signal from anywhere on the body surface. Generally, the subjects were recorded while lying passively, meditating, imaging, being Rolfed or healed. Although the baseline signal we wanted was not altered by the amount of movement, if the subject was very active, the accompanying heart and muscle electricity was so strong that it overshadowed the small constant energy field on the oscilloscope.

On every recording taken from the body where there are muscles, there is a resting baseline of electrical activity between muscle contractions. I believe that this is produced by all living tissue and can be described as life activity. This has been generally considered to be a rough indicator of muscle tension and therefore not very important. Yet I noted that after Rolfing, the baseline was higher or stronger, while a manual tension test used in physical therapy showed that the subjects were actually more relaxed.

By amplifying the baseline on the oscilloscope, we found that it was a rich and changing energy. When we filtered the baseline data to remove the brain, heart and muscle frequencies (0 to 250 cycles per second), we discovered that there is a void (no electrical activity) between 250 cycles to 450 or 500 cycles per second. But from 500 cycles per second up to 20,000 cycles per second, the frequency information was continuous. Our telemetry instrument was not capable of recording frequencies beyond 20,000 cycles per second, at that time (Exhibit 3.)

We observed that every recording using body surface electrodes contained all electrical activity of the body. If taken from the heart, a powerful generator, the heart frequencies were the strongest. If taken from the muscle, the muscle depolarization frequencies were larger, and so with the brain. But all electrical activity, including that of the auric field, was present in all telemetry recordings.

In other words, beyond the electrical frequencies of muscle, brain, and heart, there is another field of energy, smaller in amplitude and higher in frequency. This electromagnetic energy is eight to ten times faster than the other biological electricity sampled from the body's surface, and about one-half to one-third as strong as the millivoltage of a resting muscle. While numerous researchers have studied extremely low biological frequencies

(ELF) and the magnetic current associated with healing, tissue health, and disease, the extremely high biological frequency (EHF) electrical currents associated with mind phenomena and human consciousness were first researched in my laboratory at UCLA.

Excluding unicellular organisms, all living systems produce an electrical current in the order of millivoltage (one-thousandth of a volt), a relatively strong signal that is considerably larger than the random microvoltage (one-millionth of a volt) of white noise. This encouraged us to further explore shamanic healing, Emilie's movements, emotion and field interaction. We questioned why these signals had not been reported previously, only to remember that telemetry was a product of the space age. Earlier recording equipment was incapable of detecting this small signal of the energy field.

Probably the primary reason scientists had not discovered the human energy field before, even with telemetry instruments, was because they believed that biological energy existed only to make a muscle shorten, a heart beat, or to create brain activity. Data such as a dynamic resting baseline were considered to be only an artifact of the instruments but not real data.

Because our field recordings were faster than neurological signals of muscles and nerves, although of similar amplitude, and because these correlated with aura readers' visual reports, we considered the possibility that these might point to the elusive auric field. Gradually, I began to see how my experiences with hands-on healers, acupuncture, and Rolfing related to my research on the electromagnetic field of emotions, environmental electromagnetism, hands-on healing, meditation, transfer of thought, and the interaction of people and animals.

Upon my return from Asia, the Rolf Institute provided a grant to study emotions, energy fields, and the neuromuscular effects of Rolfing. For the study, there were 24 men and 24 women divided into carefully matched pairs based on age, sex, height-weight, education, occupation, general physical activity and body structure. One of each pair was randomly placed in an experimental group and the other in a control group. The experimental subjects were given ten Rolfing sessions by two Rolfers, each subject receiving five sessions in staggered order with each Rolfer.

Two men and two women from the experimental group were selected by aura readers based upon the color and dynamics of their auric field. These four subjects were to be Rolfed in the laboratory with simultaneous electronic field testing and aura reader reporting. Although the muscular changes from Rolfing were substantial (Hunt, 1972), the energy field data were spectacular. The findings established clear-cut parameters for future study and provided consistent results that have held up in ensuing research.

From the first session, each individual showed a unique pattern of amplitude and frequencies in chakras and in the synchrony between chakras. Although there were changes during later sessions, each individual kept his unique pattern, such as its strength or weakness and its variable frequency over time. For example, a physiologist, a meditator, had a more active third eye. A dancer carried hyperactivity in the legs and feet. An actress showed more energy in the heart and abdomen. A businessman demonstrated energy in the crown.

We noted individual differences in the complexity or variability of the wave train of the field. Some had a narrow repertoire of vibratory patterns over time—a more closed system—while others showed an open system with a greater variety of field interactions.

The upward energy flow in chakras progressively increased during the ten sessions. In the beginning the energy was small, dark in color, low in frequency and amplitude with an uneven flow. During later sessions the energy was even, light in color, with higher amplitude and frequency. When the aura reader observed a secondary aura five to ten feet beyond the body, the amplitude on the body's surface lowered and the color became a steady blue. The person appeared quiet and at great peace, probably in an altered state in which awareness is focused upon mystical impressions and not upon ordinary happenings.

The aura reader noted that closed or weakly operating chakras opened during the session. Likewise, the data confirmed that the amplitude of the chakras increased after opening. By the seventh and eighth sessions, all chakras and the composite field were light blended colors of pink, peach, ice blue and violet, containing the higher frequencies of white (Exhibit 4.)

When subjects occasionally reported illness, the aura reader described their field as muddy and unclear. We discovered chakras were not synchronistic, a measure called "anti-coherency (Exhibit 5.)

Most women displayed decreased energy in the feet and legs with increased energy in the upper body. Men had a more even pattern, top to bottom, but a weaker electromagnetic field in the trunk.

Often aura readers reported the classical chakra colors described in the ancient metaphysical literature as red in the coccyx, orange in the abdomen, yellow in the solar plexus, green in the heart, blue in the throat, violet in the third eye, and white in the crown—although this was not always the case.

The stretching of connective tissue by Rolfing sometimes brought pain and a rush of energy to the area, always in the red frequency. This common red dimension seemed to indicate that the entire body was alerted to danger (Exhibit 6D.) However, there were differences in how subjects handled this pain. Those who became emotional changed their field to red-orange, while others who "slipped out of their bodies" brought in white along with the red. Some apparently tolerated the pain without color change, but with an elevated amplitude of red.

When subjects experienced spaciness or coldness in their feet and legs, there was a decrease in electromagnetic energy in the lower body with an increase in the throat, third eye, and crown.

The heart and crown chakras were consistently most active in subjects when they felt anxious. This is not surprising since we live in a time-oriented culture, dominated by a stress syllable language. There is also tremendous emphasis placed on linear thinking and material achievement. Of course, we know that all of these factors are associated with cardiac disease.

Subjects reported numerous emotional experiences, imagery and memory recall when different parts of their bodies were being Rolfed. This corroborates Wilhelm Reich's beliefs that memory is stored in body tissues. When imagery or spontaneous pictures occurred, there was a strong cyclic energy shift back and forth between the throat and the third eye. Only during imagery did this pattern occur. Noting that the literature refers to these chakras as centers of psychic and creative energy leads to speculation about the role of chakra activity in human memory. There are no other electrical body measurements, including brain waves, which exclusively predict imagery during waking states.

We also discovered information about the Rolfer-Rolfee interactions. Generally, the Rolfer's hands carried a large blue and white corona with only minor changes during the sessions. If subjects expressed pain, Rolfers' hands changed to violet-pink, which seemed to calm the pain. When subjects reported higher consciousness states or imaging, invariably the Rolfer's hands were white. This apparent constant interplay between the fields of the subject and the Rolfer indicated that a transaction took place which facilitated energy exchange. Such an exchange probably occurs during all successful body therapy treatments whether by massage, acupressure, chiropractic, or orthopedic manipulations.

We observed that before the brain wave was activated and before stimuli altered the heart rate, blood pressure or breathing, the field had already responded. This led us to postulate that a person's primary response in his world takes place first in the auric field, not in the sensory nerves nor in the brain.

We believed that the auric field hangs around the body, sometimes loosely and sometimes firmly, but it does not dissipate like smoke in a wind. However, several times our instruments failed to record the field at the same time that the aura reader lost sight of it. When she found the person's field again, she described it as separated from the body by about six feet. Apparently, some bonds which attracted the aura close to the body had weakened, again, we speculated, due to the positive skin valance and the negative charge of the auric field. Nonetheless, when the mass of the field separated from the body's surface, we had a very weak signal. The aura reader could not see the aura until she moved outside the orbit and looked back at it. Although we observed the apparent separation of the aura from the body, we could not record this with surface body sensors.

Another interesting finding is that during the Santa Ana winds which rush down the mountains in southern California with strong positive ions, the human field becomes small. After many days of these winds, people become irritable and sometimes ill. It is as though the negative auric field splits away from the body, attracted by the high positive charge of the atmosphere.

Likewise, we found that the field expanded when the person was in the mountains or near the sea, possibly because of the increased negative ions present in these environments.

After subsequent study, if a person's field was particularly small, we would send him to the pool to swim or to a cold shower, or have him walk barefoot on the grass of the university campus. These increased his field and improved his feelings, probably because of the increased negative ions.

Once during a Rolfing session when the subject had sensors on his upper back and was lying supine, I asked the aura reader to report on his back chakras. She stated that she couldn't see them because he was lying on his back. I suggested that she read his back field by looking under the bed, which was covered by two mattresses. To her surprise, she saw it, and to ours, it confirmed the color wave shapes on the oscilloscope.

As a result of the Rolf study, we discovered energy emanations from the body's surface beyond the frequencies of the neuromuscular system. At the present time the only appropriate explanation is the existence of a bioenergy field. These data were obtained in quiet, resting states, isolated, and analyzed by scientifically accepted data analysis procedures such as Wave Shape Analysis (Exhibit 4), Fourier Frequency Analysis, and Frequency Spectrogram (Appendix Exhibits 7), all of which produced the same results, differing only in the fineness of detail.

Furthermore, the sensor readings from chakra locations corresponded directly with aura readers' descriptions of amount of energy, its color and the dynamic quality. In addition, there seemed to be a close relationship between these measures and the emotional states, imagery, and interpersonal transactions of the subjects.

As stated earlier, the dynamic details of the auric cloud, if it separated from the body as reported by readers, could not be corroborated by our instruments or techniques.

Although sensitives throughout history have described auric emanations, this is the first reported objective, electronic evidence which validates their subjective observations of auric color discharges.

In many ways, more questions were raised than answered by the Rolf study. For the next 20 years we conducted many pilot studies of hands-on healing, various types of meditation, and energy field transactions on a non-verbal level. Throughout these studies, we established the reliability of aura readers' reports by comparing simultaneous readings from eight experienced readers. All readers completely agreed on primary and secondary colors. With exotic or blended ones such as turquoise, puce, vermillion, amber, and mauve, they gave similar but not identical names.

To obtain some measure of the validity of the electronic recordings, we compared these with the purported measures of the energy field described in both ancient and modern literature. In every instance, wave shape analysis revealed a unique pattern for each basic color. In other words, we could differentiate between primary and secondary colors by reading the electronic signal shapes. Red, blue, and yellow exhibited strikingly different shapes, while orange, green, and violet appeared to be combinations of two primary shapes. (See Exhibit 4 - Energy Field Wave Shapes.)

Primary studies with hands-on healers verified the uniqueness of the transaction between healer and healee. For example, healers who specialized in treating pain and quieting hypertension had strong blue-white-violet fields when healing (Exhibit 8.) Healers most successful in improving hypo diseases, such as hypoglycemia and hypothyroidism, or weak tissues and functions, created a strong red-orange-amber field (Exhibit 9.) Red was predominant with healers who regenerated muscle, bone, and nerves. A green-yellow field proved most effective with nerve disorders such as Bell's palsy, cerebral palsy, or nerve degeneration. (Exhibit 6C)

Some people, particularly those with barrier diseases such as multiple sclerosis, Lou Gehrig's disease, and scleroderma, seemed to have such a rigid field that they were unable to receive energy from most healers. We realized that a transaction between the two fields was essential to hasten healing. When experienced healers had finished a healing session, the two fields of the healer and the healee showed an identical pattern. Apparently, when healers sensed that identical pattern with the healee, they terminated the healing session (Exhibit 10.)

We decided to test our belief that the auric field projecting anywhere from several inches to several feet from the body was probably where the first communication contact occurred between a person and the outside world. To explore this transaction, we placed two blindfolded people back-to-back in chairs so that only their auric fields could touch. Neither subject was consciously aware of the other. Each was instrumented to record auric changes. Simply the proximity of two fields did not guarantee a transaction. With amazement we watched the interface and the change of each field. Some people did not interact well through their fields; in fact, sometimes two fields would remain absolutely separate, retaining their individual patterns. With others, one field totally dominated the other, that is, one changed while the other did not—common with successful healing. Sometimes both fields changed to become identical, yet unlike either beginning field. This new, shared field appeared more elaborate than either person's prior one.

Later, we explored the effects of sensory stimuli, that is, light, sound, touch, and environmental vibrations on the human field. As might be expected, individuals' fields were more sensitive to some kinds of stimuli, regardless of the intensity. Without touching the body, we stroked the aura with a feather while the person was blindfolded. In other tests, we varied the intensity of light vibrations and created sounds both above and below the known range of hearing. We discovered that the energy field sometimes responded even when the person experienced no conscious sensation. Even more dramatic, the field responded before there was any increased activity in the brain or in the circulation, and sometimes even when the stimulus was too weak to activate the nervous system. (See Chapter V, "Mind-Field: Residence of the Consciousness and Soul" for further discussion.)

Another line of thought followed. Objects are believed to interact with atmospheric fields. Traditional Buddhist breathing techniques are based upon the idea of *prana*, an exchange between air and the body. Though there is no scientific confirmation of this exchange, our research led us to believe that a field transaction did not result from activity of the five senses, but indeed from interaction of the biological field with atmospheric ones. To test this hypothesis, we needed to manipulate the atmospheric electromagnetic field while recording the human field.

First, we studied the auric field in the near sound-sterile environment of the Anechoic Room at UCLA where sound is absorbed by baffles projecting from the walls and ceiling. A wire grate covered floor baffles. The room had no light or outside sound to provide electromagnetic energy. Four of us sequestered ourselves in this sterile room with the intention of stimulating ideas for future research design. Immediately, we felt strange sensory aberrations; we lost the sense of time. After several rather vacant hours, we became aware of three strong, pulsing rhythms in our bodies that we had never felt before. These were in the extremely low biological frequency ranges and appeared to be rhythms of the neurological, circulatory, and muscular systems. Actually, we never did make any electronic recordings in the Anechoic Room; our consciousness altered so rapidly that we were unable to operate instruments.

Later, we recorded the energy field of subjects in a Mu Room (named for the Greek letter, *Mu*.) This is a shielded room located in the Physics Department at UCLA. where the natural electromagnetic energy of the air can be altered without changing the level of gravitational force or the oxygen content. It is about seven square feet and high enough to stand up in. Using instruments inside the room, physicists could alter the quantities as well as the specific frequencies of the electromagnetic field. They could also direct electromagnetic frequencies to and from various locations in the room.

During the recording an aura reader read the auric field by penlight while physicists manipulated the environmental field. The subject's auric signals were broadcast by an FM radio telemetry system to our outside recording instruments. Subjects gave a continuing audio report of their personal experiences in the room while we monitored their physical field and the physicists manipulated the field in the room. Emilie Conrad, the dancer, performed simple balance and dance movements, as well as hands-on healing of a subject.

The findings were amazing. When the electrical aspect of the atmosphere in the room was withdrawn, leaving less electrical energy, the auric fields became randomly disorganized, scattered and incoherent (Exhibit 11.) Sensory feedback was so impaired that subjects were totally unaware of the location of their bodies in space. The aura reader described the energy as no longer flowing, but rather as jumping between people and chakras. Inside the body, she saw energy flowing in an extensive mesh network, described as a fishnet energy flow that did not correspond with meridian pathways. We believed it was flowing through the connective tissue which binds cells together. The connective tissue is the extensive structure which holds the body parts and cells together and composes bone, hair, nails, and skin by organizing cells into functional units. Without connective tissue, the body would be specialized protoplasm without unique shapes or functions. Connective tissue is also known to conduct electricity, although it is unknown what that energy is. The aura reader exclaimed at how easy it was to see into the body when the auric cloud was absent in the depleted electrical environment of the Mu Room.

When the electromagnetism in the air was depleted, the only other electrical energy available for the subjects to interact with was the fields of other subjects in the room. As they drew upon one another's fields, both fields were weakened. In this absence of an atmospheric source of electromagnetism, the interaction increased between their confused fields. At that stage general disorganization of both fields increased. The subjects burst into tears and sobbed, an experience unlike these people had ever endured. Although they reported that they were not sad, their bodies responded as though they were threatened, as they might be if the electromagnetic environment which nourished them was gone. Any sense of body boundary, the body image was absent, as though the field was searching for another electromagnetic field to which it could react.

When the electrical field of the room was increased beyond the usual level, the auric fields were restored to normalcy. The subjects' thinking became clear and they reported an expansion of their consciousness. Their auras became light in color with increased white vibrations.

On the other hand, if the electrical aspect of the room environment remained normal but the magnetism was decreased, gross incoordination occurred. The entire neurological integrating mechanism was thrown off. Subjects could not balance their bodies; they had difficulty touching finger to nose or performing simple coordinated movements. They lost kinesthetic awareness. Contrariwise, when the magnetic field was increased beyond the normal state, subjects could stand easily on one foot, even on tiptoes, or lean to previously impossible angles without falling. Motor coordination had somehow improved.

Apparently, the whole process of movement and coordination is related to interaction with the environmental electromagnetic field, not only to gravity. A change in the field transaction profoundly affected sensory-motor capacities. These findings caused us to speculate about the possibility of training athletes and rehabilitating those with muscular disabilities in a strong magnetic energy field.

The sensitive subjects in the Mu Room reported accurately through microphones the directional source of energy and the approximate frequencies introduced by the physicists. When the frequency generated into the room was 500 cycles per second, the two subjects and the aura reader described their auras as red. Later, we confirmed that in a normal electromagnetic atmosphere, when the aura reader described the field as red, our instruments detected 500 cycles per second from the body's surface.

Subjects were fatigued from the extreme manipulation of electromagnetism in the Mu Room. At the end of the ten-hour experiment, all subjects' fields were spent and their bodies exhausted (Exhibits 11.) Fortunately, their fields returned to normal the following day.

At this point, I would like to summarize what we had learned thus far. In a normal electromagnetic environment, the human field is nourished; physiological processes are carried out efficiently, and emotional experiences occur with clarity of thought. When the level of electromagnetism reached a critical saturation, there was evidence of improved motor performance, emotional well-being, excitement, and advanced states of consciousness. However, when the critical deficit was reached, motor, sensory and intellectual capabilities diminished with increased levels of anxiety and emotion.

The literature states that external electromagnetic energy penetrates the body through acupuncture points and flows through the meridians into the whole field. We discovered that it also flows through the connective tissues. We concluded that the electromagnetic environment is a milieu in which life and physiological happenings occur. Apparently, for all systems to be "go", a rich electromagnetic field must be present.

If further studies verify these findings, the implications are staggering. The Mu Room treatment of neuromuscular disturbances and degeneration such as cerebral palsy, multiple sclerosis, and Lou Gehrig's disease should hasten recovery. Likewise, emotional disturbances, sensory confusion and learning handicaps should improve.

From approximately 600 hours of recording under many circumstances, we discovered that each person has a unique, predictable and recurring field characterized by such measures as color, the quantity of the energy, the dominance of particular body areas and the completeness of the spectrum pattern. There were also individual differences in the complex dynamics or flux of the field. Occasionally, we found a very stoic field that showed less interaction with other fields. Frequently women displayed very weak energy in the lower parts of their bodies. In an esoteric sense, these people can be described as ungrounded. Contrariwise, males more often had a spotty field with strength in some areas and absence in others. Individual fields showed areas where energy flowed more freely while others were blocked. We discovered by recording brain waves, blood pressure changes, galvanic skin responses, heartbeat and muscle contraction simultaneously with auric changes, that changes occurred in the field before any of the other systems changed.

The direct correlation of the simultaneous readings of eight aura seers with our electronic data was used to establish the validity of the energy field recordings. The Power Density Spectrum and Sound Spectrogram techniques (Exhibit 7) specifically indicated the strength of the frequencies of the electronic recordings relative to color, regardless of the individual or the specific chakra measured.

While we visually monitored incoming data on oscilloscopes, we observed that simultaneous recordings from separate chakras frequently showed a quite different pattern. To check the differences, we used a Cross Plot Analysis technique to compare two chakras for strength, frequency and sequence (Exhibit 5.) If the various chakras had a similar amplitude and frequency they were coherent, or synchronous. If grossly different, they were out of sync, or anti-coherent. In later studies, the measure of anti-coherency was associated with physical and emotional dysfunction or disease.

We speculated that if a smaller coherent electrical field of the heart existed in a larger anti-coherent energy field of the body, that over time, the heart would pick up the body's random anti-coherency and become dysrhythmic. Later, we were able to reorganize cardiac dysrhythmia by creating a coherent energy field. (Chapter X, "Healing: The Miracle of Life".)

We know that many things happen without predictions or adequate explanations. Actually, the scientific community ignores a large residuum of information when that information contains numerous factors that are blended together and difficult to separate.

As I observed energy field data on the oscilloscope, I realized that none of the known analytic techniques could unravel its complexity. I sensed that the dynamic essence was lost when we relied on standard statistical procedures. No matter how rigorous our observations, there seemed to be no available mathematical formulae complex enough to reveal the patterns within patterns evident in our data.

It seemed that we had uncovered an information system that

we could not decode completely. All statistical formulae and computer programs, including the many we had used with limited success, are based on Euclidian geometry, which can decipher only data that fell into symmetrical, regular patterns. Irregular information loses its richness when forced into regular patterns.

Out of necessity, we continued to analyze our data with Power Density Spectra and Frequency Spectrograms despite the fact that these seemed to strip away the irregular, seemingly unpredictable qualities, crunching the data into a smooth, classical pattern with periodicities that did not actually exist. In other words, our energy field data, processed by standard statistical procedures, lost the constantly changing pattern in time and space.

Fortunately for us, early in the 1980s a new fractal mathematics, the "geometry of nature," was developed. Fractal mathematics could analyze natural, irregular dynamic phenomena like the bark on a tree, a sunset, or even aspects of human consciousness, including our energy field. Now the uneven, crinkly, curvy swirls of a flapping flag, and the eddies in moving water, could be studied by pattern. Soon, computer scientists developed graphic programs to show unusual visual patterns held even within linear frequency data. At about the same time, fractal mathematics displayed a startling new concept of chaos. (See Chapter III)

One of the confounding problems with all very complex data has been that it looks chaotic, that is random, without pattern or repetition. Yet using fractal geometry, these chaotic happenings were found to have deep, profound and predictable order. With complex information, a highly ordered pattern has emerged from beneath a superficial appearance of disorder. In other words, what appeared uneven and unpredictable on a surface level is in fact orderly and predictable at a deeper level. Furthermore, when very complex information is processed by fractal geometry the orderly pattern, called the chaos attractor, rapidly appears as though it was near the data surface.

We all know how unpredictable weather is. Even satellite data can only provide short term weather predictions. Meteorologist Lorenz, using fractal geometry to analyze 40 years of weather data, discovered a magnificently ordered pattern within the seeming disorder of the data. He discovered a weather chaos attractor pattern which indicated that over the years a predictable weather pattern has emerged. (Exhibit 15)

Using raw data from our energy field experiments, Allen Garfinkle, an established fractal mathematician, obtained a perfect dynamic chaos order (Exhibit 12 and 13 - Hunt Chaos Graph.) Compare the crinkled pattern in the Hunt graph produced from living human vibrations to the computer generated Rossler Chaos graph and the Lorenz weather graph. Note the similarity, and also the difference. (Exhibits 14 and 15.) Even more dramatic is the fact that the Hunt pattern was derived from only three seconds worth of data, whereas the weather data were gathered over a span of 40 years.

Recently, a chaos attractor pattern has been found in brain wave and heart frequency data, but these require the analysis of many hours, or even days of continuous data. Three seconds worth of heart or muscle data generated a straight line, called self similar, meaning the frequency did not differ, rather than the complex chaos attractor (Exhibits 16, 17, 18, 19). Probably all data, even those that are simple and regular, will display a chaos pattern if the data are extensive enough. But this has little practical value. What is significant is that the energy field of the human, the most complex of all living systems, disclosed this magnificent order in only three seconds worth of data.

So, what is the significance of accessing the Hunt Chaos Order? It means that by manipulating the energy field we can refine and encourage coherency in all tissues and biological systems. This approach could produce results more rapidly and dramatically than could any other known medical, psychiatric, or educational approach. Furthermore, through chaos attractor graphics we will be able to elucidate definable patterns in diseases, and in emotional and functional disorders.

CHAPTER III

SCIENCE AND THOUGHT:
The Real World

Information from science and religion molds our beliefs about reality, what we consider true, what imagined, and what carries the strongest emotional charges. These pervading beliefs direct our energies, creating life patterns. To evaluate or to change a particular idea or a belief requires looking for its source as well as at how human experience has validated that idea or belief. This chapter explores some old and some new scientific realities that structure our thoughts about the world and ourselves within it.

Rather than simply exposing the limitations of currently accepted scientific laws by presenting some new information, I hope to offer readers an opportunity to evaluate their beliefs in a new light.

To classical scientists, the "softness" of mystical thought and its apparent unreality can be threatening, or disquieting at least. But for many scientists, the problem is that they must begin to redefine themselves and their notions of reality; "truth" might have to expand to accommodate the reality of such experiences as mystical visions, for example. Of course there are some who would welcome a broader notion of what constitutes truth. In fact, many so-called mystical scientists have always been the model builders, the ones who broke through the age-old barriers. Kuhn, the philosopher of science, commented that the world needs two modes of thought—one that cares about truth and intuits what it is, and one which concerns itself with the logic of truth. I believe that the new age scientists will do both.

Certainly a profitable dialogue could take place between scientists and mystics—perhaps difficult at first, but oh, so fruitful. Both would learn: the mystic to ask more incisive questions and to more carefully articulate and explain deep wisdoms; and the scientists to loosen their mental constraints about the nature of reality to explore "impossible" ideas. It is my impression that this is indeed happening. Mystically-inclined young people are now entering scientific disciplines whereas in the past, they typically chose the arts and philosophy. Some scientists are already performing research with mystics, and several medical clinics have practicing mystics on staff. Scientists and other professionals are meditating, practicing *tai chi* or yoga, and not just to offset stress but to help them access intuitive knowing. At a recent research meeting, I was struck with the realization that the pioneer thinkers resembled the descriptions of the scientist-priests of the past in their wisdom and personal commitments.

Scientists have consistently tried to present facts about the universe and to order them so that generalizations could be made. In the early stages they sought to discover pervading laws of the physical universe, of time and space and mass, and to learn how to manipulate these. This brought in the science of the industrial era. The twentieth century, characterized by the boldest scientific exploration, has produced the greatest amount of information in the shortest amount of time that we have seen in all of history. Scientific discoveries in the past 30 years have been monumental in helping to explain the physical world. And by deeper and broader investigation of phenomena, some earlier truths were expanded and some shown to be only partially true. Einstein's theory of relativity, for example, showed that space and time are not absolute, as originally thought. Understanding the atomic structure of all mass, and its splitting and harnessing with the recent discovery of subatomic particles, demonstrated that the greatest potential power source in the world lies in the smallest amounts of matter.

The magnificent accomplishments of overcoming gravity and maintaining life in hostile environments allowed us to explore the other planets in our galaxy. Of course, none of us will ever forget where we were when we heard that man had first set foot on the moon. I was in a remote section of Uganda, Africa, living with native peoples. We heard the news through radio reports. The natives had no comprehension of the scientific break-throughs that got us "there," but their conscious reality totally understood humans being "there." Some told me that they went there often in their dream time.

Our current understanding of infinite space is overwhelming when compared to that of the early part of this century when we thought we were the only world, with our stars and our sun and moon, as though this constituted the entire universe. Now we know that there are thousands of worlds, perhaps even more, and as many suns and moons.

Our capacity to communicate in all media via satellites has made it possible to beam information instantaneously to any location on the globe. Furthermore, developments in the field of computer technology have given us a glimpse of the profundity of the human mind.

Probably the greatest recent discoveries in biology come from decoding the genetic information system and the genetic engineering it fostered. Discovering neuropeptides, the ultimate biological communication system, has overshadowed the tremendous strides made in the study of neurochemical enzymes. (See Chapter X, Healing: The Miracle of Life).

As science has delved more deeply into the nature of the physical world, it has run headlong into grave questions about the effects of the human mind on matter, and the role of human consciousness in the universe. A better understanding of biochemical processes in the body has not explained man's more subtle experiences in the material world nor in his inner world. Actually, science has not yet begun to seriously investigate such questions. There may be many reasons for this fact: while these questions are not beyond scientific study, these are beyond the current scientific concepts and therefore the instruments scientists have developed. Possibly, physical laws do not apply because such dynamic happenings may play by a more complex set of rules. Currently, science deals with less than one-half of human experience, that portion of experience that is called "real" because it can be objectively measured and quantified.

No one doubts that scientific discoveries make a difference in our lives. We can enumerate the time and labor saving devices, the speed of travel and communication, the improved comfort and medical care, and the creature pleasures we enjoy. But for many of us, these improvements have not caused us to alter our concepts of ourselves, or our beliefs about reality.

So, although we readily accept the fruits of current invention, we are not prone to give up outmoded thought. Usually, we have forgotten or perhaps never knew where these beliefs about reality originated. Therefore, let us examine two parallel, often complementary but sometimes opposing ways of constructing reality, one stemming from physical mechanics and the other from quantum mechanics.

The older paradigm describing physical reality that we have validated with our experience became known as Newtonian-Cartesian concepts of reality. In this sytem, there is no such thing as consciousness. This fundamental concept determined the design of all experiments. As scientists fit new information into this jigsaw puzzle, they gained credibility, leading them to believe this was the only path to great scientific truths.

Science gained authority by discovering and promulgating indisputable universal laws that are repeatable, stable, unchanging descriptions of the nature of things and their interactions. But today quantum physics has absolutely transcended every postulate in basic mechanical science. For example, we all know that solid matter is indestructible. Yet on the subatomic level of the particle, sometimes we cannot find the mass and particles seem essentially empty. We find only a wave of energy without dense form. At the quantum level of matter, things don't exist until they are observed. Probably both the wave and the particle concepts are essential to represent reality fully.

The fact that events can no longer be predicted with complete accuracy is known as the uncertainty principle. It states that the most accurate descriptions of phenomena lie in probability predictions, revealing to us that the world is fuzzy and always a bit uncertain. The laws of gravity are perfect examples. "What goes up must come down." And yet the Voyager, shot beyond the effects of gravity will not return. Human levitation defying gravitational law, at least for a time, is being studied in Maharishi's laboratories in Switzerland and Iowa. There are even indications of lateral gravity waves.

Objects don't have well-defined boundaries. One can't simultaneously know the path and the position of moving objects. Earlier indisputable laws are now qualified, extended, or limited in application. Stephen Hawking goes so far as to say that dynamic mechanical systems resemble human behavior in that there is little success in predicting from mathematical equations.

An older paradigm states that time flows in an irreversible direction from past to future. We can't stop time or reverse it. Einstein consistently reminded us that this was not true. Actually, space and time are bins into which we place things and experiences to categorize them. Time and space are constructs derived from our experiences and interpretations of events occurring in space, which then give rise to the idea of motion. Without motion there is no time. We have observed that when people enter higher states of consciousness, they lose the sense of time.

This was brought dramatically to my attention by my experience in Machu Pichu. I never knew exactly why I was drawn to Machu Pichu, Peru, until I got there. I thought I went to see the sights—but this was only partially true. At Machu Pichu I had spent the night in a tiny room only large enough for a small bed and a crawl space to get to it, to be ready to see the sunrise over the ancient Andes archaeological site. I roamed around alone in the early morning, photographing. I was curious about what had happened here. The standard tourist information struck me as too metaphoric to have actually happened. The rarified air rapidly fatigued us sea-landers, so by noon I chose a quiet, shaded spot in the courtyard between the two building areas to lie down. I was awakened sometime later by loud conversation of French and German tourists who had come for the day. They were photographing me and the number of llamas that were lying around me, one with his head on my boot. I am sure I had chosen their special retreat spot, and my vibrations were sufficiently high that I may not have resembled a human.

I experienced such an extended state of reality at that time that my higher consciousness surveyed the area and honed in on the different parts of the ruins. I mystically saw what had happened at Machu Pichu. I realized that this beautiful old civilization was not the peoples' ordinary habitat, but it was their "Temple of Creation." On the one side were the buildings of spiritual creation where the priests conceived sounds and chants and rituals. In another area, I saw the ancient artisans pounding gold and copper into decorations, and making pottery, baskets and fabrics that I had never before seen. At a shallow cave-like niche with a long slab of stone separating the entrance from the exit, I saw dead bodies placed at the entrance and removed for burial at the exit. This was a ritual for the ascendance of the soul. I realized that Machu Pichu had been the Incas' temple where they sent their great visionaries to create models for their people. This was a very unstabling emotional experience for me because I was vacillating in a two-fold reality system. This was my first monumental reality confrontation.

On the return trip to Cuzco, I sought our tour leader, a former Catholic priest who had lived in Peru for many years, to relate my experiences. While I had no desire to convince him, I wanted to debrief myself so that I might return to "normal" reality. He listened quietly, without comment. Several days later, he brought the curator of the Cuzco Museum to hear my story while he served as an interpreter. The curator's only comment was, "Perhaps it is true," because he had heard a very similar story from two European mystics. One important part of this experience for me was that I recognized the fallibility of our usual concepts of time. (See Chapter VI, Telepathic Knowing: The Transfer of Thought).

The second law of thermodynamics describes the disorganization of matter over time; that is things become less structured and they decay. Leaves fall and create mulch, an example of the downside of nature. Increased disorder or entropy over time helps us to distinguish past from present, indicating the directionality of material things. This raises the question of how evolution could take place if the prevailing tendency is toward disorder and decay. Transition to a higher order, according to Ilya Prigogine, is universally accompanied by perturbation. He has shown that if energy is introduced to matter, the disintegration process is altered and matter takes on a higher organization. So, entropy can be both the evidence of decay as well as the first step in the creation of new materials. Jahn refers to the possibility that consciousness has an entropy-reducing capacity which creates an ordering influence on otherwise random physical processes, thereby reversing their normal thermodynamic tendency of disintegration.

The proof of scientific truth lies in replicating experiments and producing the same results. When we believed that "truth" was a single, unquestionable answer, this idea had merit. But the tenets of the quantum era show that the experimenter, as a part of every research he performs, influences the results by what he chooses to study, the collection of data, and how he analyzes it—but even more importantly, by his actual presence in an experimental situation. It seems that scientists cannot extricate themselves from the experiment. They are a part of the field of interaction and a basic ingredient of what they study. In this sense, truth on some levels is always relative.

A subatomic interpretation is that there is no universe without an observer. It has been said that there is no physical universe without our thoughts about it. Quantum physics reminds us that the moment one inquires into matter, like an electron that has no position, velocity, momentum or spin, that electron acquires character. Simply, we cannot observe the world without participating with it. Observers are part of the nature of physical reality, where matter and mind blend. Furthermore, when studying open dynamic systems, there can never be identical answers. The importance of repeating studies is not to determine "truths," but to disclose many truths—different pieces of information to fill in the puzzle.

Scientists have been taught to keep the laboratory environment controlled, emotionally sterile, and non-exploratory in an attempt to be objective. On the other hand, Jahn has very succinctly stated: " ... Consciousness defined in proper generality is the ultimate factor in any observation and therefore an intrinsic ingredient in the conceptualization of matter waves." Likewise, the rigid objectivity of controlled experiments, if carried to extreme, limits creative observation.

Mechanistic science, in its search for specific answers, has led some researchers and many lay people to misinterpret correlation or connection with cause. Correlation only tells us that two things co-exist in certain situations and may have some connection, but not that one creates the other. They may be both the product of something else. Along this line, I believe that electroencephalographers have been particularly remiss in judging that alpha brain waves cause a shift in the level of consciousness and thus in thinking. I believe that the low alpha and theta brain waves merely indicate that the brain is operating on such a low idling level as to allow the person access to the mind. Alpha waves, then, would not be the cause, but would be co-happenings with changes in consciousness.

To summarize, these older scientific paradigms have provided answers to common questions about the material level of the world, answers which are verified by our everyday experiences. The resulting model of the world has been described as a gigantic machine connected with a linear chain of events. Assuming that we knew all the facts, we could reconstruct everything we knew from the past, and predict accurately everything that would happen in the future. Such a model, from which our beliefs stem, images the universe and the world as a complex assembly of passive, unconscious, inert matter, developing and changing without participation or creative intelligence. It implies that everything will go on as it is without our having a chance to change it, except perhaps to build a bigger machine and push matter around.

What gloomy and only partially correct beliefs about life and the universe have come from these models! They say that in this material world dominated by entropy from birth to death, we are on a downhill slide. Our world is random, moving toward thermal death. We are born to die so that we can evolve. Life can only be explained by a chemical soup from which we sprang, and we obey these chemical laws.

Furthermore, we have inserted these concepts into every field of inquiry. Psychology and psychiatry considered man a machine with bestial ideas, impulsive and unconscious drives that directed him. Reality composed of these "truths" is a decidedly restricted reality, that at most is only an approximation. Such science has told us about the lowest level of reality, but has provided us with little information about the higher realms.

Arnold Toynbee's conclusion about twenty-six lost civilizations was that they all perished for the same reason. They over-protected the tenets which first made them powerful. They eventually cracked from rigidity and sterility which accompanies a refusal to yield to an evolving world view.

Fortunately for us, a major paradigm shift has brought new ideas, ideas that cannot be explained by the language of older paradigms. Thomas Kuhn, in *The Structure of Scientific Revolutions*, predicted a quantum leap in the quest for new truths that would not happen simply as a result of small addenda to old truths. Rather, he sees major perceptual change which aligns our thinking to a more enlightened framework. Perhaps it was inevitable that science explored mechanistic reality first, like a baby creeping before it can walk. But the old process persisted so long that it sidetracked our "seeing" and caused us to forget where to "look." I refer specifically to the microscopic approach clouding the macroscopic view of wholeness.

Now we know that reality is infinitely more complex than science has ever envisioned, even beyond any single religious ideology existing today. This extended concept of reality postulates an open system—where constant interactions and transactions take place back and forth between all existing systems—in contrast to the closed systems of the past. Quantum physics has heralded its birth. Stephen Hawking, one of its eminent spokesmen, commented that "... apparently common sense notions work well when dealing with material things like apples and/or comparatively slow moving things like planets; they don't work at all for things moving at the speed of light."

The advanced order basic to the new physics and all ancillary sciences was not discovered in particles of matter; it was found in the minds of scientists who had given up their preconceived ideas about the physical world and reality, as the overwhelming idea of the oneness of life impinged upon their consciousness. They saw that things moved without following the laws of mechanical motion; things moved disjointedly in a discontinuous manner, jumping almost effortlessly between two places. This was exactly how I perceived Emilie Conrad's motion when she said that she "created a wave and rode it." On the atomic scale, physicists saw that what they used to measure data "created" and determined what they found.

Disclosures that subatomic particles had the characteristics of light were exciting. But then it was discovered that when one extends material substances toward infinity, one comes up with not mass, but a process, an event, and a relationship. One expects to hear such ideas from philosophers, but from scientists, this can be a shock. James Jeans, a famous mathematician, wrote that the universe began to look less like a machine and more like a thought system.

It logically follows, then, that our thoughts are therefore a part of the universe's thoughts, and that we can and do influence them. How strange it is to contemplate that at the deepest level, the world is more like a thought system than material reality. No longer can we accept that the universe is a gigantic clock; instead, it is a unified network of events and relationships in which the mind and intelligence and the human soul are integral parts of existence, rather than the products of nature.

Most profound changes in the conception of reality came from Einstein's Unified Field Theory. This theory states that all matter is organized energy, and that field reality is one of the characteristics of the universe. The deeper one probes material systems, the more one encounters field aspects or the substances' underlying electrical pattern, the very basis of the substance itself. Whether the energy is constellated as a cup, a tree, or a human being, it has a field associated with it. The denser the substance, the less energetic and more rigid the field becomes. There are no firm boundaries between fields—boundaries belong to dense material substances. Fields, then, extend everywhere, an open system, free to evolve and grow, and as such they are frequently in disequilibrium.

Physicists have studied the interactions between two fields, but when it comes to more than two fields interacting, they bow out, leaving that to the mystics. Yet the most important level from which to understand the world and human beings is the level of the field transaction. We know that living things have dynamic fields which constantly and selectively transact with all environmental fields. In this sense, man's field is primary to his existence.

Fields that are no longer connected to a substance, but instead to behaviors and thoughts, have been classified by the English biologist Rupert Sheldrake as morphogenic fields. He believes that fields which have existed as a result of human lives still exist and have molded past events as they color what happens today. When a certain number of individuals of a particular species learn something, it seems to positively affect the learning of all other individuals of that species.

The older concept that everything progresses toward decay does not hold with field beliefs. From a field reality, the world grows and changes—it evolves. Prigogine, the Nobel biochemist, showed that when energy was introduced into a system, that substance was refined and changed. But it did not decay. Open systems are highly interactive systems. Generally the body, but also the mind and thought are considered open systems. But actually, living systems are both open and closed.

In fact, to maintain integrity, no system can be totally open or completely closed; it would disintegrate into chaos or die from lack of nourishment. The more complicated the structure, the more it requires energy transactions to maintain its integrity. Open systems have a dynamic and shifting balance, whereas more closed ones have a static balance and are more threatened by sudden, catastrophic field changes. When a system becomes closed and stagnant, structural mutations occur. Probably cancer is such a mutation.

As a result of my work, I can no longer consider the body as organic systems or tissues. The healthy body is a flowing, interactive electrodynamic energy field. Motion is more natural to life than non-motion—things that keep flowing are inherently good. What interferes with flow will have detrimental effects.

Behavioral science researchers have coined a picturesque expression, "the random rat" for subjects who nullify otherwise clear-cut results and distort correlations. Such situations show up in most closed systems research where some of the data collected are so abnormal that they seem to come from another experiment. This will also occur in open systems studies where it is not seen as abnormal, but rather a part of the dynamic pattern of phenomena.

We have held the notion that scientists ought to be able to explain all things. Why, then, can't the meteorologists more accurately predict the weather? Why can't gamblers predict a roulette wheel? A man is feeling fine, his doctor says he's in tip-top health, but he leaves his physician's office and falls over dead of a heart attack. Why? The basic tool of science, mathematics, can't even describe or explain clouds or the bark on a tree, or lightning or a fire. There are happenings in the universe that are not repetitious, continuous, or highly consistent. These phenomena are like oddballs or random rats. Simply put, science has not been geared to understand or predict any type of irregular behavior.

To summarize, we must acknowledge that we are in a magnificent era when the old is fading and the new has not been fully disclosed. But we can say with assurance that a human being cannot be likened to a gigantic clock with everything predetermined by mechanistic wheels. The reality of the world lies in fields which interact with other fields of energy in dynamic chaos patterns that are always evolving to higher levels of complexity. This is an open system in which reality is tremendously complex. What we know as truth, intuition and consciousness all operate interdependently with matter. Furthermore, they transform matter as they are transformed by it.

The eminent physicists Eddington and Schroedinger were the first to acknowledge that science is not dealing with the world itself, but with the shadows of an imaginary world. The new physics made us aware of that fact. James Jeans further elaborated that the mathematical pictures of nature which science discloses are fictitious and do not represent ultimate reality. (Fred Alan Wolf wanted to know how a simple observation could "cause" a wave to spread out over space to produce a point, a particle).

Where then do we turn if what we have believed to be the core of science, physics and mathematics, shows us but illusions of the real world? Many physicists believe it to be a fundamental event beyond physics—an act of consciousness and thought.

As Jahns and Dunne put it, physical theory is not complete until consciousness is acknowledged as an active element in the establishment of reality. But we seem caught in a dilemma. Consciousness does not fit into the time, space and mass constructs of material physics. And the old model has so successfully described ordinary reality that all behavioral disciplines have embraced it, eliminating consciousness as an acceptable course of scientific study.

Now we can begin to accept the fact that basic truths do not stem from information accumulated over the centuries. Fundamental change is not evolutionary but is revolutionary; it occurs in conceptual leaps.

Advanced thinkers from the fields of chemistry, biology, and anthropology have drawn concepts from each other about the fundamental rules that shape adaptive systems. While each searches for universal principles of world order, it was the "Santa Fe Group" which first articulated a unified theory of living systems. They called it complexity theory—a major revolution in science. (Lewin).

Somewhat earlier, physicists had introduced the chaos theory, also as a new macroscopic view of the global nature of the universe. Even in the early stages, the philosophical descriptions of these theories showed that they embraced field phenomena and holographic concepts which help to explain organized information.

We know that every part of an organized field is a hologram where each part contains the pattern of the whole. The chaos concept further elaborates a hologram to show that although each part is alike, there will be slight differences in the whole over time. The hologram then is a more spatial pattern with only implied time or motion, whereas chaos is a process containing both time and space, wherever its focus. Possibly, the term "chaotic hologram" is more appropriate for patterns representing spectrum distribution of energy over time, unrestricted by the level of energy.

Do you know that if you cut bits out of material substances they are no longer the same? But if you take a snip out of a field, a hologram, it just becomes smaller, not changed, for every particle is exactly like every other particle. David Bohm stresses that the hologram is a starting point for a new description of reality, an enfolded order. Classical concepts of reality have focused upon secondary manifestations—the unfolded aspect of things, not their source.

A field is a flowing thing. It flows within itself, through it to other fields, and as an organized unit it also flows from one place to another. It carries an ultimate level of information. Recently, we have been able to measure human fields separate from mass and describe them as energy patterns, wave shapes, wave trains, and wave packages or quanta. (See Chapter II). In the future we will be able to decode fields in other ways where relationships and patterns of happenings will not be looked on as cause and effect but a part of the transition. Dynamic fields participate as they select by attraction. (Lewin).

The unique human field does not merely react or interact; it transacts because it dynamically makes choices. Here, matter and energy, mind and spirit, are not really different things, only aspects of an expanded reality.

So far, experts have not substantially clarified the interface of complexity and chaos, their differences, similarities and unique contributions. Perhaps these merely define separate ways of categorizing elaborate data. While concepts of chaos and complexity guide a growing body of standard research, their application to the "softer sciences" of consciousness, creativity, psychic phenomena and subtle energies is essential. Years ago, I sensed such ideas when I discontinued correlation studies to focus on patterns of the human field. Chaos and complexity theories offer the first sound framework for understanding my complex dynamic data; they also provide me with new ways to interpret mystical phenomena.

Kauffman believes that complexity is not a point, but rather a quality of a spectrum which depicts overall organization. Both complexity and chaos stress patterns of information as more important than specifics. Both can be applied to linear systems but their ideas are essential in explaining non-linear living systems. I concur with Kauffman that chaos is a subset of complexity. (Lewin).

Chaos patterns appear on different scales simultaneously: the infinite, the microscopic, and the human scale of things that we can see and touch. On one level chaos describes non-linear, non-random disorder. On another level there is great order, showing the self-organizing nature of systems. Gleick reminds us, "In science as in life, it is well known that a chain of events can have a crisis point that could magnify small changes. Chaos means that such points are everywhere—pervasive."

Chaos describes the most dynamic order-disorder of everyday happenings of energy around us: a flag snapping in the wind, the wild swirls in a column of smoke, the intermittent steady-to-random dripping of a faucet, and weather. It seems that some unknown energy was introduced to account for the erratic behavior of ordinary happenings—a subliminal stimulus creating a strange response.

Gleick says that chaos describes the apparent disorganization of open systems as though they were attempting to jiggle themselves into higher order. He states, "The greater the turbulence, the more complex the solution, the greater the jump to a higher order."

The irregular side of nature, the discontinuous and erratic side, has been puzzling to classical science since its beginning. The theory of chaos helps us to appreciate the pervasive nonlinearity of our world where a system is not totally out of control; it has another control. Chaos arises in any dynamic system when a certain level of complexity is reached. It follows no known determined pattern; however, the greater the complexity the less predictable are details of its future. In chaotic systems, we know only what is or what has happened, not exactly what will happen. In the 1970s physicists expounded ideas from chaos theories that they thought could account for all complex behavior. In time, they realized that while applicable, these could not capture all of the dynamics exhibited by complex systems.

With earlier research involving specific microscopic points of information, pattern recognition was not very important— certainly not necessary. Although energy physics is basically a pattern research, it was only with chaos approaches to living systems that pattern analysis appeared at front and center stage and ran headlong into the limited capacity of scientists to observe unique patterns hidden in apparent disorder.

From this problem sprang the new fractal mathematics of nature with its companion computer display graphics. Now visionary researchers could pursue subtle energy fields where Euclidian mathematics had not worked. Chaos and complexity concepts could begin to explain things standard science could not. The word "fractal" was coined by the mathematician Mandelbrot early in the 1970s from the Latin word *fractus*, meaning broken, fragmented, like the branching, twisting organic shapes formed in nature. Fractal formulas fed to computers created fractal energy graphics—magnificent, intricate, flowing, lumpy patterns carrying both deep and global information.

Using the fractal formula, Rössler generated the first computer model of chaos, where every part of order was slightly different—an orderly non-random process with gaps. Lorenz, applying fractal mathematics to 40 years of weather data, formed a chaos pattern which he described as having a butterfly effect. He believed this pattern was so powerful that the fluttering of butterfly wings in Japan could theoretically affect weather patterns worldwide. He corroborated that at the deepest level, small perturbations over time could make things happen in a way that they could not have happened without that perturbation.

Even dynamic systems have some linear, defined order. And dynamic systems with greater frequencies are more prone to exhibiting chaotic relationships and turmoil disorganization. (Exhibit 13) presents the chaos pattern obtained from three seconds worth of energy field data. The chaos pattern did not occur from three seconds worth of neurological data from the heart muscle and brain. (Exhibits 16, 17, 18, 19.)

Chaos theory emphasizes process with levels of complexity categorized in three broad phases: (1) ordered, (2) chaotic, and (3) turmoil. This means that chaos is not a point beyond non-chaos, but rather a process of initial disorganization of data either toward randomness or toward a more static order. The Santa Fe group places specific emphasis on the phase they call "the edge of chaos" or its onset, the beginning of the classical chaos attractor. Because in my data these changes are not necessarily instant, I see the "onset of chaos" as a time dimension and the "ridge of chaos" its pattern. "Edge of chaos" and "ridge of chaos" differ in that edge implies abrupt change; ridge refers to a gentler slope.

The complexity of the data increases the opportunity for rapid change to the dynamic state, or the ridge of chaos. Beyond the ridge of chaos generally lies not an abrupt chasm of turmoil but a downward slope toward randomness. This is a vulnerable time when energy from other sources can reflect the system so that it fluctuates back and forth on the ridge, becoming neither strictly ordered nor random.

There are time instances in the ridge state when the system is in exquisite control, balanced between order and disorder. We experience this in our consciousness when we subtly shift between material, and higher or spiritual awareness, or when we are meditating and arrive at a sudden illumination or profound sense of knowing.

According to past scientific dictates, change is linear, gradual, and continuous. Now a new catastrophic theory speaks about certain critical stages in nature where a catapult or unpredictable jump occurs. We have all had peak experiences for which there was no warning. If one were to examine the macroscopic pattern of the data before the violent change occurred, one would probably find an "edge of chaos" point of disequilibrium when energy reorganized into a different constellation. Such sudden changes describe volatile weather conditions, political upheavals, and disease epidemics. Probably the apparent onset was catastrophic while its process was chaotic.

Lorenz, the meteorologist, first named the unique geometric form of the chaos pattern the "strange attractor." When the chaotic attractor appeared, there was an increasing likelihood of resonating and transacting with other vibrations. Physics and evolutionary biology describe this instance as a "phase shift" where some information drops out or changes—as when a solid changes to a gas.

The presence of strange attractor patterns indicates both time and organization when systems are evolutionary or vulnerable to being pulled in many directions. There exists a proclivity for one part of a field to be drawn to another field, not regularly, for that could not be called strange. We have observed that people and physical happenings seem to carry unexplained connections, like extrasensory awareness or Psi K. Strange attractors in the human field probably help to explain individual behavioral tendencies and susceptibility to some diseases. It may even be that genetic tendencies operate through chaotic attractors in the field.

In the human field, major attractors carry strong, personally emotional valences like those resulting from childhood trauma. I personally believe that mind-field attractors from other lifehoods will replace the ancient concepts of karma. (Chapter IX, Lifehoods: The Hidden Agenda). It is exciting to realize that the flexibility of the ridge of chaos can be used creatively to change behavior and thoughts to our advantage. (Chapter X, Healing).

Just as small disturbances rapidly alter chaotic systems, so can minute adjustments stabilize behaviors. Physics has found that by periodically introducing energy into chaotic systems they can be pulled back toward order. Because the human energy field is so resilient, manipulation techniques such as hands-on healing, subtle energy devices, and body therapies introducing subtle energy into the system can more effectively preserve health than those therapies using chemical or mechanical intervention. I believe controlling chaos anywhere in the body via the field will be faster and more enduring than testing specific biological subsystems.

As living systems transact through their attractors, they build a complex repertoire of vibrations, which results in a memory. I describe it as a "wave train." It is like a series of different chaos patterns strung together over time to show a gestalt or reactability quotient. We have discovered that some people's fields show such a limited wave train of energy patterns that in a few minutes they have literally exhausted their everyday reactive capabilities. Others show untold differences over time, an open, dynamic, complex field of adjustments. In other words, the nature of the wave train, a changing auric fingerprint, circumscribes the available interactive possibilities. It follows that if the human field does not transact, it loses its complexity, becomes narrow in vibrational spectrums, and thus displays a simple wave train with a diminished capacity for self organization or creative exploration.

The Institute of Noetic Sciences in *Scientific Positivism: the New Dualism* concluded that "... the ultimate stuff of the universe is consciousness." Ultimate reality is contacted not through the physical sense of the material world, but through deep intuition. Such an idea of matter emerging out of human consciousness seems quite foreign to our Western mind because we have no experiences of altering matter by "will." However, there is growing evidence that in expanded consciousness, man has access to the primary reality of frequencies. Living is a transaction, an interaction with other force fields, with an element of choice. This is a domain beyond time, space, and mass where only vibrations exist.

Jahn and Dunne, in their book *Margins of Reality: The Role of Consciousness in the Physical World* have postulated a geometry of reality, the wave nature of consciousness, and the quantum mechanics of experiences. The major hypothesis of this model is that reality encompassing all aspects of experience, expression and behavior is constituted only at the interface between consciousness and its environment. It further presumes that the sole currency of any reality is information, which may flow in either direction. "...Consciousness may insert information into its environment as well as extract information from it." In a functional sense, information can be constituted by any array of stimuli that the consciousness is capable of sensing and reacting to. Numerous theorists are trying to recast quantum physics in terms of information theory.

"The symbolic nature of physics," according to Eddington, " ... is now formulated in such a way as to make it almost self-evident that it is a partial aspect of something wider." The shadow nature of physics' reality paradoxically leads many scientists toward metaphysics or a mystical view of the world, like so many of our pioneer thinkers: Bohm, Einstein, Heisenberg, Jung, Penfield, Eccles, Eddington and Schroedinger. Jahn and Dunne have quoted Charles' Third Law, "Any sufficiently advanced technology is indistinguishable from magic." "In science we do not explain things away, but we do get closer to the mystery." (Lewin).

Actually, science and mysticism cope with the same things—the broadest extension of reality. Both are processes of handling information, but each does it differently. Indeed, they glom on to different pieces of information while seeking to define what is most important in the world. One could view mysticism at one pole and science at the other, the two most important poles for understanding the universe. Science in the past has dealt with the commonest of man's experiences—a low level of information and order. Mysticism has dealt primarily with the highest, but not the commonest level, which gives credence to the divine order and man's spiritual nature. The greatest scientists of all time say that their experimentation is guided by mystical, intuitive insight. For "when you've discovered the truth in science, it does have the most extraordinary magical quality about it." (Lewin).

A Russian cubist painter, Matyuskin, wrote in his diary, "When at last we shall rush rapidly past objectiveness, we shall probably see the totality of the whole world."

CHAPTER IV

FIELD TRANSACTIONS:
The Biosphere - Cosmosphere Connection

Cosmic and atmospheric sciences have produced a sizeable body of research about the nature of the universe. But similar research in bio-sciences has lagged far behind. Understandably, it is much easier to study the cosmos out there than to study it in here—within our own bodies where emotions confound things.

Modern instruments have made microcosmic tissue information available, but to date biology has not attended to the extensive macroscopic field information of the body. Of course, until recently there have been no models or research techniques to guide us. Now the recent expansion of chaos and complexity theories and the use of fractal mathematics to test these, have set the stage for definitive studies of macroscopic field patterns of the human body. As a physiologist, my research connects the body with the cosmosphere, not by physiological reactions but through field transactions. The aim is to bridge the chasms between the cosmic facts, the body field interaction and the resulting human experience.

Each of us carries our own elaborate biosphere within our tissues and fields. What do we know about our biosphere? We enter the world equipped with five senses with which we perceive the world around and within us and from which we create an ordinary, everyday reality for living. Do you realize that you cannot see anything without seeing your own body first? Notice that your nose is in the middle of every view. Likewise, you cannot hear sound without also hearing the vibrations of your own body.

I became acutely aware of these realities when I first studied the auric field in a near sound-sterile environment of the Anaechoic Room at UCLA. In this windowless room, sound is absorbed so rapidly that even speech is muffled and inaudible. Uneven baffles project from the walls, ceiling, and the sliding door of this huge room. The floor is an elevated grate covering floor baffles. There is no natural or electrical lighting to give electromagnetic energy—we used flashlights.

Three scientists and one artist meditated in that room for several hours to prepare for testing our auric fields after such sensory deprivation. As described in Chapter II, each of us had the same profound sense of three pulsing electrical rhythms inside our bodies—rhythms we had not experienced before. Each of the three rhythms had a unique frequency pattern and tone, which we surmised were rhythms of our neurological, circulatory and neuromuscular systems that we generally do not perceive.

This reminded me that every sound we hear coming from the outside world also contains the sounds of the living physical body. Likewise, everything we touch contains the sensation of our hand which touches. And every odor we smell, even that which is transported through the air from a distance, is perceived through the odor of our own bodies. In other words, our primary reference to the world is our physical body, and from these bodily sensations we create a reality in which our body is constantly present.

With this in mind, when we consider relating to the cosmos

experiencing higher levels of human consciousness, we recognize a very practical problem. We are locked into average sensory information from the material world, which is then filtered through a physical-body oriented perception. As a result, most people need to be re-educated in order to sense the more subtle vibrations of the cosmic world.

Not only are single sensations perceived through the physical body, but a permanent "body image," a holistic body referent, is completely developed some time between the ages five and seven. This general body image is composed of all the memories of living, moving, feeling, and sensing our bodies in every situation. It makes possible complex language, fine motor coordination, and conceptual thinking, all of which are retained in the form of images in the brain. Although these images change and expand with time and experience, the body image remains the primary image which one carries into all new experiences. It definitely binds us into the ordinary functional reality of our world.

The telereceptors, senses of sight, smell and sound, bring in "out there" information about the physical world at a gross level. But it is the "sixth sense" coming from the human field, the finest of all senses, which gives us the elaborate, distant knowledge about the happenings in the cosmosphere. This will be discussed in this chapter.

Because I personally experience the vibrations of the macrocosm and research its subtle transactions, I am amazed to read that cosmologists believe that all interactions between the human and the cosmos take place in the human brain. Obviously, when we try to understand how the energy of the universe interacts with that of the body, brain waves seem to be the primary connection. That is, of course, because biologists have not understood the real source of the body's energy field. I reject the idea that vibrations of the universe interface with our body vibrations solely through the brain waves, because currently recorded brain waves are composed primarily of vibrations of from zero to 24 cycles per second. Such a limited spectrum cannot possibly process the extensive information from the universe. This is not a grand enough scale.

Why are there not better biological parameters to describe our relationship to the cosmos? Simply, physiology has restricted its research to the physiological systems discovered many years ago. The current physical models in biology and medicine encourage studies in the interrelationship of cardiovascular, muscular, neural, and endocrine systems. Biochemistry and psychoneuroendo-crinology look for the environmental effects of temperature, pressure, and contamination on systems, tissues, and fluids. With such a restricted model, there is no reference to the fields of living tissue nor to those of the cosmos.

Let us look at the exciting new findings from physics that relate directly to the biological and physical universe. The concept of the hologram was a major discovery. A hologram is a three-dimensional representation, a picture, that can be created of any object. The holographic picture is possible when a laser beam, a coherent energy source, while focussed on an object, is separated into two beams by a beam splitter—a piece of glass with one half mirrored and the other half clear glass. When the laser beam hits the mirrored part, the light is reflected off to one side. The other part of the beam goes through the clear glass and hits the object directly. If the object is at an angle to the reflected beam, the energy from the beam will pick up all three dimensions of that object. When both the reflected image and the direct one are projected onto a photographic plate, a three-dimensional picture is created. Actually, the hologram is not visible until another beam of coherent light is projected again onto the photograph. The resultant image is like a stereoscopic view, as though one could walk around the picture.

A revealing aspect of this true hologram is that every part of it is a total representation of every other part. For example, if the hologram picture were projected on a piece of glass, and that glass were broken into a million pieces, each little piece, regardless of how small, would contain a total representation of the object—thus the name "hologram." Again, each tiny part of an object carries a complete picture of the entire object.

Pribram, a neurophysicist at Stanford, explored the idea that human memory is present throughout the entire brain rather than being located in any single part of the brain. After the discovery of the hologram, he concluded that the brain is also a hologram with each part carrying a representation of all of it.

Such a far-reaching idea won Pribram a Nobel Prize and gave us a new understanding of why people can remember things believed impossible when parts of the brain are destroyed. They are remembering from the entire brain hologram, not from the information believed stored only in specific cellular areas. Also, a holographic brain memory is a perfect template to explain dramatic neurological recoveries, or to provide a pattern for the regeneration of organs.

At the same time that Pribram was describing the brain hologram, Bohm, an English physicist, advanced a cosmos hologram model, contending that every single part, every unit of the cosmos, carries a representation of all cosmic happenings. Thus he described a cosmic memory as a hologram. It follows, then, that if we accept that the human brain contains a personal memory hologram, and that there is also a cosmic hologram of the memory of everything that has happened in the universe, and if we accept that we are a part of the cosmos, then there must exist some kind of scientifically testable interface between these two holograms.

Concurrently, an experimental physicist, Bob Beck, believed that the mystical state of psychics and clairvoyants while they were at work somehow related to the brain waves. He developed sensitive instruments that he used to record the brain waves of proven mystics. When he processed these data, he found that their brain waves during their mystical work were 7.8 cycles per second, plus or minus 1/100th of a cycle. This particular frequency reminded him of the research about the Shumann resonance.

Shumann, a German living in the early 1930s, discovered a

magnetic field that thrust upward from the earth rather than downward, as does the gravitational field. Beck reckoned that the great "hot spots," the historical power areas of the world such as Stonehenge, the pyramids, Delphi, and others, probably had strong Shumann-type vibrations. Many people have had unusually profound experiences at these locations, which are revered as reservoirs of great truths. Mystics have attested to an increased power source radiating from the ground at these power spots. Shumann recorded this resonance as between seven and eight cycles per second. Beck found it to be 7.8 cycles within one-five-hundredth of a cycle, exactly the frequency he recorded from the brain waves of mystics.

To summarize: Three outstanding contemporary scientists produced similar information from different approaches. Bohm, a physicist, stated that the cosmos is a hologram containing all the information about the world. A neurophysicist, Pribram, believed that the brain is likewise a hologram of the memory of human experience. Beck, a physicist engineer, found that when persons who possess extrasensory capacities for knowing about past, present, and future events are "tuned in," their brain waves are 7.8 cycles per second.

From these concepts, together with the information about the earth's resonance of 7.8 cycles per second, a vibratory field which contains data about all the events that have taken place around the world, a powerful new idea emerges. The biosphere and cosmosphere can be viewed as two massive holographic computers doing more than their own isolated work, for they are referenced, plugged together by a frequency of 7.8 cycles per second. This is the interface—the tuning mechanism. But in order to understand the interaction, we need an extended model of human biology, one which makes it possible to intertwine and interpret the fields of energy generated in both the cosmos and biosphere. Let me describe how current research supports such an idea.

All material substances are composed not only of observable

matter, but also of more subtle field components with organized energy patterns, boundaries, and definitions. The deeper one probes into physical substance, the more one encounters the underlying electrical energy or the energy field. All material substances—trees, dishes or animals—have fields because they all are composed of particles, atoms, and cells. Each of these fields is in constant dynamic equilibrium.

The less dense a substance, the more energetic the field with a greater potential to create a force. Living things are the least dense. (Pasteur found that electrical polarization distinguishes living from dead matter even though the chemical compositions were identical). Because fields are not random but are highly organized, they have their own integrity, vitality and life, different from, and therefore able to interact with other fields.

For some years the cosmic and ionic fields have been clearly described, but not the bio-field. We acknowledge that at the microscopic level of all cells there is a tightly composed energy system capable of transactions with other energy systems. But we have failed to recognize that the composite field also has its own integrity which differs from its parts.

Not until we investigated practices of Eastern medicine and acupuncture did we give serious attention to human energy fields. Still, Western science does not consider the human auric field a credible area for research. If one cannot see the aura and discussion of it is couched in unfamiliar language from other cultures, one doubts its value. Ancient writings claiming that chakras are the auric field source with meridian pathways the circulation route do not fit snugly into the current understanding from structural anatomy. Nonetheless, the few who have chosen to research this uncharted human field area discover facts unique to living fields that also correspond to universal laws. The human field looms as primary to life.

Resonating frequencies are primary physical bonds in nature. For every frequency or frequency band, there exists natural or created resonators. In other words, a field's frequency pattern at a given time is a resonating structure that determines the energy it will absorb or by which it will be affected. Theoretically, all frequency vibrations exist in the universe (which includes the body)—from sub hertzian to as high as modern instruments can measure—billions and trillions of cycles per second. Nonetheless, each material substance, living or inert, mineral or chemical, has its own vibratory signature carried in the structure of its field. There are dominant and recessive vibrations in each field, giving it character. Field interactions result from the strength and pattern of these field vibrations. These constitute windows, or thoroughfares for transactions.

A sound general principle states that interaction between fields occurs when there are compatible harmonic frequencies. Yet this is not always the case with human fields. I have recorded transactions taking place between people with mathematically dissimilar dominant fields in which the prevalent frequencies differed and should not have resonated. Yet they did. Likewise, I have found others who appeared to have a perfect resonating compatibility and yet the fields did not interact. Possibly these fields dynamically shift so rapidly that transactions are unpredictable, or perhaps a similar frequency pattern is out of phase and leads to nothing. Also, there is something about a living field that even though plugged into the 7.8 cycles per second circuitry of the universe, is not passive, but an active agent. There is a strange attraction or repulsion of fields which may result from the surface electrical potential at the boundary of each field, or from the fine organization of a chaos pattern which has not been decoded.

On the practical side, new frequency generators still being tested show great promise for treating disease. Specific generated frequencies introduced into the feet for a short time apparently can counteract viral and other disease frequencies. One researcher found that the frequency programs of most of these healing generators was nearly identical to some of the upper harmonics of the Shumann resonance, 7.83 cycles per second. Likewise, the dominant frequency patterns of "healers" when healing was closely correlated with Shumann harmonics. This raises the question: is the Shumann resonance a universal vibration—the key to the primary harmonic resonance of our planet? And, does the extensive increase in the electromagnetic atmosphere of the electronic age significantly change the harmonic properties of material substances and with it their resonating capacities? The science of field constellations is too young to provide adequate answers, but it does seem clear that we live in a sea of force fields all being absorbed and altered by the human mind. (See Chapter V, "Emotions, the Mind Field Organizer").

Sources of universal electromagnetism exist at all levels of nature because chemicals, minerals and atoms are the same wherever they are found. When the tiny mass of an electron spins around the nucleus of an atom, a magnetic field is created by its spin. Even the center of the atom is said to contain a crystal in the magnetic domain. All living tissues contain magnetism from iron in the cells. Magnetic flow at the nerve synapses transports electrical signals down nerve routes. This natural magnetism inside the living tissue is directly influenced by the prevalent electromagnetism of gravity.

Furthermore, gravity seems to lower the body frequencies toward the red spectrum, particularly in the feet and the lower body. The higher frequencies in the atmosphere seem to occur more often in the upper body or head. Such patterns are considered "normal" on Earth. The classic case of "ungroundedness" with decreased electromagnetic energy in the lower body, often resulting from meditation and high thoughts, can be improved by increased earth vibrations—barefoot walking on the ground, gardening, lying on the beach, entering caves or being near volcanoes. Tapping into the red end of the light spectrum grounds the human electromagnetic field. Bacteria use their magnetism to create their own north and south poles, to orient themselves and to swim to light and food. Pigeons and bees direct their flight by a magnetic substance contained in their heads and bodies. In humans, magnetism from iron in hemoglobin may account for our directional sixth sense.

Wherever there are strong electrical forces released in our environment, large magnetic fields are created. Today in this electronic age, the electromagnetic energy of the environment is the strongest, highest and richest in the history of our planet. Electromagnetism is spewed out constantly by the radio and TV stations, high tension lines, industrial electronics, the many electrical household appliances such as microwaves, heaters, coolers, dryers, moisturizers and ionizers, as well as the convenience gadgets we acquire to save time and to entertain ourselves.

While most reports point out the destructive aspects of electronic contamination, I believe that there are both positive and negative effects. To adapt to a more volatile electronic soup, a higher vibrational mix, challenges the human field to broaden its spectrum. This increased complexity in turn facilitates higher consciousness encouraging flights into the ether which enhance both creativity and a healthy sense of escape.

On the other hand, unsuccessful adaptation to higher levels of environmental electromagnetism always leaves an incoherent random field, one in which the edge of chaos has been exceeded, leading to turmoil.

Of all animals, it is the human who gravitates toward stress; it taxes the organization of his field and in positive cases, leads to greater coherency and higher refinement. If one does not respond successfully to stressful simulation, the body suffers—probably first in the energy field with anti-coherent patterns. It behooves us, therefore, to recognize that the health of the electromagnetic field is critical because this leads to the health or disease of the entire biological system. Emphasis on clean air, food, water, rest and exercise are incomplete without retuning and strengthening our energy fields.

Let us look into the positive side of electromagnetic enrichment. Remember Prigogine redefined and extended the second law of thermodynamics which states that all matter progresses from organization to disorganization and then to turmoil. According to this law, humans from birth progress to disorganization and finally to death. Everything is downhill. Prigogine found, however, that when energy was introduced into any field, its complexity increased with concomitant refinement. It did not disintegrate rapidly by entropy.

In human terms, when energy is introduced into the body, it becomes more complex and refined; it "moves" upward toward light and life, and away from death. Perhaps this helps to explain the long productive lives of symphony conductors, as well as how living tissue can regenerate. Becker found that by introducing energy with a frequency of 8 cycles per second into fractures and injuries, they healed more rapidly. Note again the similarity between the 8 cycles per second regenerative field, the 7.8 cycles per second of the mystic brainwave when channeling universal information, and the Shumann earth resonance. (See Chapter X: Healing, the Miracle of Life).

There are other practical examples of increased production of living organisms in heightened energy fields. Crashing waves deliver a mammoth amount of energy to shoreline plants and animals—energy estimated to be as much as 15 times greater than that provided by the sun. Proceedings from the Tropical Research Institute of the National Academy of Science disclosed that abundant wave energy allows marine organisms, algae and mussel beds to maintain exceptionally high productivity—even greater than that which occurs in the rain forests. The report concluded that wave action facilitates the flow of light and nutrients, an important contribution to the overall richness of this type of environment. To take a step further, we have known that tumbling water produces negative ion particles and amps up the electromagnetic pool. No wonder a day at the beach is so invigorating!

Earth vibrations carry coded information. For example, underground water, whether moving or pooled, is sensed by dowsers. In rocky areas with surface strata, powerful earth vibrations often create vectors or "hot spots" from several energy sources. People gravitate there. In active volcanic areas one may sense the strong electromagnetic pulses predominantly in the lower red spectrum. The gravity of the earth also pulses based on lunar tides.

Trees seem to structure direct earth vibrations to create their own energy matrix. A group of sensitives at an old ranch deep in a natural forest studied how the shapes of living trees organize the air patterns in their immediate environment. During the study they meditated resting against different tree trunks. Gnarled, ancient apple trees and dwarfed, crooked pines at timber line emitted a gentle twist; the energy spiraled as it flowed upward. Great lofty pines exerted a strong energy suction upward, causing the consciousness of the meditators to soar—a very different effect from that in the full, contained richness of the field inside a greenhouse. They discovered that symmetrical trees planted in rows and closely growing lodgepole saplings create a lattice-like field of energy that jumps and leaps, as contrasted to the flowing patterns of isolated trees. The lattice-like field, while strong and stimulating, was too jumbled to be enjoyed for long.

Pesticides are known to produce chemical contaminants, but their effect upon energy fields is unknown. Perhaps hints are contained in insect infestation reports. When particular bugs or beetles begin to massively destroy one kind of tree, other trees become immune before they are attacked. They develop a chemical which expels insects. Apparently, either the insect vibrations alert the trees, or the already contaminated trees send out field warnings to other trees. Probably we could hasten the trees' defenses by recording the insects' fields and broadcasting this into target trees—a field vaccination to encourage a tree's immune response. This should be more effective than trying to poison insects with sprays or systemic chemicals. Insect vibration generators do exist, which can directly combat infestations without harm to plants or animals. They are not extensively used because of governmental complacency and successful lobbying by large chemical companies.

We have learned that microwave ovens create a wave vibrating at between 3 and 11 megahertz, millions of cycles per second. When the microwave is introduced to the double helix of the genetic code, it resonates directly. This means that the important information center in body cells has a direct affinity to microwave frequencies. Although we cannot predict a result, when microwave power increases in the atmosphere, the body must either adapt or suffer destructive consequences.

It appears that the fields of once-living fibers are more compatible with human vibrations than are the fields of synthetic fibers. The demand for natural fibers—cotton, wool, and silk fabrics—increases as people opt for comfort at the expense of convenience.

At a large health fair, we performed a simple test to determine the immediate effects of fabrics, chemicals and electromagnetic radiation on the strength of muscle. We selected four volunteers from the audience, one man and one woman who were vegetarians, drank no alcohol, wore natural fabrics and were meditators. The other man and woman were meat eaters, drank alcohol, wore synthetic clothes and did not meditate. We brought each person separately into an area which we contaminated by operating television, microwave oven, computers and fluorescent lights. We dressed them in synthetic clothing and asked them to sit in a chair covered with synthetic fiber placed on a synthetic rug. Then we further contaminated the atmosphere by introducing paint remover, ammonia, bleach and fingernail polish remover into the environment while we sprayed hairspray and aerosol air freshener nearby.

We then tested the strength of one shoulder muscle group using a Cibex computerized dynamometer which flashed the actual foot pounds that those muscles could generate before, during and after contamination. In each instance, the strength of the muscles dropped one-quarter to one-half during contamination. When the contaminated field was blown out by fans, the muscle strength returned but not to the pretest level. However, when we played a tape of the actual recordings[*] of the sound of the human aura, a coherent field, the muscle strength increased to a higher foot poundage than was generated during the pretest. To protect oneself from immediate sources of toxic chemicals is essential and somewhat automatic. But toxic field vibrations are probably equally as harmful and are much more insidious.

It is not just the random free chemical contaminants that affect the human field; of greater importance are the localized contaminants from chemicals stored in the houses. A comprehensive, five-year study by Harvard University and the United States Environmental Protection Agency concluded that, "... your home sweet home is a toxic waste hazard greater than the Love Canal or a chemical plant or dump site next door." They chose for their study Bayonne and Elizabeth, New Jersey, both highly industrialized areas with an abundance of petrochemical substances in the environment, and Greensboro, North Carolina, and Devil's Lake, Idaho, pristine areas without industry and thought to be clean. The report disclosed that most people spend an average of between 21 to 23 hours per day inside a building, so that whatever the contamination that exists inside has a more pronounced effect than the air outside.

Using sophisticated techniques, they sampled the air around the subjects as they moved about the rooms. Next, they sampled the air in the yards outside these buildings. Over 350 air samples were taken in each city. They also analyzed blood, urine and breath samples. Their conclusions were revealing:

Persons who live in close proximity to industrial contamination or even right next door to industrial plants have no greater exposure or bodily contamination than those who live far

[*]Available from Bioenergy Fields Foundation, P.O. Box 4234, Malibu, CA 90265, (310) 457-4694

away or in pristine environments. Finally, they concluded that the indoor field levels of target chemicals were at least 100 times greater than outdoor levels, regardless of the location where the samples were taken. Levels of contamination were equal in all four locations.

The American Cancer Society acknowledges that geomagnetic forces affect the incidence of cancer: near the North Pole and near high tension electrical sources, the incidence is much higher. They do not conclude, however, as do some researchers, that cancer is an electromagnetic disturbance. W. Ross Adey, of Loma Linda University in California, an eminent neurophysiologist, said that electromagnetic fields may cause static in the electrical broadcasts from one cell to another, assisting cancer cells in confusing normal cell development.

Santa Ana winds and atmospheric changes disturb many sensitives. When positive ions in the atmosphere replace the negative auric ions, the field is weakened and becomes ungrounded. I observed a prime example of this when a small group of us crossed the Alta Plano, a 15,000 foot high desert in southern Peru. We had ridden a train to the remote Lake Titicaca, the highest and largest lake in the world. While we were there, a revolutionary group had captured the rail lines and threatened the small city. At night we escaped by caravan across the high desert in old, ill-equipped cars which left the city at different times so as not to arouse the suspicion of the guerrillas.

I was in the first car, which was to await the others at the end of the ascent. Soon after we arrived, two women, one a prior cardiac patient, went into extreme cardiac distress. We placed them on the ground, propped them up, and watched as their conditions worsened. In desperation, I checked their electromagnetic fields and found totally incoherent, ungrounded states. The fear of the situation and the altitude had sent them into this altered state. By verbally assuring them, by laying-on hands on their feet, and teaching them breathing techniques to stabilize their fields, they quite rapidly returned to normal.

Planetary electrical storms can suddenly shock the human field. A large group of scientists was attending an international medical meeting in Madras, India, when at 2:00 a.m. some were awakened by a strong electrical shock. I sat bolt upright breathing rapidly, with palpitations, acute awareness, and a red explosive image before my eyes. Some described fear; I felt euphoric, for I was sure that the source was inter-planetary and not Earth. The cause eluded us until we returned to the states to learn that this was when the vibrations of the 1987 super nova explosion reached the Earth. Although the clock time differed on opposite sides of the Earth, the shock was identical, and so was the human response.

Let me reiterate a guiding principle of biocosmic interaction. Whenever there is sufficient energy along with compatible frequencies, patterns, and phases in the human electromagnetic range, a transaction can take place. A classic example occurred when I was on a cruise to Antarctica. During our first day at sea, I had the impulse to conduct an experiment with the passengers. I knew about the strong magnetic field of the South Pole from reading about experiments with single-celled animals. I wondered how humans would react. Although I had no preconceived ideas about what would happen in the body, I did anticipate that we would experience higher consciousness states with glorious mystical imagery.

I had not taken electronic equipment, but I did have a pendulum—a crystal ball affixed to a string which had been validated in the laboratory to show field motion when I held it over chakras. Generally, the ball would circumscribe a large or small circle, clockwise or counterclockwise, or create an elliptical circle. Or it would take a two-dimensional path back and forth, a north and south excursion in areas of pain, prior injuries or functional disturbances. Occasionally, it would remain stationary.

With this understanding, I enlisted 80 men and women, cruise members, volunteers, residents of all inhabited continents, ranging in age from 15 to 80. Although these passengers were a bit older than a normal sample of the population, of high economic status and very experienced travelers, in all other respects, they seemed to be average people. I pretested their fields with the crystal ball in the latitude of Buenos Aires. We had stopped to observe King penguins at the now famous Falkland Islands directly east of Buenos Aires. The findings were ordinary: exactly what I had found in laboratory electronic tests. Most women displayed little or no energy in the legs and thighs, with strong head activity and asymmetrical energies throughout the body, an electromagnetically ungrounded condition. The men showed strong fields in the legs and thighs, with uneven energy in the body and less in the head. There were apparently no racial or ethnic differences.

But interestingly, four men, displayed perfect fields—strong and circular in all chakra areas. Later I learned that they were our guides, and that they had traveled this Antarctic route for three months. Five days later, as we neared the Antarctic Circle, I retested the group, both on ship and again on the narrow, frozen, pebbly beaches where we landed by Zodiac craft. The results of this second test were more surprising. There was increased energy in all chakras and major joints, and the crystal ball pathway was not circular as it was during pretesting; now, it traversed a two-dimensional, back and forth path indicating an increased magnetic field from more powerful north-south poles. Furthermore, everyone had the same pattern, differing only in intensity or how far up the body the energy continued. Because it diminished in the upper body, the energy appeared to originate in the feet. I observed also that no one fell down, despite the slipperiest terrain one could imagine. Nothing seemed stable, even the smallest shore rocks were covered in moss; the large boulders were slick with penguin excrement. Ice lay in between. We disembarked by wading through water full of seaweed and walked on snow fields and ice floes. Our bulky clothing and huge boots caused us to waddle like the penguins. Furthermore, no one walked cautiously as we focused on photographing birds and sea lions. Nonetheless, our coordination was superb.

Why we were not injured was even more difficult to understand. Often we returned to the ship in landing craft when waves were so high that we were literally thrown to the gangplank to be caught by crew members. On one particularly rough day, I recalled the experiment in the Mu Room where our coordination improved dramatically when in an increased magnetic field. Did the naturally rich magnetic field of the South Pole also improve our coordination? Probably.

Likewise, I also noted that none of the passengers got ill on the cruise as one might expect when older people engaged in what was for them vigorous exercise while overeating and drinking. (Of course, there were no germs there except what we took with us). I questioned the ship's doctor about my observations. He confirmed that the passengers were healthier and had fewer complaints during the Antarctic cruises. We discovered that chronic problems were almost absent in this environment. In fact, some passengers remarked that they remained on this ship, tour after tour, throughout the Antarctic summertime because this was the only place where they felt totally healthy.

When our ship approached the tip of South America on its return voyage two weeks later, I retested the field. The Antarctic pattern, a two-dimensional north-south path of the crystal ball, remained. Several weeks hence, while five of us were in Peru and again in Los Angeles, I retested this small group to find that now their fields were flowing evenly throughout their entire bodies in a clockwise circle—a perfect pattern. This was not the case with any of the passengers before or during the Antarctic cruise. Now it was apparent that my early deduction gave additional weight to the idea that electromagnetic environments in which we live powerfully affect our biological fields. I recalled again the work of Robert Becker who introduced magnetic current into body tissue to hasten healing. I remembered my laboratory study of "healers" who when healing, generated a stronger magnetic current. Obviously, the magnetic energy of the South Pole had a healing effect upon the chronic backaches, insomnia, prostatic and cardiovascular difficulties of the ship's passengers, at least diminishing the symptoms.

Sensitive people often complain about the noise and crowd contamination of large groups and conventions. I believe that these scattered, yet concentrated, energy fields are more debilitating than the actual decibel level of the noise. Because we respond so immediately to human field happenings, these can push us past the dynamic edge of chaos into a disintegrating anti-coherent field.

A perfect example of such contamination occurred in the laboratory one day when a national TV crew came to shoot a broadcast film. They brought nine technicians with an array of lights, cameras and power generators, and of course, their own individual energy fields. By the odor of the alcohol still on their breaths and their groggy states, they had apparently been entertained at a party the night before.

As the crew set up their equipment, we prepared to instrument a person's energy field for direct on-line filming of the oscilloscope and the computer displays. To our amazement, a glitch occurred in our equipment. We could not obtain a signal. I asked the crew to turn off their equipment, for I surmised that their video lights and generators overloaded our instruments. Still the energy field signal was absent. Then I asked them to leave their equipment on while they went outside the room and down the hall. This was a strange request that worked. In a few minutes, the normal field recordings occurred. When the crew returned and approached the subject, the recording signal failed again.

We had had enough experience studying human field transactions to realize that the problem was not incompatible instruments, but rather incompatible human fields—a sensitive subject and a contaminated crew—or even possibly a field reaction from sensitive staff. We circumvented the problem by playing old data tapes where there was no new human interaction.

I believe that all diseases are caused by a break in the flow or a disturbance in the human energy field. Eventually, this disturbance is transferred to the organ system creating functional, and ultimately, destructive changes. By the time the organ systems are involved, degenerative changes are occurring.

In the future, it should be possible to diagnose field disturbances and to treat them months or even years before they are manifested in the physical tissue. We should be able to increase normal biotissue growth in healing by using the normal vibrational fields of the universe, for example, by replicating the powerful, yet harmless, field of the Antarctic. The fields of the South Pole, emanating from a land mass separated by water from other land masses, are apparently more powerful than the fields of the North Pole which are generated over water. There are probably other important field differences. The South Pole has been called the "hot pole," or the "female pole," where energy flows up to the North Pole. On the other hand, the field of the North Pole may have positive healing effects of its own.

Let me return to my initial comments about the relationship of the human energy field to the outside cosmic and ionic fields. Because it is easier to study the world out there than the world here inside us, information about the fields of the universe has advanced beyond those of the human energy field, or our understanding of field transactions.

At the cutting edge of biological science is the understanding of vibrations and the transactions of fields. Here is information currently beyond total comprehension but from which will spring a new biosphere/cosmosphere model, a wedding of the world micro- and macrocosms, a true understanding of bio-complexity in action. I have accepted a challenge to try to understand the mind aspects of our field where we decode field information. It is in this arena, that by our actions, we can change our internal and external worlds.

I would like to close on a slightly metaphysical note. There is an imaginative study of predictions reported by Wilson in his book, *Cosmic Trigger*. A group of computer scientists from Stanford University were fascinated with the tremendous explosion of technological development and scientific knowledge coming into the world today. Because they were adept in programming computers to answer intriguing questions, they decided to categorize and chronologically plot the great technologic and scientific discoveries in the world, starting from the beginning of urbanization at about 4,000 or 5,000 B.C.

They traced developments such as the discovery of the wheel, the printing press, the steam engine, splitting of an atom, and computers.

As they surveyed the computer printout, the discoveries fell into a hyperbolic curve which flattened out at the top at about 1975. At the speed at which these discoveries were occurring, they requested that the computer project into the future and predict the great upcoming discoveries. The projected pattern took a sudden upsweep and went completely off the computer graph at the year 2011. This was the end of the computer's predictions.

During the last thirty minutes of the year 2010, the computer predicted 18 discoveries that equalled the splitting of the atom. While the specialists were amused, they could not understand. Suddenly, one of the researchers recalled the Mayan calendar, which ends at 2011. This date, according to the Mayans, is the end of the Fifth Age of Man, the Age of the Intellect, and the beginning of the Sixth Age of Man, the Age of the Gods!

I believe we are leaving the Fifth Age of Man, the age of our great intellectual development, a development of our magnificent capacity for higher reasoning, creating and manifesting our greatest abilities into a world of material things. I hope and trust that we lose none of these profound skills and abilities as we move into the power and wisdom of the Sixth Age of Man, the Divine Age of God.

CHAPTER V

MIND FIELD:
The Residence Of Consciousness And The Soul

Have you ever thought that your mind played tricks on you, soaring too high for comfort, or getting you into trouble with commitments you thought you did not want—keeping you in the dark, like it had its own remote existence?

It is interesting to notice the language we use when discussing our minds. We don't say "I am a busy mind," but rather, "I have a busy mind," or "my mind feels slow," "dull," or "so forgetful I think I'm losing it." When people think narrowly, we comment about their rigid, unexercised, or unimaginative minds. Those who challenge our traditions we label as radical minds. On the days when everything works, we tap into our creative minds.

These comments indicate deep beliefs that there is some master operator someplace who runs us and our lives, occasionally letting us glimpse the master plan, but rarely soliciting our advice. The "I" both enjoys and has difficulty with what we call mind.

When we refer to our minds, we gesture to our heads.

Everyone knows that mind resides in the skull. Science and logic tell us that if the mind is encased in the head's bony cave, then it must be a closed, imprisoned system to be understood only by microscopic study of brain tissue.

Controversies about the mind have existed since the early Greek philosophers argued about the nature of the mind-body relationship. None of these disputes has been solved even today, although we have shifted the emphasis to the brain-mind connection. Not that the ancients had a lesser idea about the mind than we have today, but without brain research they did not attempt to explain the mind as a brain phenomenon.

Let us examine these early philosophical ideas about the mind that are still with us today.

Pythagoras commented many centuries ago that the mind is a substantial reality and somehow it exists in the body, but not in the head. Plato, like Pythagoras, thought that the mind was an important entity inside the body which separated from the body at death. He likened mind to the soul that brought life to the non-living body.

Socrates stressed the separation of mind and body, commenting that mental things occur in a non-physical environment.

To illustrate the mind's uniqueness, Aristotle said that he believed it was possible to have thought with no brain, but he did not think that one could walk without legs or hear without ears. He guessed that the mind was in the brain, but he felt that studying the brain as an organ did not answer questions about the mind.

Rene Descartes, the eminent French mathematician and philosopher, reactivated the controversy, taking a strong stand that mind and body were not the same.

John Dewey, around the turn of the century, expounded the educational importance of the whole person's experience, which he justified by a belief that the mind is everywhere in the body.

Wilhelm Reich further strengthened the belief in the unity of mind and body by noting that memory of traumatic episodes is stored in body cells. Physical therapists have discovered that deep joint and skeletal massage does in fact release memories of emotional episodes.

William James, the father of psychology, reiterated his conviction that the ultimate problems of man came from the mind-brain connection. Such thoughts contained in the extensive writing on psychosomatic illness early in the century cemented the belief in a cause and effect relationship between emotions and body malfunctions. Here, authors professed a mind-body unity for which there was growing evidence from the new Gestalt ideas promoting the "wholeness" of behavior. The mind directly affected the body, and vice versa. Furthermore, the cause and effect logic of the oneness of mind and body required that the mind be located in the body.

Neurologists located the mind in the brain. By electrical stimulation of brain cells, researchers were able to chart for the first time the functional contributions of various brain areas to sensation, movement, affective behavior and recall of sensory experience. Surgical destruction of animal brain tissue and brain surgery left motor-sensory disturbances and often caused loss of memory of both animate and inanimate objects. Observations of behaviors following cerebral strokes, brain injuries and tumors showed alterations not only in motor performance, but in thought, memory, emotions and awareness—all thought to be mind functions.

Prefrontal lobotomies, severing hemisphere connection, and other brain surgery were used to cure acute persistent emotional disturbances. These many findings tightened the knot of proof that mind and brain were synonymous. It became very clear that the brain is a specialized body tissue with the unique functions of the mind. Obviously, it seemed the mind and brain were therefore identical.

Nonetheless, along with the mounting evidence of the oneness of mind and brain, there were growing observations to the contrary. Neurological research showed that electrical stimulation did not activate what was considered to be the higher mind. Researchers concluded that there is no neurophysiological research which conclusively shows that the higher levels of mind are located in brain tissue.

When parts of the brain are stimulated, there is a perturbation that the person becomes aware of as emotions or feelings. If we believe that it is the brain stimulus which causes this experience, it follows that it must be the brain which is also aware of the experience. I believe that such proof of the mind-brain's oneness is a result of faulty logic. That which causes something to happen is not the same as the consciousness which experiences the happening. Furthermore, not all conscious awareness should be lumped together. Although some levels of awareness occur in the brain, higher levels of consciousness have not been found there. To the contrary, some philosophers surmised that consciousness is on a continuum from material to non-material reality in which the mind is always involved, sensing non-material happenings primarily, while the brain taps the material ones.

You may ask whether these arguments about the unity or separation of mind-body are simply academic questions. My answer is an adamant "no"—as we have already determined, you think and operate as you believe. If quantum mechanics cannot be understood by mechanical theories, so the higher mind of man cannot be comprehended by neurochemical brain studies.

Early in this century, Sir Arthur Sherrington, the leading neurologist and one of the primary voices of dissent, allied himself with the ancients' view that the mind, thought and feelings were difficult to bring into the class of physical things. He doubted that the mind and body were one.

Karl Pribram, the Nobel Prize winner for his brain hologram research, commented that the holographic images that we see are existing in the mind somewhat outside of the brain machine that produces these—as though the mind hovers like a protective entity beyond the brain's machinery.

Three eminent contemporary neurophysiologists, Penfield,

Eccles, and Granit all agreed that there is nothing in the brain to account for the high level of experiences and capabilities of the mind. They further qualified these higher capacities as intuition, insight, creativity, imagination, understanding, thought, reasoning, intent, decision, knowing, will, spirit, or soul. These are the mysteries of the mind that have been relegated to psychiatrists and theologians, because we believed that they do not lend themselves to scientific study.

Penfield became the most convincing spokesman as he extended the concept of mind to a distinct reality. In his provocative book, *Mysteries of the Mind*, Penfield shared with his readers his experiences and thoughts as he created the brain charts still used today. After studying with the pioneer neurophysiologist Sherrington early in the century, Penfield became an eminent neurosurgeon specializing in the treatment of epilepsy. During the latter part of his career, after many observations, he still claimed that the mind was an entity within itself, although he did not know where it existed or where the energy of the mind came from. He accepted, but with some doubt, that the active brain neurons supplied the mind with energy when the brain was awake—but on that basis the mind should have no energy and be inoperative when the brain was asleep or during anaesthetic. Except, he knew also that people can remember what happened when the brain was dormant. He sensed that the mind operated as though it were endowed with its own energy. As he pondered the source of mind energy, he wondered also how one could account for a soul when the nerves of the body died and with them all energy dissipated.

Penfield found that during anaesthesia the human mind continued to work in spite of the brain's inactivity. The brain waves were found to be nearly absent while the mind was just as active as it was in normal states. Here the mind experienced everything that happened during the surgery, contrary to the belief that this was impossible. Upon coming out of the anaesthetic, the patient recalled even minor details about the surgery, including statements made by the surgical team while he was supposedly unconscious. Since Penfield's work, numerous other researchers have discovered total and acute awareness in comatose patients.

Penfield also discovered that the brain was predictable. A stimulated brain cell gave a consistent response. Stimulation of the cerebral cortex brought memory of early childhood experiences. These memories were as vivid as when the events had actually happened. (Such stimulation did not bring past life recall, however). (See Chapter IX, "Lifehoods: The Hidden Agenda"). He found, on the other hand, that the mind is totally unpredictable by any known criteria.

He likened the brain to a computer where the memory of man's experience is stored—more like a data bank for information retrieval. He strongly expressed the view that the brain is not the location where experiences are known or altered. Experiencing the world is an activity of the mind. Succinctly, Penfield concluded that "... it is the mind which experiences and it is the brain which records the experience." The brain can store memory, but it is the mind which makes decisions. The mind is independent and contains the will of man. In other words, the mind takes the initiative in exploring the environment. It enters into transactions and is aware of what is going on. The mind understands, comprehends, reasons and has judgment. It is aware of self.

Penfield offered illuminating accounts of the responses of 53 patients during an experiment in which he electrically stimulated their brain neurons during surgery under local anaesthesia. When primary sensory locations were stimulated, patients reported gross sensations or light flashes. But stimulating the neurons of the cerebral cortex provided dream-like experiences with flashbacks of long-forgotten episodes—memories of events in this life. His conclusion that the mind has no memory, or needs none with the effective brain memory bank, probably stemmed from his inability to find the mind's energy source, which he felt was essential for memory storage.

Although during his 30 years of intricate brain study Penfield did not solve the mind's mystery, he did clarify some cloudy issues. He taught us that the highest level of the mind contained the capacities of insight, imagination, creativity, and spirit that did not exist in brain tissue. Beyond that, he brought to our attention the mind's role in monitoring one's stream of consciousness; in fact, it IS the stream of consciousness. The mind is primary to thought.

A new group of studies declared that thought, feelings and dreams, all workings of the mind, are the product of chemical, electrical activity of nerve cells in the brain. This came from findings that perception, memory and self-awareness become scrambled when chemistry goes awry. These studies point to neurotransmitters as possible culprits in Alzheimer's disease, depression, schizophrenia, and other psychological disorders. While I acknowledge the soundness of this research, I urge that neurotransmitters not be misconstrued as the source of higher mind functions.

Today, more and more scientists are expressing doubts about the brain-mind model because it leaves unanswered so many questions about man's ordinary experiences, as well as evading his mystical, spiritual ones. Some say that philosophers and scientists operate by different sets of rules: the brain operates by physical laws and the mind by principles as yet undiscovered. But today we look to scientists more than ever before to interpret linear facts with higher wisdom. It is as though all scientists who visualize their unique research in the larger scheme of things owe the world their speculations about ultimate things: life and death, mind, consciousness and evolution.

One such scientist is Candace Pert who while with the National Institutes of Health, extensively researched neuropeptides. She disclosed that until recently she viewed the brain in Newtonian terms with the neurochemicals and their receptors operating like locks and keys. Now she visualizes the brain and its functions as a vibratory energy field with its locks and keys only ways of perturbing the field. The brain is no longer the end of the line—it is a receiver and amplifier of collective reality.

Hooper and Teresi in their book, *The Three Pound Universe: The Brain*, told about a neuroanatomist who was known for his methodological vigor pausing during his nerve cell study to comment, "I doubt we'll ever get to consciousness from here. Who knows if the mind is even in the brain." Along this same vein, a prominent pharmacologist said that we may find that the brain is unnecessary for consciousness.

Primarily, the brain has been studied in an airtight glass jar, a closed system; while we have tried to deduct from it an open system—the mind. Still, it is quite evident that the human mind is the enigma of our time. Of course, the mere acts of splitting and putting the mind and brain back together again is futile. I believe the evidence is clear. They differ—one is a physical entity, and the other is something beyond the physical state. Both inherently serve the body's existence, but not in the same way.

When a problem has remained unsolved for so many centuries, the approach and some of the fundamental tenets are probably incorrect. Our long-held basic premises about the mind are probably wrong because the linear, frontal attack has not answered many questions about the mind and human experience. New approaches loom where the mind is explored through extended realities, consciousness, different types of awareness, thought, and spiritual experiences.

To summarize: Some aspects of reality—the mind is one—cannot be explained in a material framework. Mind has energy since it causes things to happen. Many of the experiences that we casually attribute to mind are clearly brain functions: reflexes and responses to material reality that are recorded in and recovered from the brain. Other experiences and capacities such as thought, insight, imagination, and soul seem to be properties of the higher mind. The higher level mind seems to be outside the domain of material reality as we have been able to measure it. The mind is more a field reality, a quantum reality, or a particle reality.

The idea that the mind is unique from the brain and that it has its own consciousness which monitors awareness outside the realm of material reality intrigues me. The idea that the mind experiences non-physical reality quickly led to the thought of the mind as a field. Einstein stated that all the only reality is that of energy organized into fields. If all matter were disintegrated, we would be left with a field, the primary source.

Questions about the "location" of the mind during anaesthesia, coma, or in the last stages of Alzheimer's disease, in psychosis or trance states where it seems lost, could be answered by understanding the mind as a field. Is it possible that the long undetectable energy of the human mind springs from the electron energy of the body's atoms? Energy in this form, permeating all tissues, does not need to be conducted through the nervous system. The mind-field would then be a literal super-conductor. If the electron spin-off from the body atoms is the source of the mind's energy, then the mind might also reabsorb free electrons from the universe. Since there are no mechanical losses in such a system, the mind energy is literally recycled in the environment.

We already know that the mind is capable of energizing and communicating with matter, including the brain, the body, and other material things. Electromagnetic waves from the universe and those from the atomic structure of the body in field form could meet these requirements. At some level, all material boundaries are permeable. Electromagnetic energy in the form of waves constitutes information circuits which can penetrate physical boundaries and, like "worm holes," flow through and back into the environment. These qualities of an energy field also describe the mind, that is, the mind is beyond material substances yet interactive with them in an open system.

Yes, I believe the mind is infinite; it can be everywhere. The "Mind of the Universe" may be more than a metaphor. The human mind, if it wills, could have distinct contact with other fields now.

It could be here and there simultaneously. This agrees with the thoughts of Gregory Bateson, a cultural anthropologist, who saw mind as a set of relationships realized by the individual organism, but also by the social and ecological system. By the same token, there are individual, group and collective minds which likewise are embedded in the larger mind of the planetary ecosystem. Such reasoning concurs with my thoughts about the two massive holographic computers, the reservoirs of information and experience of man and cosmos that are interfaced by 7.82 cycles per second, giving them access to the same informational network. It is the mind, not the brain, which selects and reads from this informational pool, making partners of logical and conceptual thinking.

We know that the behavior of a purely mechanical system, like the steam engine, can be accurately predicted. Mind functions and field interactions are unpredictable. While both the mind and the brain can shift to "automatic pilot," we can predict only the function of the brain. With the mind, "automatic pilot" means only that there are degrees of probability in predicting function.

In the field, there is no immediate cause and effect as we know these, but rather meaningful coincidences or probabilities. Fields and minds are characterized by the unpredictability of chaotic dynamics. The mind with its vast complexity can explore far beyond a closed-circuit brain. Actually, attempts to understand the mind send us to research the nature of biological field transactions.

I recall the difficulty I had when thinking about material mass and the brain in non-material ways. From the beginning, I had the impulse to junk the old mechanistic ideas and to acknowledge mind as a field concept. As I edged toward a mind field model, my biological training made it hard for me to totally accept this new model as more than a theoretically sound thought exercise. I realized how difficult it is to believe that all the human experiences carried in a fluid, chemical brain cell are like a computer memory on a tiny chip. Think of the shock at first learning that the DNA, the genetic code of cells, carries extensive, basic instruction for the entire human organism, or that each cell carries a holographic replica of all cell groupings. This knowledge did give credibility to my belief that positing a mind-field was at least logical, and probably even true, but for awhile my acceptance was purely by faith. There was no research evidence to support my ideas.

Actually, there is no direct means of studying reality, but we can approach reality by observing field transactions. Likewise, we cannot judge what is "normal" except by determining what is an average or central tendency on the scale of reality. Metaphysical views of reality show that usually the mind and consciousness are more universally distributed and in tune with human experience. These offer us ways to comprehend our place in the scheme of things, as contrasted to the scientific picture of the brain.

After many years of listening to the higher nervous system's Morse Code-like sounds, Sir John Eccles was convinced that this was not the location of consciousness. He added that the complex neuromechanisms of the brain continue to function regardless of any co-existing consciousness. The unity of conscious experience comes from a self-conscious mind, not from a neuronal mechanism of a neocortex. He ended a series of lectures at Harvard by admitting that evolutionary processes could account for the brain, but that only something transcendent could explain consciousness and thought.

Eccles' ideas are confirmed by observations that tumors in certain areas of the brain do not affect the higher levels of consciousness, only the lower ones that deal with experiences of the material world. Likewise, poor circulation in the brain will create a change in consciousness, but again, only in material awareness. Poor circulation creates absolutely no problem in non-physical awareness, nor in the chaos-reducing capacity of consciousness.

The right-left hemisphere findings of Sperry and Bogen, so

popular a few years ago, were over-publicized, wrongly, as the final explanation for behavior and learning. The research did demonstrate that, depending on hand dominance, subjects' hemispheres are specialized for different modes of consciousness and information processing or retrieval. We have since learned, however, that one's mental life is not neatly zoned along right-left lines, nor is consciousness. Abstract experience and thought do not rely on the function of sensory nerves.

This is when my reckoning took another turn. If higher mind could not be studied directly like the material brain, then why not focus on mind's unique functions—extended reality and broadened consciousness? Basically, reality is neither fact nor fiction but is the emphasis we place on various parts of our stream of consciousness. My starting point was accepting that consciousness is a continuum extending from material awareness to higher awarenesses. I also knew that the mind experiences by means of its awarenesses.

Prior Western research has dealt with the material end of consciousness relegating the non-material realm to philosophical investigation. On the other hand, Eastern philosophies describe complementary modes of consciousness, yet they stress the non-material modes.

Do you realize that if you move into an altered state of consciousness, your brain may not be aware of that consciousness? If this is so, then whatever takes place in the altered state cannot be remembered until you return to that altered state.

I had such an experience when my wisdom teeth were removed. Two of my laboratory assistants had taken me to an oral surgeon's office. I promised to show them how to remove the light, general anesthetic I was to have once I became conscious again. After returning home, I showed them how to contact the body field with the hands, using short outward movements away from the body, to literally pull the anesthetic from the field. At first, I had no recall of what took place during surgery. But as my assistants worked, I reverted back to the altered state induced by the sodium pentathol and actually re-experienced the dentist breaking my gold crown while removing one tooth. I remembered how upset he became because these teeth were not easy to extract. A second shot of sodium pentathol was required to keep me under. (Actually, people who operate in higher consciousness do not stay "under" easily). His comment when I returned to his office and described what had happened was, "How did you know? I kept you asleep."

These are the mentations that I had had for some time. Always, my approach to an intellectual problem was to look first at the larger integrating factors, that is, the nature of the forest, to insure that I did not get lost in the trees. My working philosophies were Gestalt and Holism. Field theories excited me because these had a sufficient theoretical and mathematical base to entertain a mind-field. My earlier research looking at emotional and cultural correlates of neuromuscular activity patterns had led me in a similar direction.

As previously described, my first studies of the human aura involved hands-on healers who simultaneously reduced symptoms and altered energy fields. Most surprising to me, the auric field responded—it changed before the sensory nerves told us what was going on. For example, an inadvertent sound stimulated the field seconds before the brain waves altered. Light flashes were instantly recorded in the field—in too short a time for the brain to receive them. Stimuli that did not even reach the brain affected the energy field, such as a feather touching the field but not the skin, or one person changing vibration and affecting another person's field. The process had already taken place; the transaction was over by the time the brain finally got the information; and sometimes the brain never did "get it." This affirmed Penfield's oft-repeated statement, "The mind experiences and the brain records."

But still the questions loomed. Is this where the higher level of mind resides? Is this the energy that Penfield could not find? Is this why Reich described the brain as everywhere in the body? I was recording the energy field from the body's surface and aura readers were seeing it outside the body; some saw it inside as it traveled through connective tissue. Pert had found that when brain neuropeptides were stimulated, body cell neuropeptides in remote areas were immediately activated—again, too fast for chemical or neural signal transmission. This could only happen in a field transaction where there is no material resistance to create a time delay, or a loss of power or information.

There were other extraordinary field happenings. The experience of imagery first appeared in the field, and was only later evident in brain wave recordings. Turmoil in the energy field signaled the experience of emotions and physiological manifestations before they happened. The auric field of a healee changed when the healer's hands were placed over the healee's body. Field transactions required no physical contact.

I discovered that a person's intent also could affect another field. If I thought about easing pain or changing a physiological condition, that's what happened, whereas if my intent was to release repressed information without knowing or sharing my intent, the person remembered previously forgotten early childhood episodes and other lifehoods—even if he didn't believe that this could happen.

It began to look as though energy field patterns were related to streams of consciousness—a function of the mind. Along this line we discovered that when a person's field reached higher vibrational states, he no longer experienced material things such as bodies and ego states, or the physical world. He experienced knowing, higher information, transcendental ideas, insight about ultimate sources of reality, and creativity in its pure form. Thoughts were grander, more penetrating and global. All of these experiences we attribute to the higher mind because they are not available through the ordinary senses at lower field vibrational levels. In fact, the consistently highest vibrations were recorded from people who were accepted "seers" and "knowers", people whose perceptions occur at cosmic field level; they know things about us and the world without the usual sensory clues.

Now another universal question loomed before me. How is it possible to read another's intangible mind-thoughts unless these are expressed in some form? My explanation is that a person must be decoding our mind field with his, resulting in a direct mind or field communication. He is not "reading" the information stored in the brain. We had already seen that average people who could reach higher vibrational states participate in this type of communication. Conversely, when their vibrations lowered as they returned to material consciousness, our average state, such skills subsided.

These discoveries led me to hypothesize that the energy field is the highest level of the mind of man, and that it is through this level that we interrelate with the cosmosphere. This model allows us to investigate scientifically the interface and interdependence of man and the universe at the level of mind. Equipment as sophisticated as the mind itself would be required to completely validate such a model. It would require the mind to know itself rather than just to experience itself. It is unlikely that either of these requirements will be satisfied. But even considering these restrictions, the research possibilities are enormous.

Thus far, my theories about the mind field were based on recorded field data. But my strong conviction arose from clinical observations as I laid-on hands with the intent to expand or open the mind field. I started slowly, even reluctantly, for although I was trained and had practiced physical therapy in hospitals, I did not want to be a mystical healer. Rather, I chose to study the phenomenon of field healing as I continued as director of the Physical Therapy Division at U.C.L.A. and taught physiological science courses.

While writing up the Rolf Study in a state of exhaustion, I contracted a serious polio-like virus which left one leg with sensory and motor paralysis. I could not stand or walk. During the six long months it took to recover, Rosalyn Bruyere came daily for three weeks to treat me and later at my home. I learned to meditate for the first time by visualizing the transport of oxygen to the injured tissue and watching the nerve light up with energy. My condition improved slowly, but consistently, until all sensation and motor strength returned.

But other strange things happened. I awakened at night with my hands pulsing with energy. When I placed them on my body, it enlivened. What should have been exciting actually annoyed me, for constantly I felt as if my literal hands had been replaced with big, warm, glowing mitts. Finally, I timidly told a dear friend about my problem, asking her to let me lay-on hands to get rid of these excessive vibrations. She hesitantly consented, saying, "I don't believe in that stuff."

But in spite of the reluctant subject and a doubting healer, something profound happened. As I channeled energy to her—and my mind seemed to know how—she imaged a large pink lady in a forest, the same pink lady she remembered playing with as a small child in rural Canada. She vividly and emotionally recalled what she had forgotten years ago. Now this friend was over 80 years old, quite a long time since her childhood. Although she loved the sensation of energy transferral, she accused me of "hokey-pokey," and of manipulating her mind. Because I believed my mind was neutral with no such intent, I easily passed off her experiences as happenstance.

Later, while teaching graduate students to record the energy field, I again laid-on hands merely to demonstrate energy exchange. A similar thing happened, although the experience was not as pleasant. The student remembered her brother locking her in the bathroom and setting the next room on fire. She was very emotional. This time I wanted to know what was happening. In the weeks that followed, I reconstructed the incidents and arrived at these ideas.

These memories that had been stimulated "resided" in the subjects' fields. The strong vibrations from my hands assisted the subjects in raising their vibrations so that they assumed the states they were in when the experiences first occurred. This is where the memory existed.

This was the beginning of my 20 year journey studying the mind field and working with it to bring about healing. I discovered that by using energy field biofeedback and guided imagery, we could powerfully communicate through the mind field. When John Dewey first proclaimed that a variety of experiences was essential for a child's education, he must have contemplated this level of experience. Now I knew that teachers, instead of just providing the physical aspects of experiences, also should provide the high level vibrations to activate the mind fields of their students.

As we continued clinical and laboratory research, "out-of-body" experiences were numerous. Invariably, the person's body frequencies rose higher as energy in their feet and legs decreased and energy in the crown increased. The expressions "in" and "out-of-body" refer to the awareness of the person. It does not mean that the mind physically separates from the human tissue. One's mind field is always experienced as being either in or out of the body, depending on where the awareness is focused. When one believes he is out-of-body, he simply has no direct connection with certain material levels of consciousness. This is a consciousness experience and a vibrational one with a shift of frequencies and locations. Some people enjoy this shift, others become frightened that they may get lost and not be able to find the way back to their bodies. Yes, if you think that the mind is in the brain, and you experience what you believe is out-of-body awareness, it is easy to believe that you are too far from the "gas station" and that you can get stranded. The answer is, if you know you are "out", you can always get back because there is some awareness on the brain-material level to tether you back. A similar situation occurs just before you drop off to sleep—you are shifting consciousness and minimizing awareness of the material level but not the mind level. In this sense the mind is then freed and can go anywhere to dream in different places and times.

Many popular books offer ways to free one's mind, implying that it is restricted. This reflects old beliefs about the mind. But if we consider the mind as a field, then it is free by design, as fields always are. Eastern philosophies present ideas and exercises purported to clarify the mind, that is, to sharpen it. These techniques in fact subtly reorganize the field rather than mechanically change the brain.

Popular psychotherapy also stresses the importance of keeping the mind in bounds, meaning controlling emotions, because most of us fear deep feelings. Unfortunately, it is difficult to close an open system. It is dangerously repressive and restrictive. I prefer to solve the problem at the higher source level by freeing the emotions which so tightly stricture the mind, limiting its explorations. (Chapter IV, "Emotions: The Mind-Field Organizer").

Theoretically, I accept that the mind is the most powerful force in the world, more powerful than the split atom—because it is beyond physical force. The Bible tells of Moses parting the Red Sea and of the men marching in cadence around the walls of Jericho who, stopping together, caused the walls to come tumbling down. I wonder if they had their minds focused on destroying the walls or, if, as implied, did it result from purely mechanical vibrations? My guess is that the former was equally true.

Many of us firmly believe that if enough minds concentrated together, we could stop floods, hurricanes, tornadoes and perhaps even earthquakes. There have been some organized groups which created weather changes. Many individuals have experienced such mind-power which can be measured through the field. We need to determine if this power is released only when people believe that they can make these major environmental changes or when emotion encourages it. (See Chapter X for evidence of healing through prayers). Thus far, we have not been able to get enough people of like mind to concentrate and to test the mind's power adequately. I accepted these ideas as true for people in general but not necessarily for me specifically, until my own personal experience with mind over matter occurred.

I was traveling with a friend in the Vale of Kashmir, India, among the beautiful lakes and gardens of Shalimar in the lower Himalayas. It was November, dangerously late to be in this land of early snows. But it was glorious; and so we lingered. On the day we were to leave, I for Egypt and my companion for Israel, a major snowstorm hit; it was frightfully cold as we sat waiting in the tiny airport. The natives carried little clay pots full of active charcoals under their huge parkas to keep their hands and tummies warm. The few planes there were grounded, the officials suspected, for the entire winter. We were concerned, for we both had close connections to make in Bombay.

As we sat looking out the window into the stark whiteness, we both had the urge to alter the storm. After a short discussion about whether we could do it, we settled down to meditate and stop the snow. In about 30 minutes, the sun appeared briefly to the south. We were hustled onto a plane and literally shot out a hole in the storm. We were the last plane out, we later heard. It is a great and true story we sometimes share socially, but still in our deep thoughts it was an "out there" fairy tale happening even to us, until it happened again.

This time I was on remote Bora Bora island of the Tahitian group, lying in the sun, oblivious to the cares of the world, when a sudden violent windstorm with threatening black clouds seemed to come from nowhere. My doctor friend and I discussed whether to leave or take a chance on getting our books, recorders and cameras wet. When we saw the sheet of rain coming at us across the water, it was too late to move. Our only chance was to stop the rain. To physically push back all of that force of wind and water quickly seemed impossible. I chose instead, to try to split it. Both of us saw the rain part in a V-shaped wedge passing on both sides of us in a downpour that lasted for many minutes.

Again, this was hard to believe, although it was not really different than bending spoons or moving impossibly heavy objects during an emergency, where small amounts of focussed energy have yielded large results. I was more intrigued with how it happened than with the fact that it had happened. To believe that mind had created a counteractive power sufficient to offset the storm energy was unacceptable to me. So I searched for other explanations. If a storm is a chaos pattern of change in weather, teetering on an edge where an anti-integrity or anti-cohering force is set in motion, then there also exists an integrity force which reorganizes it into a coherent state. This can explain a pattern of vibration which starts the storm, and another which stops it. This would mean that we would not need physical force to blow away or to stop the storm because the factor which created the storm was not mechanical but vibrational. All we had to do was to use our minds to manipulate the forces which exist for change. By the same token, rain or snow can be created and objects can be moved.

So it follows that any mind which accepts its power completely and can focus thought can do profound things. The mind on the non-physical level has eminent power.

Thoughts are fleeting and non-physical. They contain information about both physical objects and non-material happenings. But thought itself can only be understood as a field regardless of where you think it originated—from brain cells or from the mind field. I hold the view that thoughts are transactions of one mind field with another field (or fields). And although the brain cells are activated to remember and respond, the active thinking experience is in the field.

Thoughts, then, are structured vibrations—some fleeting and others which are recorded and become permanent. Some thoughts display an intellectually intimate connection with information stored in the brain. Some thoughts are so strong that they color the entire environment in which they occurred. These create what Rupert Sheldrake describes as a morphogenic field, or Gregory Bateson calls individual, group and collective minds. Stated more simply, there are thought fields in the home, the office, and in organizations and groups, by virtue of the thought vibrations of those who created these institutions and those who live there. Each one of us has experienced these unique fields, perhaps with pleasure, doubt, or hostility.

The first time I knew about place-fields was in Jerusalem in the 1960s, when it was a divided city. To visit the historic, religious part of Jerusalem one had to enter Jordan by way of Syria. One could only go through the Mandelbaum Gates separating the two countries one way, from Jordan to Israel. One day as my niece and I wandered in the Old City on the Jordan side of Jerusalem, we found ourselves walking along an ancient high stone wall on a rocky, dirt path inside the city walls proper. The longer we walked, the more depressed I became, until I was morose. Although I couldn't imagine what was happening, I knew I wanted to get out of this place as fast as possible—the vibrations were too heavy for me.

That evening I learned this was the "Wailing Wall" where the vibrations of the Jews' sadness over many centuries still exist today. Years later I returned to Israel to find the "Wailing Wall" now in Israeli territory. I was with a young rabbi friend exploring the Old City when we came to the "Wailing Wall". The local buildings have been restored with beautiful pink stone from that area and a new flagstone court led to the Wall. The Jews still come in large numbers, davening, chanting, and wailing, facing the Wall. I asked him why so many Jews returned to this place to talk with God. He explained that it was so easy to contact God from the Wall because the Jews had done this for centuries, somehow paving the way. He intimated that Jews went there when they were troubled. There they could pour out their sorrow to God and receive divine help. When I asked the rabbi where Jews praised God for the beauty of the world, and for life and happiness, he answered, "That is in the temple." Truly, I had experienced the sadness at the Wall on my earlier trip. The sad thoughts were still in the field where they had been created.

Another time, when I first visited the Dome of the Rock, the holy Islamic temple also in Jerusalem, I knew little about its history other than that it was the place where Mohammed was said to have ascended into heaven. The structure is magnificent. It carries high vibrations and is further beautified with ancient tile and Persian carpets. The Arabs are proud and reverent about this temple—second only to Mecca. They insisted that tourists keep moving and not stop to admire or become curious. Travel guides spoke only outside. But despite such restrictions, I was enjoying this unique temple built around a huge rock on a lower level, open to the main floor. I took the ramp downward to be nearer the holy rock and walk the pathway around it. Before I had finished, I became nauseated. Perhaps it was the heat, but nausea was not one of my usual reactions. Suddenly, I realized that I smelled ancient blood of animals. It was so repulsive that I rushed up and out into the air.

The rock, I learned, was where animal sacrifices had taken place. Yes, the stone was stained with animal blood which I thought was the natural color of the rock. I have smelled fresh human blood in surgery, which gives me no concern, but the field here carried the thoughts and the information of sacrifice. That was what upset me. Many others have smelled the same odor while there, and unless they knew, as I did not, or decoded the vibrational information, as I did, they just think it is a strong, unpleasant odor. Odor is a pattern of vibrations that the mind can decode.

I believe the focused mind-field has the power to tap into everything going on in the world. Many of us intellectually accept this as true, but our experience does not confirm it, and our brain is so busy with things of the day, that we don't even test it. Besides, most of us identify the mind with the cellular brain; we don't recognize it as a wireless transmitter and receptor. We acknowledge as commonplace that we can send and receive radio waves, bounce them off satellites, unscramble them and materialize information transmitted over a distance. How strange that we cannot accept that all the marvelous things we invent or discover "out there" are really prototypes of the body and the mind-field. The power of the human mind is such that we could monitor and decode all major "goings on" in the world. Without the news media, we could sense starvation and catastrophes when they occur. The mind-field has the capacity to have known about the Jones' group in Guyana. With mind-field knowledge, we would have less need of the CIA or FBI or satellite spying. The mind-field has the capability of sending instantaneous thought messages. Most of us try and are surprised when this works. We shouldn't be.

On the basis of my experience with deciphering and broadcasting thought from a field, I believe that all the great and profound ideas ever expounded, the tenets of advanced cultures, the deep and meaningful spiritual happenings around which religions are organized, all of these are available to us today in their original vibrational forms. They can be retrieved directly, rather than passed on with the distortions of time through writing or story-telling. Socrates at the Forum, the Sermon on the Mount, Moses and the Ten Commandments, and Buddha at the Bodhi tree, will someday be experienced by present-day people. So far, we have not created the adequate instruments and we are not sufficiently developed to receive and decode these with our minds. But we will do both in time if we know we can.

Are these ideas really so preposterous in light of the fact that we landed on the moon by manipulating and controlling physical forces? No, we can go beyond the stars by harnessing the non-physical power of the mind. The open mind-field concept says that all important thought is ours for the taking.

If you can accept as truth, at least tentatively, these ideas, or if you have been stimulated, or even shaken a bit, then perhaps you can imagine how difficult it was for me, a didactically-trained researcher, to arrive at such opinions. I had to weaken my material referents and reevaluate much of what I had learned as truth from "holy" science.

Now I take a further step to join the ranks of a growing body of philosophers who believe that thought and mind precede physical substance, and that when matter disintegrates after its form has changed, the mind and soul are freed and the power of thought still remains. You see, I really do believe in the power and greatness of the mind as a field. No, not believe; I know its power, for I have experienced my own.

Recently, when I was meditating, information came to me that I deemed contained great wisdom. There were no guides or teachers to tell me that I had tapped into a universal source. I paid attention to my thoughts and was very pleased, but also a bit annoyed—irritated because I could have used that information many years ago. And so my mind complained. Why did I have to wait so long, as though someone or something held up my knowing? The answer came quietly and firmly, "You needed seasoning." My higher mind was speaking to me. Perhaps I am more seasoned now than fifty years ago when I thought my students and I could change the world. Now I know that we can, because this time I think I know the way, through the education and freeing of the mind-field. Fifty years earlier, I had only the inspiration.

I will close with an appropriate statement from *The Bhagavad Gita*, the ancient Hindu book of wisdom: "If you understand your own mind completely, you are not just a human being, you yourself are God."

EMOTIONS:
The Mind-Field Organizer

Since the advent of written language there have been more words recorded about emotions, in every language, than about any other single subject. Why not, when emotions are the experiences we know most intimately. They are etched in our minds, indelibly recorded in our awareness as pleasant or distasteful. Emotions carry the essence of our unique and collective consciousness. Our thoughts and behaviors are basically directed by emotions which either permit or prohibit what we can think and how we can act.

Each of us is an expert in human emotions—from our extensive experience with our own, we know them well. Therefore, any discussion that challenges our beliefs or strays from accepted philosophies will be controversial. In this sense, the information presented here may be controversial because it offers a new model of human emotions. I suggest that human emotion is the organizer of energy fields.

In my process of rejecting ordinary ideas for strange, yet possible ones, I remember the Buddha's wisdom:

Do not believe what you have heard. Do not believe in tradition because it is handed down many generations. Do not believe in anything that has been spoken of many times. Do not believe because the written statements come from some old sage. Do not believe in conjecture. Do not believe in authority or teachers or elders. But after careful observation and analysis, when it agrees with reason and it will benefit one and all, then accept it and live by it.

I suggest that we adopt a similar attitude as we explore ideas that may fall outside the range of our current beliefs. I also advise that we assess their truth in light of the material evidence and their rational soundness in the context of our own experience.

Current ideas about the psychology of emotion need to be re-evaluated. Psychotherapy as it is practiced today is only partially successful. Freud admitted this with the statement, "Successful psychotherapy is changing the extreme suffering of the neurotic into the normal misery of human existence." Carl Rogers' study of an extensive array of psychological treatment modalities further demonstrated the incompleteness of psychological techniques. An extensive questionnaire asked if participants had profited from their psychotherapy. Fifty-one percent responded that they got some help; forty-nine percent said that they were no better after psychotherapy. Statistically, both figures are too close to chance to be significant. We may then conclude that if one had embarked on any new healthy endeavor, they might have come out as well—not a very good recommendation for current psychotherapy. Of course, this study does not indicate that the therapy was worthless, but that it did not change what people wanted changed. It may have prolonged their lives, or even benefitted society, but there was something that those respondents sought that was beyond what they received. I believe that the source of the problem was not addressed, and I reject the standard belief that they did not want to change.

In the last 25 years, 100 new schools of psychology have been established. But there has not been a revolutionary new idea about human emotion since the early part of this century. While it is true that transpersonal psychology is pointing to higher spiritual aspects of consciousness, it is still with a weak voice that is not commanding the attention paid to the old models. Actually, even transpersonal psychology is not radically new; it is merely an extension of older concepts.

I first began to realize the gaps in theories about emotions when I studied neuroanatomy and pathological neurophysiology at the College of Physicians and Surgeons at Columbia University, where we dissected brains. Simultaneously, I was in graduate school studying emotional and behavioral theories, learning that both seemed locked into new discoveries about the brain. Reflex and emotional responses were researched using EEG recordings when brain neurons were stimulated. Emotional centers were thus charted with state of the art scientific instruments. I still remember how confused I became with this approach. Regardless of my then-amateur status in brain studies, I sensed that reducing emotion to physiological reflexes and behavioral responses was an inadequate explanation for what humans experienced. Human emotions carry a personal element—something of the mind, they are not merely brain activity. Even then, the great neurophysiologists, Eccles and Penfield, stated that the mind and emotions were some kind of organized energy, although they too sought this in the nerve cells of the brain.

My quandary about emotions arose again following my eclectic Freudian psychoanalysis when I knew that something was unfinished, but it seemed unconnected to my personality. I began to realize that the current information about emotions was grounded in the scientific emphasis on material existence, upon presumed causes and cures. This yielded the belief that emotions were rooted in the nervous tissue and biochemical substances of the brain. This, the programmed aspect of the emotions that is shared with animals, is instinctual. Even the uniquely human super-ego, advanced by Freud as that aspect of the psyche that modulated our raw desires, still was geared to the survival of the body and personal existence.

Finally, it was during my work in higher consciousness states while opening the mind-field, and in the laboratory when I researched human electromagnetic fields, that my long-awaited questions found answers. I was beginning to peel the emotional onion.

But first, let me review old and new insights about emotions. Current psychotherapy suggests a closed system—a perceptual world that is bounded by the function of the ordinary five senses, the ego, body image, and selfhood. Verbal, free association techniques are geared to probe a closed system to find specific causes for emotional problems. Of course, the many brain monitors which screen word association themselves exist as a closed system. Here, emotion is a tool—to keep us alive, to protect our bodies, elaborate our selfhoods, and to perpetuate our kind. They protect us from injury and danger and they guide us toward experiences in the arts, education, and nature which do make our lives richer and give us pleasure. We know that emotions motivate us, and that unless we "will" to do something, we will not do it. Those acts which are heavily encrusted with emotions are willfully intense—actually, emotion is present every time we care about something enough to take action.

Protective emotion is strongly attached to the physical body; when something is seriously wrong with it, most of us get upset, particularly if the problem is life-threatening. Emotion is linked with our selfhood or sense of identity—the me I know as me. Any attack suggesting that I am inferior or not worthy elicits strong protective emotions. Emotion is embedded in personality and its behaviors. Some of us with particularly fragile personalities care more deeply about how we appear to others. But emotion goes even farther; I also transfer emotional energy to possessions that I identify with, both things and relationships with others, my mate, my friends, my children, or my pets. In a broader sense, any classification with which we identify, whether it is race, sex, ethnic group, or neighborhood, carries emotional charges. Real or imagined threats to our group may be interpreted as personal threats.

All of these beliefs about emotion and psychotherapy point to a closed system geared to the ordinary reality of the everyday world. These beliefs indicate that emotions organize physical existence.

Information that emerges from higher consciousness states helps to explain the profound emotional connection with traumatic episodes, intense spiritual experiences, and threats to the soul. Although these emotions are similar to those connected to physical existence, they are simpler, purer, and possess greater charge. When not released at the source level of higher consciousness, the effects of these energies seem to filter down to be discharged at the personality-body level of existence. Thus, higher emotions often become locked into the material closed reality system.

In contrast to the emotions at the material body level, in altered states there is evidence of an open emotional system that is dynamically in touch with deep needs and subtle happenings in the universe. Here in the no-time/space realm, one discovers free emotional energy, a super-consciousness state, the home of the peak experiences that we never forget. Here the closed system opens, revealing a broad continuum of emotions that explain things we knew about ourselves, particularly the schisms in our awareness.

I began to see the current model of emotion in a broader context when I realized that the emotions connected with the self are the synthesizing mechanism of the body, and the emotions connected with the soul are the organizing medium for the mind. Depending upon the organization of the field, transactions are selected; these transactions constitute humanity's experience.

Somewhere within this emotional continuum, each person finds his own identity, his patterns for handling reality. Ideally, we should be able to focus on any aspect of the continuum without needing to block any other aspect of reality. All emotion should flow on a continuum, one merging into the next. Actually, because emotions, the guardians, determine how our mind-field is organized, we generally hang on to one reality at one time while hanging on to another under different circumstances. Ideally, we should be able to focus consciousness on any portion of the spectrum without losing our identity within the larger system. We should be able to remain grounded in earth reality while another part of our awareness is soaring to higher states. And we should be able to experience emotions materially and metaphysically and to intellectually process both simultaneously. This is a sign of higher evolution that all of us seek and few of us command. Here, rigid emotional resistance fades and our self-identification broadens to include full access to all realities.

As a prologue to specific examples of the organizing power of emotion, here is a summary of what we have discussed:

New paradigms of the physical world, new concepts of living matter cause significant shifts in the beliefs about reality and how to incorporate inner experience. The power of these beliefs will shake up every institution in modern society. These brilliant new ideas about life and societies spring from the concepts of complexity theory. "Complex adaptive systems are pattern seekers" (Lewin).. Behavior on all levels, from tissues to individuals to societies, displays characteristic organization patterns. And what cells, individuals, or communities do is the result "of the internal dynamics, not the response to anything external" (Lewin).. I strongly believe that the internal dynamics of the most complex biofield, the human energy field, are based on its emotional organization.

At the deepest level, all things are composed of vibrations organized into fields that permeate the entire structure. Fields, whether biological or otherwise, have their own integrity. They are organized, not random, and they have the capacity to selectively react, interact, and transact—to respond passively, and to cooperatively unite with other fields. In other words, the mind aspect of the field, the aspect with the highest vibrations, dynamically guides all choices and transactions as it influences and is influenced by all other fields.

Emotion provides a force which flows and fluxes; it captains a field organization to maintain its integrity. Whether the mind-field can continue without becoming disorganized is determined by the strength of the emotion.

Patterns of the mind dictate complex human behaviors; brain patterns activate simpler ones. Every experience has concomitant emotions, and every emotion temporarily restructures the field. Activated emotions increase the electromagnetic flow of the field. Likewise, emotions arise from an altered electromagnetic environment.

We don't know exactly how the mind-field operates, but we are aware of some of the vectors. At any given time, the pattern and power of the mind work as a strange attractor to determine which fields we resonate with. Strong emotions and decreased field vibrations often limit the range of transactions but when the field broadens, interactibility increases. In other words, interactive opportunities of the field create the final action arena with its freedoms, limitations and directions. Dynamic fields on the ridge of chaos can reorganize more complexly with revolutionary transactions and evolutionary outcomes. If, however, that window of opportunity is missed or is clouded by disorganization, chaotic behavior can result until the field is more simply organized.

My research shows that human energy fields display a continuum. The extremely low frequencies (ELF), are directly involved with life's biological processes. The extremely high frequency (EHF) patterns ally with the mind-field and awarenesses. The general pattern of ELF is similar for all people, while the EHF reveals a personal signature of emotional patterning for each person. Therefore, an individual's mind-field patterns may show unique clumps of energy at different frequencies with breaks in the frequencies along the total mind-field spectrum.

To understand the individual emotional signatures, the steady state to which one returns, requires a search in the EHF patterns of both ordinary people and of the gifted during different states of consciousness, as well as during abnormal states such as psychosis and coma. The variables are frequency and power (or amplitude), and where these clump on the energy continuum. Lower vibrations exist with material reality, higher ones with mystical reality, and a full vibrational spectrum with expanded reality. To describe it another way, one's experience of reality is a direct measure of the vibrational organization patterns of that individual. Emotions can be fleeting, lasting only a few seconds. Or the pattern of an instant can prevail with enduring feelings, moods and affects lasting for hours or days. These are the forerunners of habitual emotional patterns of a lifetime, or even many lifetimes. These define the individual's emotional field signature (Exhibit 20).

The extreme ends of the consciousness continuum describe two foci of reality and their frequencies. A grounded state in material reality shows energy field ranges from about 350 to 600 cycles per second, while an altered state exhibits ranges of frequencies extending as high as 200,000 cycles per second. This range accompanies non-material awareness apart from earthly time-space. Here, experiences are not locked to now-time; they seem to exist in any time, now, then, forever, and whenever. Providing the person is simultaneously grounded, thoughts occurring in the higher states can be intellectually screened for their potential relevance and usefulness to his physical life. If he is not grounded in these lower frequencies, his thoughts have little reference to the material world and he has trouble recalling his daydreams.

In grounded states, the energy is located in the feet, legs, and lower torso, while in ungrounded or altered states, energy is truncated in the upper trunk, limbs, and head. Electronic recordings often showed energy pouring out the crown in great plumes, sometimes four and five times the amplitude of ordinary states, making the top of the head feel extremely hot. This is a characteristic of most young children, the seriously ill, and the psychotic.

Expanded consciousness encompasses a complete spectrum of vibrations with grounding in the lower frequencies combined with great power in the higher ones. Here any level of reality one desires is available.

If you happen to be present when a person is "channeling," I encourage you to pay attention to the kinds of information the channel expresses. If the facts or predictions are about an individual, a thing, or the physical world, the channel's strongest vibrations are in the low to mid-ranges on the consciousness continuum chart, referencing common reality. We refer to these channels as "psychics." However, if the information has the essence of ancient wisdom, great truths, spiritual knowledge, and lifehoods, their vibrations are in the highest range. (Exhibit 20, Consciousness Spectrum). This is the pattern of those we call "mystics."

Oftentimes during meditation, one experiences a sudden shift in body sensation and awareness, like breaking through a barrier. The field takes on higher vibrations with a sudden increase in amplitude—a phase shift. With more experienced meditators, one shifts unknowingly into higher vibrations. Also, when a powerful channel or healer comes into one's field, dramatic changes in consciousness frequently occur.

Repressed emotions create huge gaps in the frequency spectra; these are sometimes called "chakra blocks." In these cases, the power of the electromagnetic vibrations is increased or decreased, particularly in body areas associated with emotional trauma. This is the source of psychosomatic disorders. If the emotion is abandoned and not just repressed, there is inactivity in some chakras.

I saw a dramatic example of repressed field emotions in a young woman who presented a long history of major neurological disturbances and gastrointestinal surgeries. She had worked patiently and unsuccessfully using many therapies and medical treatments. I found that she imaged so freely that she rapidly uncovered many childhood sexual experiences, some of which she had known, with adults and other children. Generally, she freely participated in or instigated these. The frequency and unusual character of her experiences differed from those of sexually-molested children I had worked with previously. Hers seemed to be in a more mystical vein.

This young woman's past lives also disclosed extensive sexual activity, both traumatic and pleasant. What struck me was that even in the higher consciousness where emotion generally flows freely, she was emotionless. At times I wondered if she had created these fantasies, until I realized that the flowing quality of her speech and the unusual details reflected that these memories were not creations but were in fact valid memories; also, she was amazed with what came from her mouth, for she was always grounded.

Throughout many sessions, we uncovered extensive factual information without any change in her symptoms. Sometimes, in fact, her psychosomatic conditions worsened. One day after numerous mind-field sessions, she discovered another lifehood so bizarre that it seemed unreal—it was something one might read about but certainly not experience. Day after day for weeks it unfolded. She had been a baby victim of a sexual fertility ritual in an ancient culture somewhere near an ocean, in a tropical country with many Greek columns. She recalled with sensitive detail how temple virgins lovingly cared for her as they prepared for her special mission. When the three-day celebration date arrived, she enjoyed the elaborate ceremonies during which she was the star offering to the gods. At this stage she did not seem to know that she would be killed, only that she had been chosen for the special role—a gift to please the gods and to bring fertility to the leader and his wives.

While this story was unfolding, Dr. Walter Frank, a professor of cultural anthropology at Bonn University in Germany, visited my home. We had worked together in India. Because he specialized in "ritual" meanings, I started to tell him in detail this fantastic story. Before I could finish, he excitedly told me the end of the story and that it was a real ritual of Tripoli from around 400 B.C. He exclaimed that I had given him far more details than he had ever found written. We wondered if this kind of recall, whether conscious or not, provided the stimulus for great novels. We speculated that history could be updated by this real life memory as more people reach this consciousness level and recall lifehoods.

As we continued our work, the subject passively enjoyed the elaborate music and dancing of this colorful pageant until just moments before her death. When she was sacrificed by fire, her emotions exploded into rage and resentment at their acts and at her own passive acceptance. It was then, when these emotions were freed, that the energy field became hyperactive and chaotic. Over a period of weeks, as understanding and integration took place, her field stabilized, and became strong and flowing. The major symptoms subsided and her health improved. She has since been happily married.

While we acknowledge that we are emotionally conditioned by childhood experiences, most of us do not acknowledge the imprints we carry from other lifehoods. I did not fully accept the reality of lifehood conditioning until I had a dramatic experience. I was attending an international biomagnetic medical meeting in India. This was a pleasant, relaxing time for me with a group of friends from the States. Early one morning I was suddenly awakened with a great physical shock and emotional excitement. The entire heavens, as far as I was concerned, were streaming with bright red light. I was euphoric. The remainder of the night I was awake, not wanting to sleep; it was too dramatic. Although I did not know what had happened, the energy seemed to come from a far galaxy, not from the Earth. Of the many people I questioned the next day, only a few had experienced my "red shock." Every following night for two weeks I was awakened at the same time by the "big shock." Each time, I enjoyed the euphoria, my body tingled all over with the full spectrum of frequencies, and I was aware of my hyperconsciousness. Four days later when we returned to the States, I learned the answer. That was the exact time when the energy of the supernova of 1987 reached the Earth.

I asked a friend, a hypnotist, to break my habit of awakening that had been started by the supernova. Under hypnosis, I recalled the same experience occurring in another lifehood in India when I was "strung up" like a butchered goat because I had killed two men. In the middle of the night, when witnesses were gone and I, from guilt, had passively accepted my impending death, suddenly something happened. My energy became so great that I broke the sinews without effort and eventually escaped. Ten years earlier I had remembered this lifehood. Nothing was new or different so far. But this time under hypnosis I experienced that same red bolt of energy. Although I doubt if there were records of such astral happenings, there must have also been a supernova in the 8th century. My field that day in India was emotionally programmed to cosmic happenings.

Under hypnosis I also remembered the many nights I spent under the bed as a child in this current life, seeking protection from the intense lightning and thunderstorms in the Midwest where I lived. Understandably, I was hypersensitive. After these hypnotically induced memories, my sleep returned to normal and sudden noises shocked me less.

When a person catapults into higher consciousness without smoothly raising his vibrations, the body frequently goes into shock with muscular paroxysms, pain, and emotional disorientation. Probably these are due to sudden phase shifts which release strong energy, possibly forcing the field past the edge of chaos. Powerful activation of the Kundalini (serpent energy rising from the spinal tail up the spine to the crown) is an example of the sudden, full-scale release of the EHF. Literature and neurological clinics have cited numerous examples of the rising Kundalini energy over powering the nervous system with destructive consequences. Poorly supervised Kundalini breathing classes can move people to powerful chaotic disorganization, not only of the field, but also shocking its biological counterpart, the central nervous system.

If you are curious about your emotional field organization, ask yourself these questions. The answers will give you clues about what easily stimulates your field. What types of situations really alarm you? What characteristics of a person immediately upset you? What kinds of persons do you gravitate toward? If we recorded your energy signature under these situations or along with the person who stimulates you, we would see that either your fields were very similar and resonated well, or they contrasted and clashed. These emotionally programmed field situations occur before you are consciously aware of "there it goes again."

Do you have any prevailing affects that you frequently experience, like sadness, anxiety, depression, or happiness? Do you have persistently intense traits, compulsions, aggression, or perseverance?

Your energy field signature will show dominant patterns just like a fingerprint. Modern psychology relates these to childhood trauma. This offers some understanding, but it rarely eliminates the problem. Regardless of so-called insight, the field will remain the same until the emotions which have organized it have likewise changed. Psychological understanding rarely insures such deep change. Remember, energy fields should change in concert with different situations. Complex ones do, and encourage fluid emotions. Does yours show a very limited change? Are your likes and interests small? What is the worst thing that ever happened to you in this life? Do you remember vivid details or only vague impressions of this experience? If the memory is still intense, your field will show anti-coherency in parts during the recall. And some time afterwards, the field will reorganize in a more coherent pattern.

Do you have any regular extrasensory experiences or abilities? And do you pay attention to these by thought or action? Are you insensitive to things others experience? In both instances, there is increased power in certain frequencies in the field and/or areas where there are blanks. If emotion is generated from material concerns, the lower levels of ELF are affected most. If emotion is activated from metaphysical thoughts, more action occurs in the upper ranges of the ELF.

Without external stimuli, one can experience heightened sensations from memory stored in nerves. But these differ from memories held in the field. Mystics easily read field memories, but rarely nervous tissue memories. In other words, they read material thoughts in vibrational patterns or experiences held in the field state. The clairvoyant capacity of "reading minds" is more understandable when we accept this fact.

All of us can experience an odor coming from a field, regardless of whether its source is a chemical or a thought form. This impulse is carried to the brain, activating memory. I remember when I first sensed odors connected to a field. Alegra Snyder, a professor of Dance and Ritual Anthropology at UCLA, and Buckminster Fuller's daughter, and I were personally exploring mind-fields. As she went up in vibrations and started to image, we both smelled the unique odor of sandalwood. I thought she was wearing sandalwood perfume, but she was not. The odor became stronger and stronger until we adapted and no longer sensed it. Some time later, we both left the laboratory at the same time, but I returned after a few minutes to turn off some equipment I had forgotten. Upon entering the room, I was struck again with the intense odor of sandalwood.

The next time we worked, we discovered the source. She had been a temple priestess in Siam during another lifehood, where before each celebration they put on face masks which had been impregnated with sandalwood smoke. The odor emanated from her field from experience in that other lifehood.

While working with an older man, we strongly sensed ether before he recalled his numerous childhood surgeries. He described the mask over his face and the agony of believing that he was being killed. Emotions are particularly intense during inhalation anesthesia and near-drowning. The sudden loss of oxygen sends one into the life-death panic. In both instances, the strong emotions heightened the sense of smell.

Once when Rosalyn Bruyere, the skillful aura reader, mystic and healer, was scheduled to give a lecture she became very ill with strep throat. She asked me to lay-on-hands to ease some of the congestion. As I worked, we both smelled gin. I knew the distinct odor of gin from gin martinis I had enjoyed in my younger days. But now, neither of us could find an ordinary source for the odor in her house. Somewhat later, she remembered a lifetime in Europe when she and her alchemist father crushed juniper berries for a medicinal formula that they were creating for the plague. She didn't know that gin is made of juniper berries.

I relate these experiences, again, to demonstrate that intense odors were experienced from vibrations in the field connected to thoughts. In two of the examples, the odors were carried in the field from other lifehoods, in another example, the odor was projected into the field from neural memory in this lifehood. All come from patterns carried within the mind-field.

Cosmic awareness with a completely extended reality is rare. Pseudo-cosmic awareness is legion with ungrounded people. Cosmic awareness always is devoid of personal reference with a field so expanded, so large, that it literally flows into the universe. The mind expands, becomes hyper-alert to divine global happenings, not to the physical body or material reality. Not that one has left the body, but the body image has expanded into an undifferentiated state which has no me-ness.

The boundaries of the human field become more permeable as the positive charge on the skin's surface weakens, loosening its grip on the aura. This is like allowing a kite to float away by uncoiling the string. It is still attached but is more distant.

Although I have experienced this cosmic state of being in total unison with the universe, it only occurred once while I was recording the field of a subject. This condition cannot be planned or predicted. Rosalyn Bruyere was reading the auras that day when the subject had just finished the tenth Rolfing session and was in an ungrounded, altered state. Suddenly, we lost the vibrational recordings for three or four minutes. Rosalyn commented that she couldn't see or find the aura, nor feel it with her hand although she was standing near the person. Finally, as she walked around the room to get a different visual perspective, she ran into the field hovering about eight feet away from the body. This should not be confused with an eight-foot expanded field in strong contact with the body. Visually, this aura seemed disconnected from the body's surface. During those minutes, the subject's electronic sensors recorded only a few microvolt vibrations (millionths of a volt), rather than the 20 to 80 millivolt range (thousandths of a volt) routinely recorded. Generally, we do not consider such low recordings because these resemble the ambient background of universal electromagnetism. But in this instance the sudden drop in voltage apparently signaled a state of cosmic consciousness. During this state the vibrational patterns were similar to, but of considerably lower voltage, than during a coma.

Coma, believed to be a state of prolonged unconsciousness, is actually a state of extremely high, ungrounded consciousness. I believe as long as any life exists there is awareness. In a coma, the individual can receive and decode information, but there is insufficient emotional energy to stimulate the will to act or to communicate by ordinary means. The mind-field, however, is sufficiently active that mystics who decode thought can obtain information and communicate with them. Whether the source is violent physical injury, emotional shock, anesthetic, self-induced drugs, or starvation, there is always an emotional element locking these memories in the field, freeing the self from the tragedy.

Connections are severed; the field is temporarily reprogrammed so strongly that ordinary consciousness is delayed or never recovered. In a coma, the individual is protected from memory of the experience which sent him there until he unlocks the memory by returning to that expanded state of consciousness in which the traumatic event occurred.

My coma studies have taken two directions: by assisting normal people to open their mind-fields and access their coma experiences, and by working with persons in a comatose state. In both instances, while in a coma, both the lower ELF and the higher EHF ranges of frequencies were extremely weak and equal in all body areas. The physiological body processes were so closed down that body functions idled. The awareness was high and weak, but not related to material things. However, this is not a simple, ungrounded state where healers can change a coma field by simply feeding it with their own energy. It seems that only strong, uncomplicated love energy crosses the coma barriers to make contact.

While I was teaching at UCLA, a physician friend, a professor of pediatrics at the medical school, asked me to work with a seven-year-old girl who was mute and cerebral palsied following anoxia, a lack of oxygen, during an extended anesthetic for an ordinary tonsillectomy. She was receiving daily speech and physical therapy, but could walk only a few steps with long leg braces. She spoke little. I found a sharp break in her energy field with great amplitude of lower and higher vibrations and no connections of the middle vibrations. As I lay-on-hands, she quickly went into an altered state where I was able to passively move and reeducate her limbs without the rigid or clonic contractions of cerebral palsy.

I relayed this information to her physician, along with my doubts that she had a classical cerebral palsy with central nervous system destruction. She improved rapidly in walking. Speech came in sentences and paragraphs. One day while we were working, she dropped into a deep altered state. I casually remarked, "Did something happen to you during surgery?" Almost instantly, she stopped breathing. With fear, I started mouth-to-mouth resuscitation. In a short time when her breath returned, she was in a rage, flailing her limbs and screaming. I held her, asking her to remember and tell me about what happened. As she calmed down, she relayed her anger when her father "dragged" her to the hospital the morning of the surgery. She tried to escape from the car. She was so upset when they reached the hospital that the surgery probably should have been delayed. But it was scheduled and the show went on. She told me that she believed that they tried to kill her with the anesthetic. She fought a lot. Apparently, in this hyper-emotional state, more anesthetic was required. Her heart and breathing had stopped, requiring electrical cardiac stimulation.

When I checked her memory with what her doctors said happened during surgery, she had remembered correctly. Her emotions had caused her field to be so reorganized that memories were frozen. It was this field block which created the major part of her neurological and speech handicaps. She learned to walk and to run again. From a child who could not learn, she became a verbally assertive little girl who progressed well in school.

I was once called by the brother of a man who willfully, at the suggestion of his guru, fasted into a coma. The man told me that there had been a great deal of stress between his brother and an Asian teacher whom he had brought to this country in connection with his business as an herbalist-acupuncturist. This was in the 1970s when both treatments were becoming popular. Apparently the guru had taken over the young man's practice, his house, and his woman friend, telling him that he was not a high being and was thus unworthy to continue his work. This is when the student started a total fast.

In the beginning, his brother agreed not to interfere. But when he became comatose, the brother called me. I found a man lying under covers on an outside porch surrounded by trees and California brush. He was unable to move, to take in nourishment, and was oblivious to all stimuli. I tested eye, body and pain reflexes, and found them absent. My first and strongest response was anger. Professionally, I had known this handsome, highly educated and brilliant young man for some time, so my emotions contained a personal aspect. I verbally berated him for trying to solve his problems in this way. I told him that I would see that he got one more chance to straighten out his life.

I contacted the U.S. Public Health Service, which immediately sent a doctor and an ambulance. The young man was hospitalized and after several weeks of intensive treatment and intravenous feeding, he came out of the coma calling out my name in rage. He had comprehended my attitude and what I had said to him. The coma problem was an emotional block in the mind-field.

To end the story on a better note, weeks later he discovered his anger at his guru and recognized his passive acceptance of his guru's behavior. He had the guru deported, took back his practice, his woman friend, his house and pursued a more normal life.

Near-drownings frequently produce long-term coma where the actual loss of oxygen causes neurological destruction in the brain. From work with three little boys in comas following near-drowning accidents, I obtained some additional information. I sensed a reluctance on their part to return to normal circumstances. I wondered if, to fill in the gaps in their consciousness, they needed to recall the horror of their near suffocation—to go back through the door they had closed with the coma. Rather than do this, their wills seemed to become dormant, wishing neither to cross over nor to return.

I had found that if someone sits with a comatose child, quiets his mind to tune into the child's field, the stories of their near-drownings can be communicated. One does not need to know anything about children or comas; in fact, that knowledge may hinder.

One little boy gave me information through his mind-field that his sister became angry at him and pushed him into the swimming pool while their mother was in the house. From another, I sensed that his mother had left him in the yard too long when she went to answer the telephone. He became angry and accidentally fell into the pool when he ran to find her. Information these boys relayed to me revealed how the incidents had happened, all of which was confirmed by the parents. But the third little boy said that he did it purposefully because his father had preplanned his life so rigidly—he did not communicate how he had the "accident," or possibly I could not comprehend it. When I asked his parents, they told me about a party starting around their pool. They and other guests left the pool area after securely latching the gate. One other adult had also checked the latch, which was believed to be too high for a child to reach. Sometime later, when they missed their son, the gate was open and he was floating in the pool. The father emotionally told me that his son would have followed him in his business; he had already picked out his university, and he would choose his son's bride from the "old country"—strongly concurring with what I had learned from the son.

My work with these boys was totally intuitive. Consciously, I didn't know what to do, but somehow I sensed I was there to learn and to help with another problem—a problem of the will. I lay-on-hands with the intent to strengthen their wills to take action—to come back or cross over, but not to remain in limbo. In either case, the will had to be strong enough to direct the energy.

Small things happened at first. They smiled when I came into the room—later, they smiled at their nurses. They started random movements, slowly, but progressively. The first little angry boy came out of the coma state in a few weeks. At first he babbled, then raged about being a soldier in a war he was against, and about his dying on the battlefield with head wounds and no one to help him—as though he had died tragically before, in a way similar to suffocation from this near-drowning.

Again, I wondered if comatose patients needed to go through a window of death to return to normal consciousness. I speculated that the war memory could have come from a prior lifehood because of the vivid detail, but I could not confirm this—the little boy did not respond to these questions. Over months he grew in consciousness, went to special teachers and physical therapists, and became a more spontaneous and outgoing child. I did not continue work with him—apparently my role of intervening in the mind-field was completed. When last I saw him, he had some physical weakness, but he spoke and attended a regular school.

As the field started to organize and become stronger, the child who may have tried to drown himself suddenly died. Although he never resumed ordinary consciousness, he crossed over, not at the weakest time, but when strength and awareness were returning. Probably a strengthened will enabled him to act. Apparently he chose to move on.

The third little boy whose sister pushed him into the pool was progressing steadily, according to the nurses, when the father said that he did not want a conscious but imperfect son and requested that I stop seeing him.

What are the important learnings beyond my memory of these little yearning faces? Into each experience we take our old programs. There are no simple drownings. A person emotionally organizes his mind-field as best he can, given the circumstances of the time. In comas there is a weakening of the will which makes any course of action difficult. I believe that someday we will know how to assist victims in making their choice to free their souls or to reestablish their lives. These stories may point the way.

Drugs do create changes in the energy fields giving emotional experiences, but the source is chemical, not emotional. Only a few generalizations can be made about drug reactions because of the many drugs, the purity and individual reactions to dosages. Bad trips always result in massive stimulation and disconnection of the body from both higher and lower consciousness. This makes for an incoherent field with large quantities of very high and very low vibrations with no medium-range frequencies. The EHFs may be very strong or, in extreme coma cases, very weak.

On the other hand, if the field contains large quantities of very high frequencies from drugs (without corresponding lower vibrations), there is a smooth electromagnetic pattern with pleasant feelings. The person is ungrounded and unable to form coherent, rational thoughts about the real world, but exists in a euphoric state. When comparing drug-induced with consciously-induced higher states, drugs act faster, can be stronger and more frightening, require no active participation of the person, and are not under voluntary control. Finally, drugs do not help the evolutionary process; they hinder it.

Aura readers are called by police departments to "read" the auras of drug-induced comas so that they can be quickly treated. Rosalyn Bruyere states that drugs lend a metal appearance to the aura, unique for each drug. In the future, computer techniques should enable us to analyze the drug victim's field, hastening treatment and providing sound evidence for law enforcement records.

Benett, of the University of California Medical School at Davis, California, did some interesting research with surgical patients showing that a surprising amount of awareness does exist during anesthesia. During surgery he played a tape asking the patients to rub their ears upon awakening. Nine of 11 subjects did, although they did not recall being told to do so. He also suggested that upon awakening, one hand would become warmer than the other. This indeed occurred. He concluded that anesthesia does not totally turn off the nervous system. The brain surgeon, Penfield, similarly concluded that the mind is active during general anesthesia. He discovered that patients consistently recalled exact details of incidents during surgery. He noted, however, that the EEG brainwave was totally inactive during anesthesia, ruling out the idea that an active nervous system produced the memory. From my research, I found out that this memory is held in the mind-field, where the new emotional organization limits its retrieval.

Trance mediums who lose normal awareness and have no memory of what happens during their "reading," generally channel "real life" information. They diagnose disease at a distance, predict world disasters or changes, and remotely see people and events—a psychic type of manifestation. It is as though they operate a powerful telephoto lens which they focus in a narrow range to illuminate highly specific information. Edgar Cayce and Jane Roberts were examples of this deep trance mediumship. During normal states, trance mediums pose questions that are to be answered in the trance state. But their findings are recorded by others. In deep trance they have no recall. Although it is somewhat unique for each medium, the energy field during trancing shows massive explosions in a narrow range of EHF, not the highest frequencies, and with no apparent connection to the lower frequencies. This explains why they cannot remember. Although some mediums are also higher beings who bring wisdom to bear on these predictions, this is not a part of trancing *per se*. Unfortunately, their current popularity has exposed many trance mediums with neither sound predictions nor wisdom. (Exhibit 20)

If trancing is a narrow pinpoint of awareness, hypnosis is a powerful wide angle lens that is capable of surveying a broad range of information—to bridge a gap in memory and recover forgotten information. Generally, like trancing, the information from hypnotic states is about material happenings, since that is usually the motivation. The frequencies are strong and broadly spread in the low- to mid-ranges of the higher frequencies. Occasionally, this consciousness overlaps to higher vibrations where lifehoods are experienced.

I was measuring neuromuscular coordination changes in patients from the UCLA Neuropsychiatric Institute who were participating in a dance therapy study. Individuals had different psychopathological diagnoses and were on different medications. All were sufficiently disoriented to require attendants to bring them to my laboratory. While I instrumented their muscles, I had time to casually chat with them. Each gave me the standard complaint, which, of course, is very true: we average people do not understand what they feel. Many complained that they were "wired," plugged into an electric light socket, and they described how painful it was.

Their metaphors seemed somehow correct—their bodies literally buzzed. So I decided to place electrodes also over the chakras to check their electromagnetic fields. All of the recordings from the crown (or top of their head) were so intense and of such high frequency that even without amplification these sounded like the buzzing of a bee. We could feel the electromagnetic energy pouring out of the crown in plumes that actually stung our hands. Also, no patient showed any recordable vibrations below the waist. The acute truncation of energy in the head with absence in the body made them literally electromagnetically top-heavy. There was a very narrow banding in the extreme upper ranges of human vibrations and little in the grounding lower ones. No wonder they were out of touch with Earth realities; they were out in the ether!

I do not know how much of the patients' physiological depression was caused by sedative drugs. But I doubt whether depression or drugs altered the field pattern except to decrease its strength. The larger quantity of high vibrations probably kept them in fuzzy consciousness rather than in a true comatose state.

To witness some of the treatments for psychopathology today causes us to realize our limited understanding of the process. We have not envisioned psychopathic behavior as a break in the vibrational continuum tied to a consciousness split. Probably when a person's mind-field slips over the ridge into chaos, a gross disorganization occurs, forcing him into an altered state devoid of everyday reality. Here we treat only his symptoms—not the cause.

I was impressed when I visited Epidarus, the ancient Greek center in operation many centuries ago to treat the mentally ill. They must have intuited even then that the primary problem was consciousness, not a disturbed physiology. Then they isolated patients in solitary, padded rooms where they were protected from self-injury and removed from reality, encouraging them to reach their extreme aberrant state. Diagnosis and treatment were planned by observing them in this acute altered consciousness. Treatment involved full days of heightened sensory experiences and participation in athletics, symbolic plays in the Greek amphitheaters, music, and other creative arts. Reports indicate that such a regimen was very successful.

Fears of insanity occur with average people when they move into sub- or superconscious states and are not in touch with the other realities. Particularly when one is reaching out for other awarenesses, there may be fear of not returning, as though one might get caught in the rapture of the heights or the depths. I believe that every single soul now existing in human form has had during some lifehood a schizophrenic episode—a splitting of reality so that the person was no longer functional. Such episodes are very frightening if we realize that our will is not in command—if we cannot consciously monitor what we do.

After we open the mind-field and move these persons through a schizophrenic episode, fears lessen. I recall working with a 35-year-old illiterate woman sent to me from the UCLA Neuropsychiatric Institute. She could neither read nor write. Her psychiatrist asked me to help determine whether she was a deep mystic or a psychotic. He said that she had been hypnotically regressed to age five, where she got stuck and would not communicate. They had had difficulty bringing her out of that hypnotic state. When I first saw her, she announced that she was a mystic, to which I responded, "So am I, we should have a good time together." She described that she had been an Army "brat" whose family had moved so fast from place to place that she never had time to go to school. And besides, she had to care for her younger brothers and sisters.

When she appeared comfortable after telling bizarre stories about her strange, yet skillful drawings of people, I suggested, "Let's take a consciousness trip." I explained that she should close her eyes and start imagining that she was walking on a path, and then to look around and describe what she saw. After some rambling, she saw herself as a young girl with a whole rack of new, little girl clothes of all colors and styles. When I asked her which of these she wanted to put on, she chose a black and red one, not the colors chosen by most little girls. She put it on and went back to a play area. There she found a boy who was "playing around." Instantly, her vibrations shot up, leaving a vacuum. She escaped something frightening by entering another state of consciousness. I made contact with her in her higher state and suggested that she was "out of her body" and should come back so that we could work. Finally, I was able to gradually lower both of our vibrations and literally, while talking with her, to "walk her back down" in consciousness.

Soon she again remembered the little boy and started to vibrationally escape. This time I knew that I must get her cooperation if we were to continue. I told her that she was "going away" so often that I needed her help. I asked her to grab one of her feet in her imagination when she started to escape, while I would grab the other. Together we would keep her grounded. She liked that; she could do something about her escape. Later, I gave her the job of monitoring to see when she was about to pop out of her body. She was then to pull both feet downward. It worked fabulously.

Throughout a long session, we discovered that the age five episode was a sexual attack where, to protect her from her rage, she went into a high mystical state which she enjoyed so much that she did not tell anyone about either experience. Furthermore, if she stayed in that mystic state she could not remember the attack. She also verbalized that she did not want to read or write because it was not any fun. I told her psychiatrist that the emotional program of her consciousness and electromagnetic field had blocked their diagnosis and treatment. It should be easier now that we had made some connection.

Another woman was referred by a local priest because of her intense debilitating fear that neither he nor a psychiatrist had been able to change by working on the many material problems in her life. I chose to concentrate on the fear. Intuitively, I suspected that she had been insane in some other lifehood, although this was not the present diagnosis. When she started imaging and going up in vibration, she poured out the crown chakra until I could no longer feel her energy field, as though it had slipped from her body. This condition existed off and on for many days. When I brought down her vibrations by contacting her field, it was like trying to ground a helium balloon.

In this state individuals do not know the way back and many do not will to return. Different from comatose patients with a weak will, they have an energized will which misdirects all their energy into the altered state. Finally, I helped this woman to know how to put on the brakes so as not to lose consciousness. We walked up and down the vibrational consciousness scale until material imagery came. There were many skirmishes with lifehoods, none settling on any significant information—until we hit pay dirt. She laboriously relived being a wizened old woman in Egypt who at one time had been a simple mystic who channeled information that the priests had rejected. When they threw her out of the temple she went to live in a small rock cave. There she became insane. At night she crept out to steal people's dogs to cook and eat ceremonially.

Gradually, she began to recognize this horrible experience and to acknowledge how her spiritual nature had been rejected when she was a temple priestess. She confided that she had always been afraid of insanity and had known that she was insane before. Indeed, her life has changed, her mystic nature is returning, and her fears have lessened. More importantly, she no longer fears insanity, for she had relived insanity and returned. We helped her to reprogram her energy field. In the process of reprogramming she found the emotion which organized the field and the behavior which resulted.

All of the examples in this chapter have demonstrated the direct relationship between emotion and vibrational patterns in the mind-field. In order to heal and to evolve, we must learn to coherently organize our emotions and to use this emotional energy to expand the mind-field. This is often slow and tedious work, but when we have done it, we are free to evolve into the magnificent beings that we are capable of being.

CHAPTER VII

TELEPATHIC KNOWING:
The Transfer Of Thought

Jacob Bronowski in *The Ascent of Man* stated, " There are many gifts that are unique in man, but at the center of them all, the root from which all knowledge grows, lies the ability to draw conclusions from what we see to what we do not see."

Telepathic knowing requires tapping into remote information sources. Since we can't explain clearly why we know things when logic says that we can't, we attribute our knowing to ill-defined skills like mind reading or intuition. We have all experienced intuition—an innate way of processing information—but still it remains an intellectual mystery.

Sending and gathering subtle information does not involve an act of will, but rather a high level exchange between mind fields, minds that are selectively organized by emotions. Telepathic communication of thought requires decoding and bringing to awareness information held in frequency codes. While philosophers are concerned with thought as reason, I am more interested in higher thought as a mystical process.

Human thought has always been a philosopher's enigma.

Scientists don't touch it except to record brain waves, the activity during thought; but brain waves do not resemble anything as mercurial as thought. I believe that mind reading and thought transfer will remain a conundrum until we envision a *field* of thought occurring in a larger mind field.

Thought is an organized field of energy composed of complex patterns of vibrations which consolidate information. If the accompanying emotional energy is strong, the field is energetic and integrated. It persists and stimulates other fields to action, both the dense world of matter and other human beings. If one uses auditory memory skills to decode an information field, one hears sounds or voices. If one translates thoughts through visual memory, one sees pictures or print. And if one processes vibratory information via olfactory or kinesthetic memory, one smells odors or has a motion sensation. If one somehow integrates all of these, one *knows*.

We have been aware of our thoughts since childhood and we know that most occur spontaneously. They come and go so quickly, and they are like quicksilver when we try to capture them. Have you ever wished that you could put your finger on a thought to hold it for contemplation or remembrance? But thoughts are peripatetic, constantly on the move, non-static, and non-rigid, the machinations of a dynamic, restless mind.

Some of us keep a tape recorder handy for important thoughts, or a notepad near our bed. Isn't it interesting that our gem thoughts occur often during daydreaming or preceding or following sleep or meditation? This reminds us that the field never sleeps; sleep belongs to the brain.

Transient thoughts, those most difficult to anchor, are of an order beyond simple thoughts. The slippery ones can be kept intact throughout several lifetimes by emotions which give them flavor and persistence. These tell us about our inner self—a different reality—the non-material reality of the higher mind. Isn't it interesting that our thoughts about physical reality are themselves non-physical?

Thoughts are events in the mind field that are available not only to the consciousness of the creator, but also to other minds. Does it alarm you to know that your very private thoughts are not private, but field-public? As we can read others' minds, so too can they read ours. But remember, this is a special situation. Since the part of our mind which reads others' minds is non-material, it requires a higher reality to decode thought vibrations. I believe that sleeping partners are aware of the other's thoughts. When one is ill and the other healthy, the ill one should benefit; the other may not. If there are discordant thoughts, particularly if these concern each other, it is better to straighten these out or at least to clear up the fields before trying to sleep.

I was involved with several dramatic experiences of telepathic knowing and thought transferral. While I superficially acknowledged that sometimes things happen that could only be explained by telepathy, like most normal people, I laughed and did not accept that reason. In my work as an academic kinesiologist, I studied the postures, gestures, and movement of sub-cultures and racial groups on every continent and taught university classes on non-verbal communication. It was obvious that each group had its unique patterns of movements, rituals, and the rhythms of speech, and there were no universal gestures except gross facial reflexes that were programmed by the nervous system. I discovered, however, that the dominant pattern and location of a movement did give me an initial impression which preceded verbal communication. For example, the Asians had small, quick movements, some smooth, some staccato, with accents upwards. American Indians on reservations moved slowly with a sustained disregard of time and a downward emphasis binding them to the earth. The South Sea island peoples displayed a rhythmic, undulating movement of their limbs, flowing with nature, with gestures out and away from the body towards others and an expanding world. The movements of tribal Africans incorporated a great variety of slow and sustained to bursting and explosive movements outward from the body—a pattern common to hunting cultures.

These observations were so general that I did not explore them further until I discovered energy fields. Here I conducted specific laboratory studies of the Southwest American Indian Corn Dance, the Japanese ritual warrior dances, and African war dances. By simultaneously comparing energy fields with the actions of muscles, I was startled to find that each predicted the other. When the movement was light, continuous and exaggerated in the arms and neck with little movement in the legs and torso, those were the same locations of the continuous low energy field recordings. Both movement and energy field patterns coalesced during the African and Japanese war dances with strong, sustained, explosive, muscular activity and intense, very changeable field patterns with sharp amplitudes and continuous strong ones.

My curiosity was so piqued, I asked one class to put on blindfolds and sense the quality of movement (without music) of these three cultural dances and improvisational movements performed by three modern dancers with unique styles. Beyond chance, the students predicted the quality of the movements and the feeling states these communicated by sensing the field. These experiences implied three things: one could sense the field without seeing it; the field communicated some affect flavor; and the communication effectiveness of ethnic, ritual movements and individual dance styles were probably equal. While most people accept that the quality of movement seems to carry messages, now it appears that the unseen field carries the same non-verbal, non-material message.

These findings were interesting, but still I was not inclined to pursue the role of thought in the transfer of field information. One could hypothesize motion all the way upstream to a source in thought, but that was a remote jump for my rational mind. Then I experienced something I did not forget.

Some 20 years ago when I attended Brugh Joy's 17-day workshop, I dramatically participated in the transfer of thought exercises. The scientific part of me ruminated over it. I didn't just buy it; I dissected it. And it went like this:

On a Saturday evening we all started a three-day silent fast. I was rooming with an attractive psychologist who was as curious as I about what we would experience. To reduce material thought, we were encouraged not to communicate in any way by gestures or sign language—to try to rule out the existence of the other person.

The first night my roommate and I quietly went to bed without the usual patter, and with no recognition of each other. I relished the period of silence to explore my inner states. But the moment she turned out the light, she began to snore. This surprised me, because she had not snored during previous nights; but now this energetic young woman ripped and bucked stronger than any large man I have ever heard. I was conditioned to be sensitive to snoring because my father snored so loudly that he was heard through doors and walls. During my childhood, I slept with a pillow over my head to muffle the noise. Now my pleasant thoughts of a quiet fast changed to annoying ones of a noisy starvation. This irritation kept me awake. If I spoke to her, I would break my silent pledge, and if I shook her, I would communicate non-verbally. With frustration, I thought, "Dammit, Susie, stop snoring!" My imagination disclosed my emotions when immediately I saw a huge, black, snorting rhinoceros pawing the ground. In Africa, I learned that they can hear, but they can't see. Symbolically, I was hearing things while not seeing around the problem.

Finally, to calm down, I went out onto the porch to smoke. This was years ago, when I still smoked. As I closed the door, Susie stopped snoring. That really alerted me, but I rationalized that it was a coincidence, of course. When I finished the cigarette, I was more relaxed and eager for sleep, but as I opened the door, she started again. My analytical mind again insisted on a coincidence. But still, I began to wonder if on a subconscious level she had somehow heard the door opening. So outside I went while I opened and shut the door, and she stopped. No longer a coincidence, my anger was gone and my curiosity up. Strangely, she was turned away from the door, yet somehow she knew when I went out and when I was inside, unrelated to the door opening and closing. Back in bed, I still wondered what was happening, but decided I would consciously block out her noise.

Again, imagery disclosed what was going on with me, even if I didn't know what was going on with her. Now I saw a big, black hippopotamus stomping the ground. Hippopotami can see, but they can't hear. In Africa, rhinos and hippos help alert each other. For me, I was still angry but at least moving beyond hearing to a deeper seeing stage. Despite my attempts, I was not successful at blocking my hearing. In exasperation, I sent her a telepathic thought: "Dear sweet and sensitive Susie, I love you, but you are keeping me awake." She stopped snoring immediately. Now it was quiet and I could sleep, but I was wide awake.

Something important was happening and I had to understand it. For about five minutes, all was calm except my racing mind. Then she started snoring again. Again, I thought non-verbally to ask her to stop snoring. Each time she responded, and each time it lasted a bit longer, but she always reverted to snoring. My mind fought the possibility of conscious transfer of thought.

Eventually, I realized that I would be awake all night long, telling her to stop snoring so that I could sleep. I somehow knew I had to get the cooperation of her higher consciousness. Only then did I realize that I already had access to her mind. Deliberately, I sent a message. "Dear sensitive Susie, I charge your mind to monitor your brain to keep you from snoring." And to my utter surprise, she stopped snoring for that and all ensuing nights.

For one who was basically a disbeliever in such non-material transfer of information, I was in awe, confused, and a bit anxious. In some way I had intervened in the mind of another, had changed a behavior by my willful thought. To me, that was exceedingly dangerous. Seemingly from nowhere came the thought, the words, "You will study the transfer of thought." In a heated dialogue, I spontaneously answered, "Oh, no, I won't; that can be dangerous and manipulative." The other voice rejoined, "No, it's not dangerous if you follow the divine law." Hastily, I countered with, "But I don't know the divine law." The rebuttal came, "You will know the divine law as you grow in consciousness." This was my first conscious transfer of thought. The words and thoughts had come from the higher reaches of my own mind. No outside force had created them. But two levels of consciousness, generally separate, had fused.

By now I was convinced that thought was a major communication system between self and others. I was shown the power of thought when I was in Jordan just after Israel was declared a nation. I was visiting a sabra, a native-born Israeli woman, who was instrumental in starting neighborhood conversations and social gatherings among the Jews and Arabs in Israel in the 1970s. She had made friends with influential Jordanians and Palestinians, whom she loved and admired, and she was concerned about their peoples' struggle since Israel somewhat controlled their lives. She wanted us to meet and to talk about their concerns and my work.

On the appointed day, she secreted me on a circuitous route so that we were not followed, across the pink and mauve rolling hills of Judea, beyond the Jordan River to a small town outside the then-Israeli border. The modest Arab house was in the center of a small dust-swept village. The Arabs' greetings were spontaneously warm. Assembled were about 15 ranking magistrates, lawyers, judges, professors, and spiritual leaders, who all spoke English fluently. For our meeting they had prepared a special lamb feast.

I was touched by their intelligent, sensitive discussion of their concerns for both Jews and Arabs. When they asked me about my work, I hesitated, expecting that they might doubt or be disinterested. On the contrary, they totally understood about non-verbal communication, emotions, lifehoods, healing and spirituality, and although they had never heard of energy fields, they did know about auras.

Our conversation lightened. I thought up an experiment to

give them an example of communication by field vibrations. One man had brought his little son who was about nine months old. I asked if the child had known any of these people before. When he answered no, I asked if he would place his son in the middle of our circle and then leave the room. I predicted that the child would crawl to two men whom I had already observed had the highest vibrating fields. The child did methodically crawl only to the two men I had predicted. One accused me laughingly that Americans always manipulate things.

When the father returned to the room, we praised his son's brightness, to which he rejoined that his child cried a lot at night. Then he complained that if he got up to comfort the child, the child stopped crying but started again when he left. Remembering my experience with snoring, I suggested that he send a telepathic thought to his son broadcasting his love and intention to keep the child warm and safe. With a quizzical expression, the father said that he had done just that the night before, not really believing, but it had worked. You see, he did know the answer; we only confirmed it, and encouraged him to acknowledge it. Again, we all too easily get caught in thought patterns that must be broken to allow for new information.

Thoughts are created from transactions with other fields. We do not think in, or from, a vacuum. Thought and mind have been said to precede the existence of matter, to continue through matter, and to exist at the termination of matter albeit in new forms. This implies that thought and mind do not disintegrate because they are not subject to physical laws. Matter is the denser of the vibrations, mind the finer of them. Mind should probably be reserved for organisms of higher complexity, but not just humans.

One's thoughts, especially when amplified by intent or emotion, leave an imprint on matter , that is, will directs all energy. Previous thought forms may remain as fields in places such as buildings, powerfully affecting susceptible people who resonate with them. Actually, such thought forms can be removed by powerful counter-thoughts or made impotent by persons who do not need to resonate with them. I believe fire can disintegrate all existing thought forms, including the destructive ones.

I was invited to assist an exorcist on an Atlantic island where a plantation farm was supposedly inhabited by entities. Now I went with considerable doubt about exorcisms and the existence of entities. The farmhouse was old and musty, full of clothes and papers of a former owner who had been a slave on this sugar cane plantation. The property had been given to the current owner's grandfather by his English "master" when he was freed.

The first night I witnessed a Kabbala ceremony during which black and white candles were burned and the house was cleansed with fire pots. A ring of salt was placed into a long-handled tin skillet, which was then doused with alcohol and set afire. We moved about the rooms carrying these low burning pots, raising and lowering them under tables and chairs until the small flame flared. With these little flame explosions the exorcist exclaimed, "We got another one!" She thought that we were burning up souls, beings, entities.

Her comments startled me because I don't believe that a soul can be burned up; it is forever. Theoretically, the fire flare came from some form of organized energy; some strange attraction created the unpredictable. I wondered about thought-form as a source, but had no proof of my strange idea until the last two days of our work.

During the days that followed, the house smelled cleaner, the windows had been opened, and gone were the depressed feelings I first experienced—like the sadness at the Wailing Wall. I believed that we had cleaned up some of the thoughts left there by the slaves, but I wondered if the present owner, the grandson of the slave, also had something to do with the so-called house possession. He allowed me to help him open his mind into higher consciousness to see if he had a part in creating the problem.

During this process, he remembered being a small boy in the hospital with acute typhoid fever. His father, a reserved, educated man, was separated from his mother, a warm and loving, more primitive native woman, who stayed with him throughout his illness. He remembers her wailing at the foot of his bed, "The voodoo has got you." This probably made him susceptible to the thought forms which remained in that farmhouse. Still, there was only minimal proof of my beliefs until the last day.

To conclude our work, we checked out each room only to sense a problem in one bedroom that the owner said was never used. Actually, no one lived in the farmhouse—the owner used part of it as an office and a place to rest when he was at the plantation. As we meditated in that room, we picked up new thoughts of a woman's fear. When questioned, the laundry woman admitted for the first time ironing in that room. She went there, she said, because we had not "messed" with it. She was afraid she would lose her job—something superstitious about the Kabbala ritual and candles burning all day.

Now, the ideas all seemed to come together. The difficult vibrations we experienced first in the house and later in the back room were emotional thoughts to which the owner was particularly susceptible from his boyhood hospital experience. Thoughts are passed down to future generations not just by picture, print or the spoken word, but by the strong thoughts remaining in fields.

I remember my great-great-grandmother, an Irish Romany Gypsy herbalist. Even as a child, I ran from her. Later, I learned that she professed black magic. At that stage I couldn't describe why, when all the other family members "bowed down" to her, I got sharp pains in her presence and evaded her.

Thoughts, of course, are not material; they do not occupy space with size and weight, but each has its own energy pattern. The gross energy may resemble a whirlpool, an octopus, an arrow, or a meandering stream. It has space-shape like words do. If its emotional strength is sufficient, it will travel any distance like the speed of light. If decoded correctly—or even incorrectly—there is a transfer of information.

Transference implies a distance; somehow, thoughts get from

here to there. When we try to understand how, we create a package with our sensory telereceptors—our eyes, ears, and nose—with their antennae which bring in information from a distance. In other words, these sensory nerve endings put us in touch with distant information. This is our way of materially reaching out for information in the space that extends from our own bodies; but our sensory apparatus can give us information about only local space, not infinite space. Infinite space belongs to field transactions. Local happenings perceived by ordinary awareness belong to the senses and the brain, and they exhibit a superficial cause-and-effect relationship. In telecommunications, unseen, unheard and unsmelled essences come from infinite space where energy flows back and forth in patterns of interrelationships.

Telepathic communications, however, often referred to as a "sixth sense," are entirely different. These have nothing to do with physical nerve endings; they are field transactions. As a result, I find it so much easier to explain my ideas about telepathic communication by lecture than by the written word because during a lecture, I place my thoughts in my field and literally broadcast them to my audience. Then, the audience has four methods of "listening"—my posture, gestures, words, and thought fields.

In order to decode human thought vibrations, we must leave behind the constructs of space and time as we know them. We must enter the neutral state, neither past nor future, but now. We must extend our consciousness to experience through fields directly so we can grasp the inner content, the nuances of information, as well as its external form. In extended energy field recordings, we found dynamic shifts that may come from the energy fluctuations of thought waves themselves. We know the frequencies of thoughts are neither consistent nor constant; they exist, cease to exist, and exist again, in a continuous on-and-off pattern.

Transfer of thought implies a transaction. As one becomes more skillful in tapping one's own field and projecting thoughts, one is better able to decode rapidly the information from others' fields. Such is the capacity of the great healers, lecturers, clairvoyants, physicians, and spiritual leaders when they enter expanded consciousness states.

On a more mundane level, one day in the laboratory we were studying simple transfer of energy between two people lying with the soles of their feet in contact. An aura reader reported a strange pulsation in the field of the leg of one participant. Although the other could not hear this comment, apparently the incoherent energy passed into the other's leg, causing a major muscle spasm. This was an energy transfer across space, through fields interacting on a biological level.

Because we know how powerfully we communicate through our thoughts, I suggest that we use them consciously and creatively to get help and information when we need it. If we actually believe that we can get what we ask for, we will. Many times I came upon a research problem that I could not solve—I had no idea even where to turn. Help from the usual sources was inadequate. So I broadcast my need to the universe, asking for the most knowledgeable people to assist me. They came, four of them, a physicist, an engineer, a pharmacologist, and a chemist. Some called almost immediately to ask what I wanted. Strangely, I didn't even know them. Others asked to see me and didn't know why until we met. A telepathic communication system had brought us together.

Most thoughts never leave the auric field of their creator. Only those firmly structured and vitalized by emotion have sufficient power to be broadcast. This implies that random thoughts go nowhere, but announces that the great thoughts of our civilization are still available. We know that when emotions are stirred up, earth fields react more potently. Plants respond positively or negatively to strong emotions. All therapy and rituals activate and release energy carrying both individual thoughts and group beliefs. Some people with dynamic fields excel in communicating thoughts very convincingly. We hail them as the "great communicators."

When we refer to the inner work requisite to evolution, we mean communication with the self, or our higher mind. We cannot escape the driving insistence of our own thoughts—our inner life. And yet, such self-knowing does not come easily, for we must focus attention on our own fleeting thoughts, decode these, and then emotionally experience the content and our "now" reaction. There are many techniques to assist us. Here is one that broke my reserve.

At the same 17-day intensive workshop in the 1970s (mentioned earlier), Brugh Joy told us to find an animate or inanimate object to relate to. Because I like animals and grow plants easily, I chose instead to commune with a rock, an inert piece of matter. I was instructed to go into the desert and look for a rock until one rock somehow chose me or spoke to me. To put it mildly, this was a bit far-fetched for me, but I passively played the game. I walked back and forth for a long time in the desert. No rock chose me. No rock said, "I'm your rock." Finally, I had to return to the retreat for lunch with no rock communicant, so I decided to quickly make a choice. I would choose a rock, not it me. Up loomed a big, nondescript one, to which I mumbled, "You're my rock, whether you like it or not."

Later that afternoon, I returned down the same path to commune with that special rock, complaining under my breath about having to go back and talk with a dumb rock. I personalized the rock to berate it as a dull, insensitive rock lying on a sandy desert for all of its existence. What am I doing making a trip to talk to you? And as I neared my nemesis rock, confronting it with, "Who do you think you are?" I heard a wee voice saying, "I am a rock and the source from which you will build your temple."

This only strengthened my defiance. I thought, how dare that rock try to instruct me to build my temple—much too metaphysical for me. I muttered, "Dumb old rock, what do you know, you've never done anything in the world but lie there and get moved around with the shifting sands." The answer came, "Of all the things you know, you don't even know yourself."

My game plan was over; I was exposed. My deepest mind level was communicating with my conscious level to tell me a profound truth about myself—it was humbling and quieting. I sat all afternoon on that rock, learning more about myself, my unfinished business, feeling grateful for an experience with an inert rock, which, of course, told me nothing, but allowed me to project my hidden thoughts on to it so that I could become aware on another level. This is a powerful technique for removing barriers to self-communication.

Thought communication by group dreaming has become popular throughout the country. Dream incubation with helpers was started in 1970 by Henry Reid; now many thousands of people are involved. To do this, a group of people concentrates its dreaming on an individual and his problems, which are never described to the dreamers. The next morning, when the group members gather to recount their dreams, they are often surprised to find similar details in their dreams, yet with their own self-illuminating details.

Today there are extensive practical reasons for tapping into universal thought. We know that the brain alone cannot absorb and retain the current explosion of information. But telepathic methods also provide simultaneous access to the unusual and great thoughts of many people. Time has fostered the popularity of "channeling," with both its good and bad features. When psychics stress that all information is available to everyone, and when they teach people how to access it, channeling is constructive. The emphasis is destructive when people sense its importance as a tool, but believe that it belongs only to those who have some gift or quirk of birth. Believing that all channeled information is the gospel truth is another negative feature. In fact, a great deal of information proffered by famous channels is from lower sources and lacks wisdom.

The most disastrous aspect of channeling occurs when individuals give over their power to guides and accept without discrimination all information obtained as God-ordained. Many believe that guides choose us and actively communicate with us, when instead we are the active agents—we have to reach the vibrational level to tap this information; guides can't drop down to contact us. The use of guides is merely a technique to help us get our intellectual, rational mind out of the way so that universal information is available (perhaps a step up from my rock experience).

Yes, I have used guides. I have seen them, heard them, and for a long time, was sure that they instructed me. I contacted Einstein, Pythagoras, Aristotle and Christ, each time obtaining unique information. It was fun to play the "guide game" and it made interesting conversation, replacing what my psychiatrist and I uncovered. Now it was my guides and me. I even got vignettes that convinced me that I had directly contacted these people, not just their thoughts. I saw Carl Jung at a magnificent waterfall— before his interview with the British Broadcasting Company disclosed to me that he lived beside, and spent much time on the banks of, a fast-flowing stream.

When I contacted Einstein after his death, my questions were creatively answered by graphic imagery. Some weeks later, a physics professor told me that Einstein did not think in words, but rather in images.

For a healing problem, I sought to contact Aesculapius, whom I knew to be the father of medicine and the teacher of Hippocrates. I received the information, but never saw or heard him. A Greek philosopher friend told me that Aesculapius was a god, not a human.

In these and many other instances, personal information about the "guide" comes along with the requested information. We can indeed tap into the vibratory fields of those who have crossed over. But remember that channeling occurs at a soul level, not at the level of physical beings, and we must not become emotionally dependent on a personality that doesn't exist on this level. But the question arises: how can we see these guides? Remember, we decode information visually, auditorily, and olfactorily, which means that we can see, hear, or smell the information. While there is some truth in this manner of decoding, we will progress faster and farther if we don't dwell on the sensory process. It is not important. At most, these experiences can be valuable to assure you that you are never alone.

The children of Fatima and the recently publicized Chinese children with highly developed sensing capacities have encouraged the writing of many popular articles and books about their predictions and feats of remote seeing. They are mentioned here only because a special physics research team from the High Energy Institute announced that these children could expose film in a lightproof container. When channeling information, the children seemed to emit light quanta and electrical waves that could be picked up by special biodetectors. The exciting dramas associated with these manifestations do not really concern me. The value lies in the clear-cut examples of the human capacity to experience higher consciousness.

Is there research evidence of telepathy? In a series of controlled studies, the Russians demonstrated sending and receiving specific factual information between two people over a distance of hundreds of miles. Several of my laboratory staff were able to predict the color changes of the vibrations radiating from a subject's body seconds before the telemetered data appeared on an oscilloscope. They were in an instrument room, unable to see the subject, or hear the aura reader's report.

I recall when four researchers met to perform some energy field experiments in an anechoic room (where there is no sound). It was early morning. We were a bit bleary-eyed from lack of sleep, having been awakened with a start at 1:45 a.m. We all agreed something must have happened in the cosmosphere. Bob Beck, a physicist, called one of his contacts in Washington, D.C. to learn that the Russians had detonated an atomic bomb at that time. All four of us had experienced the vibratory shock wave.

Elaborately controlled remote viewing experiences by Targ and Harary reported in *The Mind Race* that individuals, while sitting quietly with their eyes closed, can, by using their psychic abilities, accurately describe activities, events and geographic locations all over the planet. We have discovered that when individuals telepathically "saw," consciousness was expanded and the mind-field vibrations increased.

Dunne and Bisaha found accuracies on precognitive viewing or predicting target locations before these were chosen or known were equal to accuracies where the locations were chosen at the time of telepathic viewing. Because of their strange findings, they concluded that not all remote viewing is telepathic. I believe that their interpretation is incorrect, that both precognitive and present cognitive remote viewing are telepathic. When a person's sense of time is lessened but not absent during higher consciousness, remote viewing of current happenings can occur. However, when a person loses the sense of time, during even higher altered states, there is no now or later, no present or future, and field information is not referenced to time. Here, it is as easy to predict future events as present ones for the strange attractor fields already exist. Actually, telepathy is a kind of intuition—a direct knowing of distant facts devoid of time. The problem we mortals have in understanding the experience of knowing before things happen comes from our incomplete understanding of space-time. Einstein commented that the distinction between past, present, and future is an illusion—although a stubborn one.

As mentioned previously, growing trees communicate alarm to like trees through their fields. Willow and maple trees that are attacked by parasites seem able to communicate the news to untouched trees nearby. When trees are attacked, they try to fight off the parasite by changing their chemistry to make themselves unpalatable. Research shows that the untouched trees get the message that invaders are nearby; they respond by making the same chemical changes.

I have surmised for some time that the primary method of communication, the transference of information, is through the field rather than by written or spoken word or gesture. I also believe that the field carries as much general meaning as the more ordinary modes of communication. Now there is evidence that infants understand a great deal more than we believed they could, even before they are able to speak and supposedly do not understand the language. Hypnotic regression discloses that, at birth, the child knows if he is a wanted child, and if his parents approve of his particular sex. He comprehends the general nature of his relationship with his family members and their attitudes. This basic information is not necessarily communicated by word, but by intent and thoughts available to him through fields from which he interprets and understands the world.

Through mind-field work, I confirm what hypnotists have stated for years. There is a close, two-way communication between fetus and mother. More than a chemical relationship, the mother's field carries specific information about her emotional state and her experiences with pregnancy. In his book, *The Secret Life of the Unborn Child*, Verny offers impressive evidence of this communication. He stresses the value of the father's presence during the mother's pregnancy, and the importance of the mother's emotional calmness and happiness in the process of bonding. He encourages both parents to talk to the unborn about their love and joy at the upcoming birth. Actually, talking to the baby through the mother's tummy is appealing, but it is probably the thoughts and not the words which are communicated. Only the thoughts are necessary—the baby understands. Communication with the unborn doesn't make sense if the mind is in a brain that is not yet developed. But it makes perfect sense when we know that the mind is non-material, and that it is perfectly developed when the soul enters the fetus.

I have also learned that the field interactions of mother and child carry both nourishing and destructive content. Back before surgical abortions were legally available, some women resorted to dangerous, violent attempts to abort the child they did not want. Others wanted to abort, but for moral reasons or out of guilt, did not attempt it. It was startling to bring to consciousness the detailed information stored in the mind-field of those who lived through the attempted abortion, or in those where the thought existed but was not attempted. When re-experiencing that fetal state, the person's emotions are spontaneous, frequently overwhelming, and often doubted. It has taken time to sort these out and to discover the truth. Because of such discoveries, a new "prenatal psychology" is emerging to handle emotional problems that originated *in utero*.

Let me explore some other examples of communication through fields. Vibrations of 16,000, 17,000, or 18,000 cycles per second are frequencies which the normal ear can detect if the amplitude is sufficiently great. Above these frequencies, we can only experience through the field, but we cannot hear through the ear. However, animals hear frequencies in much higher ranges. For them, the field is their principal mode of communication. They smell and hear vibrations with senses which are much more acute, and they appear to be more aware of vibrational differences. For example, camels smell a human's breath to make judgments. Domestic animals, particularly cats, gravitate to persons with higher vibratory fields—persons they don't know, even if these persons dislike animals. Once a cat selects a person, it moves to the chakra with the strongest vortex, the throat, abdomen or crown, where they purr and knead with their paws.

Jacques Cousteau has reported that the same person has been attacked by sharks off the beach in Australia, and again in France. Do some human fields, then, attract and some repel sharks as in the example of domestic animals? I would speculate that at the time of an attack the victim is carrying either a dominant color, a frequency pattern probably red and orange, biologically vitalizing, or a fear reaction, either of which could stimulate sharks. If this were true, one could counter the attack by altering the field, either consciously or with instruments.

When watching trainers work with dolphins and seals, I wondered how much of the learning resulted from the trainer's intent and his thoughts, and how much from his gestures and verbal commands. Marine research shows that dolphins and sharks respond to frequencies up to 200,000 cycles per second, the same range we recorded from human fields.

Once on an African safari, I watched lion prides, gorged from food, lying on their backs as if asleep, oblivious to the zebra, their chosen food, literally grazing all around them. Each knew of the others' presence. Suddenly, the zebra became alerted. As a group, they moved steadily but slowly away from the lions before they broke into a gallop to escape. A few minutes after they had gone, the lions awoke and started their hunting prowl. According to our African naturalist, the lions had broadcast their intent to kill and eat again even before they awoke. What a subtle agreement between predator and prey!

When in San Diego, I often visit the famous Sea World museum. Friends and I enjoy going to the building housing the electric eels, piranha, and small predator fish. By placing our hands near the individual tanks we are able to predict which fish kill their prey by electric shock and which merely stun them. The killers that shock have a sharp, sudden blast of electrical energy from their bodies; those that stunned have a much smoother and milder discharge. The electrical information had crossed space from the fishes' field to the fields of our hands, telling us about the fishes' behavior.

This idea of attraction and repulsion as a field communication phenomenon emerged when I observed peddlers and hucksters selling trinkets and cards at tourist sites around the world. If I am on tour with others, I am not the woman they haggle. Once, several women friends who were exasperated by being blocked and hassled to buy, asked me how I protected myself. I hadn't really thought about it, but told them that these men annoy me and probably my field turns aggressively red and my thoughts carry anger, telling them that I cannot be coerced. That night I gave lessons in projecting color and thought into our fields. In the days that followed, it worked wonders for all except one woman. She said she couldn't get angry, that it wasn't spiritual. We didn't try to change her, but when passing the peddlers, we encircled her, and she was left alone.

I have assisted numbers of women who have been raped or sexually assaulted in this life to relive their fears by opening the mind-field to their emotions. In every instance, at the time of the attack, their emotional field was weak and passive; it also carried intense fear of their own anger and aggression. As society becomes more open and helpful to these women, new information surfaces. Rapists tell us that they intuitively know which women are easy targets. They describe them as passive and fearful of their own emotions—the same pattern I discovered in the victims. I, like other women who have chosen to travel this globe and, of necessity, frequently alone, have found ourselves at times in very perilous situations. But I do not believe that it is luck that we have never been attacked. I have found that, in these situations, pure, unadulterated rage is the best protection. Running announces your fear, and physical fighting, unless one is skilled in the martial arts, is nearly worthless. Remember that, regardless of the intensity of the attacker's motivation, their lives are not in danger and ours may be. If the woman is emotionally free to express powerful emotion, even rage, assailants will be shocked and frightened, as are all people when they encounter a raw, emotional display.

As evidence by the earlier examples, first research on field communications should use animals and infant subjects because they are more sensitive to field information. Also, the primacy and complexity of verbal and non-verbal communication with older children and adults cloud the experiments. Along this line, we have already started a pilot study using sharks. First, we recorded the field of a mystic while she was in an altered state, unaware of ordinary stimuli. Her field was quiet and strong, and her brain wave was *theta*. Two healers who were able to focus their thoughts broadcast specific thoughts via their field to the mystic while she was in this altered state. The thoughts were commands directed to the fish such as "come to me," "go away from me", or "remain still," all action commands. These thoughts were broadcast for a prescribed time in cadence with a flashing light. Our data show that the mystic's field responded in sync with the time cadence of the thought. The computer printout showed that her field activated while senders were thinking and quieted when they stopped. Later, the senders thought about "anger and attack", followed by "love and embrace"—emotions combined with actions. All three fields responded identically and as thought changed, so did the data from the senders and receiver. We have secured the permission to play these data underwater to a captive shark in a small pen at the Hebb Research Institute at San Diego. The thought vibrations will be introduced into the tank by auditory amplifiers while the action of the shark is monitored by video camera. No people will be in the immediate environment during the experiment, so as not to contaminate the thought field.

Studies of children and persons with language differences should follow. As we decode the primary information carried as thought forms, we should find a new approach to linguistic barriers from which a truly universal language could emerge.

Returning to telepathic knowing, psychics glean historical information from the static fields of people's rings, clothing, and possessions with varying degrees of credibility. If the owner is present, the psychics say that reading inert objects is much easier because of his active thoughts.

Just as technology stagnates without the stimulus of pure research, so human life is condemned to routine existence without the inspiration of new ideas and the power of creative imagination. Telepathic knowing is the essence of the creative act.

Have you ever had a great creative urge come over you? Or felt a growing need to create something—something you never got to? Perhaps you don't know what it is or why you are holding back. Do you believe you will in time overcome these restrictions?

Most of us don't, for we try many antidotes, generally the easier, ineffective ones, like time management, studying "how-to's" and learning new skills. Actually, the real problem is the emotional barriers that we experience as we move into the creative consciousness state.

There are no rules for creativity, but if there were one, it would be to break the accepted rules for coping with material problems and to find better, more imaginative ones. DeBono popularized creative thinking as lateral thinking—thinking around a problem and elaborating it in all possible ways before making a commitment. Divergent thinking is fun and helpful, but to achieve high level creative freedom, there is no substitute for emotional liberty.

While we accept the value of self-communication in understanding our loftier drives, we fail to realize that the energy of emotions directly activates creative potentials. Actually, the deep ties of emotion and consciousness are so bound up with acts of creativity they cause either a creative flow or a blockage. During strong emotional states, one moves rapidly away from material things and body-self reality into higher consciousness, the consciousness of the creative process and mysticism. Here, pent-up emotions are directly released, while some of the energy fuels creative acts and thoughts. If, however, these emotions are intense, unsettling, and from an unconscious source, fears may arise to turn one away, blocking creative action.

Affective emotional disturbances and mood disorders are legion among highly creative individuals. Examples are the manic-depressive behaviors of Isaac Newton, Ludwig von Beethoven, Charles Dickens, and Vincent Van Gogh. These disturbances stimulated a partial escape into an altered state. But a restless drive remained when the escape was not total. Naturally, they would gravitate to physical work or to creative acts in an attempt to organize their struggle in an impersonal way. Somehow, a neurotic drive coupled with an obsessive focus flames an otherwise normal, pleasant, creative process.

An Iowa study of prestigious writers revealed that 80% suffered severe depression or manic-depressive illness as compared to 30% of the less creative population. Studies in France and England corroborated these findings. Depression, despondence, hypermanic states and blocks in creativity are all restrictions to the coherent flow of emotions. When native people repress their emotions, they consequently repress their creativity. Remember, creativity springs from a life force. To create opens one to the deepest levels of altered states. Of course, psychosis is also an altered state. But if one can extend consciousness to monitor a vastly greater stream of happenings in the world without residual emotional turmoil, one does not get confused; clarity and creativity become heightened. This is to say creativity does not inevitably lead to psychopathology.

The remote senses of sight, hearing, and smell come closest to bridging physical reality with the creative state. Material reality dissolves into the real nature of the cosmos, a world of vibrating energy fields and resonances. Transcendent states carry experiences of worlds or tonal symbols, odors or essences, and pictures or graphic shapes. When these experiences occur, humans want to speak about them, write them, paint or compose them—to give their experiences material reality. They want to manifest and re-express their sensory perceptions flowing with telepathic ones. Creativity is, after all, an aspect of telepathic knowing. This is a process geared toward imagination and insight. What we have called extrasensory might better be called "supersensory."

During my years of university teaching, I was aware that our society and educational systems have helped to stifle creativity. But my assignments were always creative for the students and for me. I barely tolerated papers which regurgitated course information. Rather, I wanted students to turn information around, apply it creatively, and pose new questions about it. I wanted them to be so involved with the information that it made a difference to them. I spent a great deal of time stimulating and developing their creative processes. Some students loved the excitement of these assignments; they were the creative ones who spawned unique ideas. Unfortunately, many never did comprehend a creative opportunity. They kept asking what I wanted, while bemoaning not understanding.

The capacity to create remains a strong but unachieved educational goal because we have sought creativity through technique. But I believe that, rather than having mastered technique, the most all-around successful creators who live creative lives are those with the widest range of high and low vibrations, or a complete spectrum without gaps, who live on the ridge of chaos but rarely fall over the edge. Such people should be able to survey freely, play the vibrational scales, and focus on any part of the field at will. Perhaps education should try to soften the creative block, by changing the vibratory field, and allowing people to reclaim or reinstate their creativity, rather than trying to teach creativity.

Creativity involves many levels of consciousness operating simultaneously and freely. The mind is tapping into the higher sources in the universe, while at the same time acquiring information about the real world that is stored within the brain. In short, creativity requires the recovery of information stored in the brain or delivered by telepathic knowing and thought transference, or a combination of the two. When you think an original thought or you create a novel object, whether this sprang from an evolving idea or from sudden insight, you have manipulated old information in new ways. This is the highest level of thought. While these created ideas may be simple, the creative thought process was not. Skill in this process separates out the geniuses. But the interesting thing about the creative process is that it occurs when your mind is free and your brain is on automatic pilot, idling, so to speak, doing routine reflex work. Mozart and Buckminster Fuller created while walking. Darwin found the origin of the species when he was riding in a coach. Descartes' stimulus was intuitive dreams. The Egyptians incubated creative dreams with ritual practices in sleep temples.

Analysis of the creative process reveals conscious and unconscious stages. The preparatory stage requires motivation followed by defining the task or envisioning the end product. This is followed by reminiscing to bring to consciousness the memory of all information and hunches one has about the subject—the collection of raw ingredients before the slow cooking—where the process is removed from conscious reality. One does not dwell upon the process nor does one struggle to get answers. One trusts the process of higher creative thought, accepting that low level striving is not needed; involvement in routine tasks helps. The brain wave will drift into alpha, an idling state, and free the mind to soar. Some people use self-hypnosis ritually to calm the brain-talk so that the mind-field can think. And, as the mind-field is activated, telepathic knowing escalates, bringing in rich, unknown information from other fields.

From new insights in evolutionary biology we learn that just preceding the creation of new forms, there is a bewildering variety of complexity. (Lewin). The same principle is at work in creative thought. Most people are aware of the tensions, insecurities, excitement or agitation they experience before they birth brave new concepts. During these times the human field dramatically increases in strength and frequency spectra, almost to the state of chaos, before new and finer organization takes place. We can hasten it with tolerant understanding, but the process stops only with manifestation or temporary chaotic disintegration. This state (before manifestation or disintegration) has been referred to as a no-man's-land where chaos and stability pull in opposite directions. It can be likened to the period when an element is passing from a solid state to a gaseous one. It is a clear switch from one state to another. In the metaphysical world, we refer to a consciousness shift, or a phase transition in consciousness. Probably during this period of instability, new information comes to awareness, bringing a greater capacity to manipulate complex information. The state of being at the edge of chaos describes an eminently creative or universal consciousness where information seems to have a life of its own. (Lewin).

Strangely, as we grow older and obtain elaborate skills and much more information to create from, our creativity lessens. While some gifted, creatively free individuals increase in skill with age, the shocking fact remains that statistically, creativity decreases with age. Using the best prediction tests of creative manipulation of objects, children age five have 100% of their creative capacity. By age seven their creativity has decreased 50%. And by 40 years of age, creativity is reduced to 1% of one's capacity. In other words, the creative solutions to manipulating the physical environment in our culture, and the creative use of material information stored in the brain becomes thwarted with age. I wonder if, as we age, we become less tolerant of the feelings, instability and uncertainty of teetering on the creative edge of chaos. It is interesting to note that IQ scores are not related to creativity; children classified by current intellectual standards as retarded were found to be normal or above normal in some creative processes.

Descriptions of the different phases of creative states, such as belittling logic, complete absorption, increased imagery, absence of judgment, courage to take a chance, withdrawal from external realities, expanded perceptions, weakened body image boundaries, time warp and spatial distortion, trusting open systems of insight, intuition, imagination, also describe aspects of higher consciousness. Everyone experiences the loss of the sense of time and space during deep creative states—we become lost in thought. During higher consciousness, when the mind-field is in touch with other fields, thoughts are clear and coherent. Even manipulative tasks seem to be done for us; there is no conscious struggle. The "will" sets the course, then gets out of the driver's seat. We are continuously amazed that the "I" doesn't seem to be involved. The creative act is somehow illuminated when personality isn't.

Creativity is a magical synthesis. When we comprehend our creative products, we may have difficulty understanding that they happened so simply. Often we see mystical truths revealed. These facts help us to recognize that a confusion exists between what our culture stresses, that is, knowing factual information, being practical, rational, and thinking logically and realistically, but not strangely or innovatively, and the states necessary for living creatively. To comply with cultural dictates demands that we concentrate on brain activity, skirting the mind-field where creativity resides.

A very successful physical therapist uses biofeedback training to put patients into an alpha state so that they can image tissue healing. He noted that when the brain reached an alpha wave, an interactive state, the person's mental capabilities soared. They thought clearly, learned biofeedback rapidly, created all manner of unusual imagery, and they rapidly improved the injured or painful area. When he asked me why, I remembered some earlier laboratory findings. When the normal brain wave frequency lowered to alpha or theta, imagination catapulted. Information from other lifehoods surfaced and with it sometimes unusual musical, artistic, or literary talent. The mind-field data became stronger with a wider frequency range, as a repository of the soul's learnings flooded the awareness.

Elmer Green of the Menninger Clinic performed an interesting biofeedback study. Students were taken into an alpha state and then into the deeper theta state, an even lower frequency which supposedly carries a different information processing capacity, one providing hypnogogic or creative imagery. In this state, students had more vivid dreams, recalled early childhood experiences, had archetypal imagery, and were more appreciative of nature and beauty. Also in this state, they were better able to take tests, supposedly because they were more intuitive. We in educational circles have known that objective type tests are best taken while using higher conscious thinking. Test takers who know nothing about the subject frequently have higher test scores than the informed student who uses rational selection.

When studies attribute creative thought to the increased alpha waves that do in fact occur during creativity, they are in error. The alpha state coexists with creativity, but is not its cause. The alpha state means that the brain is quiet, out of the way, so that the mind-field can intuitively access facts and provide a broader vision. It's interesting, however, that creative people under ordinary circumstances create fewer alpha waves than non-creative people, but when assigned a creative task, they produce more than the non-creative ones. They move into higher consciousness states and are more disturbed by strong sensory stimuli like loud noises, bright lights, or strong odors.

Likewise, right hemisphere activity increases during creativity. This hemisphere is a processing and retrieving center for the spatial facts and relationships needed during the creative process. But brain hemispheres do not cause creativity; at most, they only support it.

In summary, during creative experiences one has freed a part of the mind from handling the world, and has reached a consciousness state where what the brain records and what the field receives simultaneously flow back and forth—a brain/mind coherency of exceeding complexity. This is a new understanding of the creative process.

The literature abounds with descriptions of the brain being an active, self-organizing system of material information. I believe that the brain is an elegant recognition and sorting instrument. But the brain is brilliantly uncreative, as are people who process information primarily via the brain. The brain is basically not a creative, thinking machine; that is the mind-field which scans for new information connections and does the lateral thinking. We might say that we have a schizophrenic split, a one-sided model of thought and creativity. When tied to the brain, there is no "depth perception," only surface happenings.

Brahms described his exalted state when he composed music as pure inspiration outside himself. This resembles a semi-trance state, where one goes through a small door to an immense new world. Trance falls into an autistic mode of thinking, where reality orientation is suspended but not lost. To create, the mind must withdraw from the physical self and everyday concerns for a time to focus forces. This is a tender, sensitive time when humans often choose solitude, or seek to retreat into the wilderness to quiet the brain in preparation for the mind's action. When intense creative urges have taken their course, one generally wishes to return to material reality.

Unfortunately, we have accepted the limitations of mind and body set forth by psychology, physiology and medicine, and by experience we have innately confirmed these norms of human capacity. Let us not confuse the limitations of material flesh with the infinite aspects of the mind. Conscious transferring and decoding of thought—what has occurred, what occurs, and what is to occur, I believe is the capacity of all people who choose to be truly human. Such an explanation of the creative nature of man describes his ascent, his evolution.

CHAPTER VIII

EMOTIONS AND THE MYSTICAL EXPERIENCE

The emotions associated with mystical experiences are those which are embedded in the upper ranges of reality and awareness. Mystical experiences differ from psychic ones. The former involve information not available to ordinary senses; this information has a spiritual quality connected with the soul, providing access to the grand thoughts and wisdom of the ages. Jung's ideas of the Self alluded to this mystical spark of the soul. Psychic experiences, which are also beyond the scope of the five senses, are restricted to information about the everyday existence of the body and personality.

Mystical experience comes first in all creative endeavors, for here we not only join the divine, but we access extremely high levels of information. The rational and logical follows. To put it another way, all great thoughts start mystically, to be later refined practically.

Albert Einstein once said, "The most beautiful thing we can experience is the mysterious. Recognition of the mystery of the universe is the source of all true science. He to whom emotions are a stranger, who can no longer pause to wonder and stand rapt in awe is as good as dead; his eyes are closed." Einstein was alluding to the metaphysical aspect of emotions.

William James stated that psychology is not a science, it is only the hope of a science, and someday when we find the answers these will probably be metaphysical in nature.

Nowhere in the scientific literature is there a comprehensive model of the role of human emotions in higher consciousness. There have been no systematic studies of human emotion connected with mystical states.

I believe that in this, the last years of the 20th century, the truly monumental discoveries about human behavior will be information about the emotions associated with the profoundly mystical qualities of the human psyche, the soul. And, I believe that we will realize finally that the origin of all emotional problems is embedded in mystical experiences. To probe these sources, one must personally tap into awarenesses of the non-rational nature of human beings. Pyschotherapists must envision this realm of consciousness as essential to an expanded, orderly relationship with self and the cosmic world. Too often, even today, mystical experiences are considered emotional aberrations primarily because they are divorced from ordinary reality. While mystical states may exist with prolonged breaks in consciousness creating emotional disturbances, mystical states are also absolutely essential for comprehending life's profound meanings.

To some, acknowledging the mystical is to return to the "outback" wilderness as though human development has passed beyond such experiences. Although great philosophers have always affirmed our mystical nature, at a practical level many of us either mistrust or spontaneously deny our personal contacts with it. Others acknowledge it, but call it "weird".

If we wish to be fully human, we must cultivate our mystical nature. This requires re-examination of our beliefs about emotions. During mystical experiences, emotions may be repressed or more intense than in ordinary states. But new information is revealed; subconscious thoughts connect with superconscious ones, creating a flow that accesses wisdom and destiny.

Socrates, many centuries ago, wisely stated: "To know thyself will set you free." Surely we have made superficial strides in that direction, but how sad it is that most of us still feel strangers to ourselves. With all the many things our mind understands, "We don't even know ourselves." Each judgment we make, each concept of truth that we embrace, each time we align with a cause, we believe we must be correct because we have logically thought out our positions. We operate as though we know our deep motivations.

Actually, we generally communicate with self in a vacuum. New age advice that one should transcend ego boundaries forgets one important fact. Successful communication with *all* aspects of self is a requisite to a satisfying interaction in an interplanetary world. True self discovery means changing our inner input of reality. The first necessary change lies within ourselves, with our motivations, awarenesses, and goals. Of all our mental processes, the most difficult is to entertain a sweeping new concept which, if accepted as true, will cause us to junk a life of training and to discard our framework for interpreting our experiences. But whether we like it or not, the process is already in motion. Things that worked in the past do not seem to work well anymore; cars break down, equipment fails, institutions crumble, and useful behavior patterns abort. When things were just a bit off, we tolerated them—now we cannot.

Anyone who tries to direct his life toward divinity would agree, I think, that to evolve is a seemingly impossible struggle. Probably, there is not one person who has crossed major barriers "on the path" who has not suffered. I believe that there is no easy route if one focuses on the ultimate.

But I do know that evolution would be easier if we were firmly in touch with our mystical nature. Too often, we relegate mystical knowing to others, but do not accept it for ourselves. So we pursue gurus, esoteric conferences, and psychic readings, or even more intellectual facts, but without success or gratification.

Sorokin, at the Harvard Research Center for Creative Altruism, became aware of two distinct patterns of creative growth in superconsciousness from a study of life histories of the greats. There were those who grew quietly and gracefully in altruism and creativity, accessing the super-consciousness, and those who had catastrophic or sharp conversions with drastic rearrangement of egos, group affiliation, and values. The Buddha, St. Francis, St. Paul, St. Augustine, St. Ignatius of Loyola, Gandhi and St. Theresa, were some of this latter group.

Early in my *Mind Mastery* work, I discovered these same two general categories without satisfactory explanation. But as I observed the progress of dedicated people, the smooth, flowing, graceful changes came to an abrupt halt. Such casual changes were much too superficial when they plunged into another, deeper level. Suddenly, fear overwhelmed them. But there were often greater mystical knowing and more magnificent manifestations just beyond. This was a major ecstatic transition, the intensity of which often brought feelings of impending danger. Many reported thinking that they were going to die. Although there are similarities to the death of the physical body, these feelings are like "death of the soul", a feeling of permanent death, a state of absolute non-existence at all levels of awareness. Fear of death is both material and metaphysical, but remember it is the self which cares whether you physically live or die; the soul is not involved. The soul is forever. Fully integrating these dichotomies, of course, is easier intellectually than emotionally.

The real struggle we experience as we evolve comes from our resistance to change, not just to move forward, but to take a new, uncharted route. Change at this level disrupts ways of thinking, making choices and behaving.

Some of us approach change with a strong will to move all manner of obstacles, others with passive acceptance that divine inspiration will remove all errors of thinking. It is correct; there are some superficial habit patterns of eating and living as well as bland beliefs that will change comfortably with more information or a new focus. However, those behaviors with deep hidden sources carry such strong emotional charges that they seemingly resist all current psychotherapeutic techniques. These stubborn blocks are more than reflexes or habits; they are agreements with ourselves and with others about who we are and what we accept. There are both active and acquiescent agreements that are beyond our awareness which keep us from changing—again, agreements we have made about what we believe about ourselves and the role we accept within a family, community, or social group. When the unnamed rules are accepted, there are no waves and little emotion, often to the detriment of all involved. The agreements, although reconfirmed in this life, stem from other lifehoods; they may continue throughout the present lifetime unless, for example, one or both people decide that some of their agreements are stifling and that they must change.

Changing an agreement involves confronting one's own feeling and those of others. I ask you to look at your relationships, your agreements. Regardless of how comfortable or materially satisfying these are, do these agreements honestly encourage the evolution of both people? If the answer is "no", be careful not to place the blame on the other person, rather than upon mutually acknowledged agreements that may have served to protect both of you from the trauma of deep change. Many people delay change by rationalizing that the reason they do not confront is because they don't want to hurt another person. If an agreement is unsatisfactory to you, you must state and discuss it with whomever it involves. Have you ever realized that you and some of your old friends have few common interests? If they bore you, you probably also bore them!

Generally, it is easier to make excuses and drop out quietly, terminating the agreement to continue as close friends. I believe this is acceptable with casual acquaintances, but with deep commitments, it is unacceptable. Only by firmly acknowledging your need for a new relationship or a better role, can you solidify your change.

Many of you are acquainted with the philosophies of emotion from research into sensation, perception, learning, brain-mind relationships, psychopathology, and currently, the biochemistry of neuropeptides and enzymes. What we forget is that we accept some of these ideas as more significant than others because they help to explain ourselves on levels that we can accept. They are not too threatening. So the explanations that we like best, we personalize. Psychology and psychotherapy, concerned with body image, selfhood, personality, ego, id, superego, do not address mystical experiences or higher states of consciousness. Instead, they deal with ordinary awareness of the body, material world, and relationships. Even the Freudian superego, the monitor of right and wrong acting to control emotions, is connected to the material world. All of these emotional concepts are time-space dimensions of reality and do not help explain other realities.

We may possibly categorize emotions as higher or lower by the vibrations we experience. With mystical thoughts, the field vibrations are of high frequencies while the body processes are slowed down. Contrary-wise, with unrepressed emotions connected with material happenings, the quantity of electromagnetic energy is increased but not its frequency, and the physiology is stimulated throughout.

Further distinctions between mystical and material emotions are based on the energy source and its supposed function. The material level of emotions we say comes from what we view as stress or harm to the physical body and ego. Its function is to protect and embellish both. Mystical emotions are responsible for protecting and elaborating the soul level of existence.

For example, pure emotions like love and joy lead to behaviors which elaborate life—anger and fear to protective behaviors which eliminate threat. Both of these occur regardless of whether the source is mystical or material. Although happenings in the material world can trigger all emotion, when probing deeper, one finds the strongest emotional charges attached to unresolved problems and attitudes at the soul's level—from mystical knowing—from spiritual thoughts. Current psychotherapy is based on the notion that the problem can be understood and solved by uncovering material childhood experiences. While some behaviors can be altered or at least the emotions discharged, the urgency of the strong emotions is not resolved; nor is there peace, emotional freedom, or spiritual evolution by the old route.

Psychotherapists acknowledge the spiritual aspects of humans by referring clients to religious counselors. While there are some enlightened leaders, there is nothing in the training of priests, ministers, or rabbis which prepares them to enter into and decode the mystical experiences of people. Remember that many of the mystical passages in the Bible were removed by Christians at the Nicean Conference in Constantinople in the 12th century. The portions retained in Catholic theology are rarely understood by grass roots priests and only a special group of rabbis is trained in the mystical Judaism of the Kabbala.

So where can we learn about emotions and the mystical experiences? There is a growing body of narrative reports about personal experiences in altered states. While some are probing, many are so irrationally esoteric (they emanated from the ungrounded state of the narrator) that these should not become a part of a model of mystical aspirations. Myths and rituals handed down in various cultures carry common themes, particularly popular in today's spiritual milieu. A great many are beautiful and enlightening, but when they contain so much symbolism that they encourage an ungrounded state, they make little difference in everyday living.

Universal mystical truths are also disclosed in archetypal images that symbolically encourage many interpretations. From my experience, archetypal symbolism is frequently used to explain irrational emotions. It is so easy when working with archetypal images to split in consciousness—to become ungrounded. When the identification is held on the symbolic level, it is difficult to incorporate these mystical experiences into one's life. But if we allow ourselves to witness the mystical part of our being while maintaining a realistic grounded orientation, we can tap simultaneously into the personal and the universal information.

In deep mystical states one often experiences contrasting ecstasy and fear. While most humans like joy, ecstasy is something else—it carries an overwhelming charge. One does not know what to think or what to do with it. An overpowering fear also makes no logical sense, yet its presence cries out for answers.

Sometimes the person has fleeting thoughts that he "may be going off the deep end" and not coming back. This protective reaction wisely keeps one from moving too quickly. It is possible, but not too probable, that an insane episode could result. If you don't accept insanity as a satisfactory escape, it will not occur. Insanity is a human experience. Except in the case of disease, animals in the wild are not insane and apparently experience no mental illness. Man can parry "madness" by developing realistic ways of handling his overwhelming visionary, illusionary, and spiritual experiences.

During mystical reaching, there may be intense anger at others who have denied you the right to feel divine. Frequently, there is also massive anger against God, who has not saved you from all manner of trauma or made you perfect.

In amnesia, an altered state, when one leaves the time-space reality, the brain no longer records the experience. It is idling with a theta wave. The mind-field, on the other hand, is in massive fluctuation. This is where memories of these mystical experiences are stored, where they constantly influence our material behavior without giving us access to the so-called files.

Recovery of these experiences comes only as one repeats the initial altered states. The closest to this in modern psychotherapy is hypnotherapy, although most hypnotherapists interpret findings on a material body-ego level, not on a soul level.

The literature does not clearly differentiate mystical states in particular from altered states in general. Altered, to me, means ungrounded, not Earth-oriented; it does not imply connection to the soul level. Generally, it means adrift and floating somewhere in between.

Research has shown that during altered states the sensory threshold to subliminal or marginal stimuli is lowered. Individuals respond more strongly to minimal intensity stimulation during altered states. But because they are disconnected from everyday reality, they may not experience pain. In most altered states, the range of environmental stimuli one responds to is constricted and the awareness may be focused upon a narrow circle of ideas. Thinking is generally subjective, egocentric, with strong precepts and no concepts. Everything may seem to be connected with everything else, but not in a rational, material manner. This is not true with mystical, flowing, complex states where information is quickly integrated.

We must understand that the current time-space ideas about emotions leave much unexplained. While these beliefs are not wrong, they are gravely incomplete.

My basic information about emotion comes from graduate academic training in psychology and from a long and "successful" psychoanalysis by a member of the American Psychoanalytic Society. Neither of these prepared me for mystical things. Furthermore, a lifetime of participation in Christian churches as a vestry member, and concerted study of the Bible and religions only informed me about man's experiences with the divine. The deep understanding about mysticism and emotion came during my own evolutionary process, and when I recovered lifehoods and comprehended my divine nature.

I acknowledge how difficult this is. As a result of my own personal experiences, my mystical capabilities increased, allowing me to enter the mind-fields of others and to read deep thoughts. I developed techniques of opening the mind-field to recover the unfinished business of lifehoods that were strongly affecting the current life.

During long sessions of mystical probing, I learned more about the soul's struggle, the universal decisions that are again replicated in the current life. My goal was to empower the individual with profound mystical understanding and to help him experience spiritual light. As a result of our work, no one ever left the same as he came, and always there was a glimmer of beauty, if not a full view of the glory of the human soul. The change is never complete with such insight, but a new course can be set—amazingly, many of the material problems lose their luster.

Because I am a teacher and counselor, I believe that information alone will not bring change, and so I refuse to give psychic readings. I learned that only through the insight available by emotionally reexperiencing past lifehoods could one remove the blocks to knowing one's divine nature. The person had to actively recover his or her own information.

During the course of 30 years, hundreds of successful professionals have given me the opportunity to assist them, to penetrate their mind-fields and recover this unfinished business. I am not interested in who you were in another life, for that lies in the ego, physical, emotional level, but rather, how you lived, what mystical experiences you had, and what you did with these. For these constitute the attitudes you hold today. This is at the soul level of change. (See Chapter II, "Spirituality: The Evolutionary Goal", and Chapter IX, "Lifehoods: The Hidden Agenda".)

Now we come to the question: what is emotion, anyway? Academic definitions of emotion have yielded two approaches: emotion as experience, and emotion as physiological process. Neither description fits the discussion of emotions in higher awareness or mystical states. Only a field concept fills the bill, as elaborated in Chapter IV. Here the human mind is envisioned as an energy field organized by emotion, where emotion is an agitation, a disturbance in the quality of flow of energy occurring as a result of field transaction. Physiological phenomena are secondary responses. Many aspects of emotion we don't understand, but we do know that all human experiences are created by, stem from, and are embedded in the energetic part of the energy field we describe as emotions. Emotion is aroused energy, a human power source. Although we have never defined emotion adequately, we know that without some level of energy arousal from emotion, there is no life. Most of us acknowledge emotion when something hurts, is grand, strange, or huge. Like all experiences, emotions have gradations which have to do with source and how the individual interprets and uses this energy. It is little wonder that we experience and interpret emotions differently.

You may wonder, if one does not experience emotion, does it exist? My answer is, if there is a field disturbance which one experiences with feelings, there is emotion. But emotional energy can activate behavior and create bodily happenings without feelings. This is the common state with mystical denial.

Wilhelm Reich's classification of emotion into primary/rational and secondary/irrational, has encouraged unsatisfactory conclusions. When we do not understand their source, we label emotions irrational. Actually, there are no irrational emotions; it is only how we use them that is sometimes irrational.

Let me summarize: emotion is an energetic agitation or condition, first in the field, and then in the body and awareness. It has a source, a response, and an interpretation in the continuum of consciousness. If focused in the time-space domain, the concern is with body and self. If out of time and in a mystical state, its concern is the soul.

There is an interesting, yet confusing, relationship between the two emotional sources. If the emotional agitation comes from the soul and cannot be handled, solved or dissipated, the energy filters down to material awareness where it creates all manner of social and sexual problems. Contrariwise, if the source is here and now, strongly tied to life, death or intense pain, the agitation may be so great that it cannot be integrated, acted upon, or resolved. The emotional force itself will catapult the person's awareness to an altered state where there is no selfhood, no body, and therefore, no pain. Here one is beyond ego. Immediate problems dissipate, one is at peace temporarily on the personality level, although behavior is still being influenced. Here the goal of emotion is to maintain the integrity of the field rather than that of the dense body. If emotions are experienced, they are connected to mystical, spiritual, or psychic things and everyday "real" experiences are absent.

Although the true source of traumatic experiences may be in this life's experiences, the altered state which results from major shock cloisters us from the memory. It creates a schism in reality. Remember, when reality changes, and with it awareness, emotional energy is not lost. Some is abated in the shift; the remainder becomes associated with the soul. Now it is ego-less.

To express it another way, strong emotions which have no outlet or solution are most often sidetracked by a shift in reality. In other words, emotion changes reality, and reality can change emotional experiences.

Here is a dramatic example of a person who recovered physical capacities by reexperiencing a mystical state. I had met socially an anesthesiologist who asked me about my communication with comatose patients to bring them back to consciousness. Several years later, he called me to tell me that his teen-aged son had been in a major automobile accident with extensive head trauma and surgery. He had been in an extended coma ever since. I encouraged the parents to talk to their son regularly as though he could hear, because he could hear, only he couldn't respond. I suggested they encourage his high school friends to tell him what was going on with them—to keep him in touch with the world he had lost. They were to have music played in his room during the daytime, also to stimulate material awareness. He came out of the coma in several months, but this brilliant student, an athlete and school leader, was now dull; he couldn't remember. The "light" seemed to have gone out. His speech and minor coordination were affected. To his parents' query about what I could do about it, my answer was clear. If it is neurological destruction, I can do nothing. If it is psychic shock, I may be able to help. Since there was no way of knowing the cause,

I chose to take him into higher consciousness to try and recover what happened during the accident and surgery.

In sessions lasting for six hours, he recovered all the information of what had taken place, from before the collision to his removal from the car, the trip to the hospital, the surgeons, and his own worried father. He remembered his rage at surgeons who did not ask his permission to "saw" into his brain. Now surgeons don't generally ask that question of people in comas. Apparently they should, because he understood and wanted to be considered, despite the fact he could not respond with words. He complained of tremendous pain, although brains are not supposed to have sensory nerve endings for recording pain, and likewise, in comas we are not supposed to feel pain. (Yet we have discovered in the laboratory that pain occurs first in the field. In altered states, pain in the field is often experienced, not pain in the physical body.) This also brought him more anger because the doctors did not stop his pain. When the brain surgery was over and he was so seriously ill that he thought he might not live, he talked to God. At this stage, he relived the intense humbling emotions of having a direct line to God, one he had never experienced before. God told him he would live "if your will is strong enough." If not, he would die. These words did not mean anything to him then.

During his long intensive care, his family and a few friends came for brief visits. His mother, a loving but not particularly spontaneous woman, wept and emotionally told him how much she loved him. His friends expressed how much they needed and missed him. They were openly emotional at seeing this stunning young man inert with a swollen, distorted face, and still unconscious. But because they thought he was not conscious and would never know, they were free to show their emotional loss. It was these many intense emotional expressions that tipped the scale and gave him "a will to live." When he knew that others cared about him that much, he wanted to recover and live. Because he relived these mystical states and recovered the emotional information held there, his mind cleared, the slowness left, and his speech returned to normal. Now he is a bright college graduate and one with psychic abilities.

I would like to return here to the intense feelings of ecstasy and fear which often accompany mystical states. You may recall when such feelings, sometimes accompanied by imagery of vicious animals, distorted gargoyles, conquering fire and blinding light upset your meditation, compelling you to return suddenly to everyday concerns. When you sought explanations from some meditation teachers, out of their own fears, they cautioned you not to proceed into this "darkness of the soul."

Psychologists frequently allude to the dark places, the demons of the human soul. Accounts and explanations of inhuman possessions and acts from earlier incarnations appear in the New Age and esoteric literature. It is unfortunate to run from these symptoms. If one gently takes the bull by the horns—brings these projected images into self and owns them—rage and anger occur and the fear is gone. Now one can begin to understand the source of these uncomfortable emotions. Fear always protects us from strong emotions, and when coupled with ugly images, their power encourages us all the more to "run" from them.

In my own and my student's evolution, fear is always present, but diabolic thoughts are not inevitable. Let me assure you that these seemingly insurmountable barriers are grossly and disastrously inflated. These so-called horrors of the emotions are machinations created by the mind to protect us from the unknown, and ultimately from change. There is no metaphysical reality in these horror images.

Because I understand the relationship between fear and mystical experiences, I refuse to empower these defenses. It is best to face them squarely as distorted and denied emotions. Rather than encourage people to work through so-called "dark spots," I ask them if they are willing to realize that they are defenses, and then give them up, because they are not the real problem. People are amazed at how rapidly the darkness turns to light.

Some psychics believe that the incidence of black magic and

Satan worship is increasing, although I have seen no compelling evidence to support that. But I have some experiences that could allay inordinate concerns. Of course, black magic and Satan worship exist. We need not fear sacrificial animal killings, as reported in southern Texas, unless we personally gravitate toward such distorted behaviors. I have seen the spontaneous voodoo sacrifices of animals in Haiti and I was tempted to observe the nightly black magic rituals on the beaches of Rio. Their so-called diabolical powers could not have affected me, but the practitioners would have known that I was not a fellow traveler, and my body might not have fared as well.

Years ago, when Rosalyn Bruyere and I were lecturing at the University of California at Santa Barbara, I was approached by an aggressive, unkempt young woman demanding an appointment. I was so uncomfortable that I literally backed away from her, evading any further relationship—not my usual pattern at all. I mumbled some excuse about not having my datebook, suggesting that she call me at my laboratory, all the while hoping that she wouldn't.

When our lectures were finished, Rosalyn congratulated me on handling that "black magic" woman. Apparently, this woman's aura was the same as a professed black magic group she had observed at other times. I didn't see auras then, but I sensed a weak, yet angry, field and that she definitely wanted something from me. Rosalyn said that such people seek out persons with vital life forces because they themselves lack the biologically stimulating red frequencies. I immediately flashed back to my "black" great-great-grandmother, a Romany Gypsy herbalist, who chased me as a small child to hold and crush me. My father had explained that she saw black witches and goblin-like creatures. When I understood my anxiety, I pursued the young woman and gave her an appointment, realizing that she was no threat to me, and perhaps I could help her. Unfortunately for both of us, she did not keep the appointment.

Later a local minister sent me a former parishioner who had

joined a Satan worship group. Admittedly, she was only partially converted or she would not have confided in the minister nor come to me. By opening her mind-field, we uncovered her extreme anger at God—anger she had not consciously known. She felt that God had abandoned her when she was unjustly accused of stealing and was flogged to death. In that lifetime, she was out to get God, using Satan as her weapon. She joined a group which performed rituals in which Satan could express her defiance and anger at God. The members of this group could vicariously vent their anger without understanding or taking responsibility.

Furthermore, we discovered that in other lifetimes she had been a mystic seer who was punished and killed for her skills. She discovered that she had set up these horrible black magic scenarios to insure her feelings of inadequacy. Now she turned her anger on the Satan group, vowing to destroy them. I encouraged her to work with her new insights to change herself. The group had actually served her need to become aware of her anger at God, her "hidden agenda." I belief that this anger at God is almost always the key motivation for participating in Satan worship.

We have simply invested too much emotional energy in protecting ourselves from imagined threats. How strange it is to employ evil thought to protect us from our greatness, to keep ourselves from the knowledge of the God within us. When people decide to give up these defenses, the change they experience is a true metamorphosis of the type Sorokin observed in the lives of those who suffered and then manifested their gifts on the grandest scale.

Reports in the literature of individuals experiencing states of being "Christed" or "sainted" are often interpreted as psycho-pathological or at least evidence of psychotic episodes. Of course, if the individual cannot differentiate these experiences and the physical realities of being a saint, then there is aberration. But to reach the level of vibrations where one experiences his divine simultaneously with his mortal nature is a goal of evolution. This state illuminates our unfinished business of lifehoods, the source of all deep problems, and the reason for this particular reincarnation. I believe that each soul yearns and has the capacity for such ascendance. All truly "sainted" and "Christed" beings have come to these experiences and have incorporated them into their lives, allowing acts of greatness.

It seems apparent that most people will not reach this goal in this lifehood, but during the Aquarian Age, more people will be willing to suffer the pain, endure the training, and make the changes—probably more than at any other time in history. More people will become visionaries, as wise as the sages, and many will manifest as divine healers. I do know that when we compare ourselves to the giants of our civilization, the ones we call masters, most of us feel inferior. Recall that we have imbued Pythagoras, Newton, Raphael, Shakespeare, and Einstein with greatness for their discoveries, creations, and intellectual capabilities, and others, such as St. Paul, Jacob, Abraham, and Gandhi for their wisdom and divine power. All of these people used mystical consciousness to tap into universal information, to use it in a disciplined way, and then to share with the world.

If we acknowledge that their true gift was divine, we must begin to accept that it is also yours and mine if our souls choose to honor its divinity. We can no longer entertain beliefs that we are unworthy and inadequate, only then can the soul recognize that it cannot be held back by negative thoughts or ego concerns. The ego remains strong and secure but humble, with the strength of this knowing.

I encourage you to find and to turn this corner. When you do, a new awareness appears. Everyday life starts to improve. There is a temptation to dwell upon these changes and to relate them to others excitedly. Actually, the improvements have occurred because you are getting out of your own way. Take time to enjoy your own change, even if it also seems only a tentative disruption of your old pattern of struggle.

But don't delay too long in reminiscence. Other subtle changes will begin to reach your awareness. You may know about future events or your wish may cause things to happen without effort. Others seek your company, want to talk with you, want to share deeper parts of themselves without being asked. Things seem good—at times, strange. You may sleep less or find yourself daydreaming or meditating more.

You may have periods of ungroundedness and get cold feet as your awareness drifts. Tolerate this latter state, but don't let it become a habit. If you remain grounded, with one foot in ordinary reality, you may still experience some emotional instability and sudden mood changes. Observe these, but don't get lost in them. In fact, simply acknowledge, but don't dwell upon them. This is a part of deeper change.

You may find that your experiences are more intense: you may dislike things more, experience greater fear, stronger joy, and more peak experiences. Auditory sensations with higher pitch sounds and music often accompany vivid imagery. Historical spiritual figures may appear.

Situations which formerly brought empathy are now super-charged. You will wonder what is happening and if it will last. Spiritual feelings will seem to come from nowhere as though old triggers such as church ritual, liturgical music, biblical verse and poetry all simultaneously impinge upon you. Even your body enlivens in a way that no drug or physical stimulant could effect. You are in motion, vibrating, with few physical barriers. Your sensory acuity is so heightened, that you can touch all thought to know all things.

From a psychiatric and material reality, these are hallucinations. When we clearly understand hallucinations, I suspect we will discover that they play an intermediary role between normal sensory perception and mystical knowing. From an expanded awareness of full consciousness, most of these so-called hallucinations will become normal, routine experiences.

If you feel bombarded with hyperstrong sensations, know that these conditions are not abnormal, just unusually new for you. They are requisite to deeper change. In the physical world, this state of vibration is called chaos—a condition appearing to be disorganized or entropic because it is new and unknown. Like chaos, this heralds a new level of organization so refined that the human mind has not yet been able to reach a level of reorganization that can incorporate its perfection.

I have been given the great opportunity of helping to support and guide many others in ascending this rocky, spiritual path. I have learned that although the work is primarily metaphysical in nature, there are some fundamental conditions that are essential to progress. The individual must have developed a relatively secure ego and selfhood and have reached some degree of success and satisfaction in society. There must be a sufficient degree of comfort with one's relationships and there must be economic security to satisfy deep needs and average human wants.

Those whose lives have been basically unsuccessful can, of course, progress slowly, but not on the level I am describing. Until these basic physical and psychological requirements are met, one's energy is too diffuse and dissipated. There is not sufficient self-strength to protect one from psychic escape when internal pressures are released into the awareness. There must also be strength of will to direct the energy and a true sense of self-worth to support it.

When people are still operating from a narrow consciousness and emphasizing physical existence, the energy from unresolved spiritual problems is truncated and leads to material problems. Since the source is not material, these perceived problems persist. Intuitively list your daily problems. Which of these, with some effort, do you want to handle immediately? Which of the remaining ones are you so sick of that you are going to start giving them up by denying them front stage? Now you will find that you have fewer problems. If those remaining are material problems, devote just half as much energy to them. This way you can double your energy for solving spiritual problems. This is a sensible approach when we remember that we cannot explain most emotional disturbances rationally or work them out intellectually.

Let us examine some widespread beliefs, which many of us have accepted, that are first line barriers to emotional freedom. Evaluate your stand on these. Have you bought the idea that happiness and bliss are the ultimate goals of everyday life? If you have, you will continue seeking superficial pleasures, all short-lived and incomplete. I believe the soul's goal is to evolve to the highest level, spiritually, emotionally, intellectually, and physically—this requires the full development of one's mystical nature. Happiness and bliss should not be the goal. These will come anyway as a result of successful evolution.

Another way to avoid emotional freedom is to blame one's culture. Ethnospiritual beliefs and customs create a framework for our lives, which do present powerful dictates, but these do not cause our problems. We know this because when customs change, our so-called problems change, but they don't go away. No culture can dictate beliefs unless we "buy" them, and unless we neurotically need them. Cultural beliefs exist to perpetuate the society, but more importantly, at another level, to protect us from our grandest emotions. This handicaps us. When people covet cultural beliefs as immutable God-ordained laws, they stifle their spiritual growth. Furthermore, they accept these dictates as "truths" instead of just as guidelines. In other words, what looks ideal has destructive potential if it encourages us to remain on ordinary human levels, ignoring the full range of mystical wisdom and the spiritual power which enables us to evolve and advance our civilization.

We have also abdicated personal responsibility to government bureaucracy, to civil laws which are frequently out of tune with higher truths. Think of all the practices destructive to our world that are protected by law. While we acknowledge how bad things are, we must be reminded that we are on the frontier of magnanimous change. Only by reaching depths of personal and group despair are we willing to reconstruct our unacceptable corporate and personal beliefs and practices.

We still have not comprehended that part of self which is so luminescent, so grandly spiritual. To recognize that we can do almost anything, that we have command, that we are larger, stronger, higher, and greater than we have ever known looks ideal. So it seems incomprehensible that these could be miserable burdens—but they are. The problem lies in the deep emotions we uncover when we remember the times when we gladly played a lesser role out of fear of overwhelmingly great thoughts and plans.

The dissatisfied ranks are growing. More and more of us want only the clearest, most harmonic total world. And we *do* know how to experience our own divine love and joy which nourishes all people and our planet as well. Our lives can turn around and turn around immediately. This is the overriding charge of the future.

So how do we get there? There are no detailed charts, but there are sure guidelines. We must be willing to discipline ourselves to avoid tangents and being lured by incomplete solutions. Urgency to "get through it" is legion, as though this is a trip from one place to another on a well-known path—going the distance but remaining the same. Human nature seems eager to be rid of annoyances in order to reap rewards, but without having to change. But change is essential. So often one hears that the problem lies in one's relationship to the world. But to change how we interact with the world is a simple approach that won't work. It shouldn't be our focus. What must change is our relationship to ourselves—our awareness, motivation, and behavior so that all levels of consciousness are in harmony.

Some people equate this kind of change with giving up their humanness, maintaining that humanness is too important and satisfying to destroy. Of course, this is incorrect thinking. Actually, humanness begins to take on a new meaning. It is true that less energy will be spent on the material aspects of existence and more upon the metaphysical, spiritual components. When awareness is complete, emotional energy flows, nourishing the mind and feeding the body with the complete realm of feelings and abilities.

Let me highlight some other widely held emotional beliefs that often become barriers. One is the emphasis upon the "lower self and the negative emotions," that is, aggression, rage, and anger, a common emphasis in the psychological literature. The Noetic Institute's study of positive emotions says that the very process one goes through to access the higher emotions may also reap the lower ones, revealing the less worthy side of oneself. This makes the discernment of inner experience problematic, as it has been for thousands of years. While discovering potentially destructive aspects of ourselves is possible, it must be deemphasized for two reasons. The "unworthy" sides of self in no way are built into the nature of humanness; these are programmed and perpetuated by us. Those who feel the so-called negative emotions are individuals who enjoy self-deprecating groveling. I ask such people if they like these unpleasant emotions. If they do, I must help them to comprehend that these are simply defenses. On the other hand, if they don't enjoy these feelings or destructive urges, then I ask if they are ready to give these up, recognizing that they are harmful baggage.

Here are some clues for becoming self-responsible and for better solving your own problems. Suppose you didn't have your problems or could replace them with others, what would you choose? Take some time to ponder this—make a list. See if your new choices resemble the old ones, also just material needs and wants, and the same old inadequacies.

Dependency is another barrier to emotional freedom. In order to be freely, securely dependent, one must be first independent. Dependency should come from choice, not from compulsion. The poet Kahlil Gibran wisely said that unless one is independent, one cannot truly love—and one has little to offer to a love relationship.

Think how appealing we usually find two people who cannot live without each other, as though this is a sign of true love. Actually, in this situation each gives away his power and choices. As one clings, one diminishes his capacity to exude a loving field. Personal growth is restricted and at the deepest level there is resentment. Gibran reminds us that lust, not love, is expressed in dependency that must possess and feed upon another, even as it offers itself to the existence it claims.

As I mentioned earlier, the importance of guides for navigating this path is often taken for granted. We are taught to call upon guides and to trust them as our special "all wise" gurus. Custom holds that a guide was chosen for you in some divine way to move you through the invariable trials along the path to consciousness; with gratitude, you are asked to humbly accept this assignment. Because the guide is deemed to be the only mystical being who can guide you, he takes on major proportions.

In much the same way, our educational system tells us that wisdom is imparted and information purveyed only from the writings and direct teachings of other people, as though our mind is an open, empty vessel waiting to be filled. We are not taught that we, too, have the ability to tap into and decode the universal storehouse of information in the cosmic field—that all great thoughts can be ours if we choose.

So, we learn to listen and heed teachers' or guides' directions, for they are always right. We accept that guides come down to instruct us. They are active teachers and we are the passive recipients. Oftentimes when we don't seek advice, we seem to be given it against our will. Of course, what happens if we follow guides' wishes is that we can also make them our scapegoats, relieving ourselves of responsibility when things go wrong. Guides then become the perfect, untouchable "cop-outs." I have never heard of people kicking out their guides, although they may outgrow them.

My major complaint is not with the guide concept itself, but with how it is misused. Some people have to check with their guides before taking action, and, like an adult tied to his parents, it stifles mystical growth. There is a subtle, yet profound, difference between "My guide told me to do this," and "On a higher level I found information which helped me to choose the way."

Sometimes we do access powerful information or deep wisdom which gives us no consternation until we create something from it or manifest something noticeable with it. Then we easily become fearful of our own power, not occasionally, but almost always. How humbly appealing and easy it is to say, "My guide did it," and what a relief to sidestep responsibility.

In past life recall, we contact many parts of self which unknowingly influence our decisions and behavior. We inevitably find that parts of self which are attributed to guides actually come from our soul's experiences in other lifehoods, but they have not been integrated. With these new insights we can reclaim the power we have given to guides.

By the way, at an early stage I, too, fell into the error of guide dependency. My first guide was Jacob of the Bible, a very popular guide whom I chose subconsciously, for he represented my evolutionary problem. He fought God to become the "Lion of God" as did I in other lifehoods.

Let me stress again, we humans can contact thoughts that seem to exist outside ourselves. We can comprehend a field of information that seems connected with disembodied souls. We can receive information from a higher source. Furthermore, these fields of information are available to all people at all times. It is not unusual to see spontaneous pictures and hear words that at one time were associated with persons who are no longer alive. Understandably, then, we can logically believe our guides are involved.

Occasionally, I have used guides as a way to focus thought, a method of accessing specific information: thoughts about Einstein, for science; Gibran, for philosophy; St. Francis, for spiritual information, and for help to pinpoint the nature of my requests and the level of information I seek. But I was careful not to get lost in the belief that these entities "gave it to me." Even this technique became unnecessary as the power to mystically know became my own. Imaginary playmates of children serve the same function. Schizophrenic voices are little different than "guides," except that guides are supposed to be good and caring; schizophrenic entities may be the opposite.

During a three-day spontaneous initiation, I made repeated contact with the wisdom of the great philosophers, scientists, artists, and spiritual leaders of the past. I learned to use them to ask questions and receive answers that I did not consciously know. But what was more important, I learned that I did not have to wait passively for them to appear. I could, at will, contact that level of information.

Regardless of how exciting we find them, I warn against dependency on guides, voices, entities, or even spontaneous writing, which can manipulate us. Remember that we are the active agents—we have the experience. Teacher guides provide us with an informational source and a motivational thrust which may be useful as long as we don't confuse it with material reality. Guides don't make us do or believe anything.

In Hinduism, the inner search culminates in self-realization. There is no charismatic leader—the higher self contacts the perennial wisdom. We must no longer rely on external teachers to tell us what to do and think. Our evolutionary work is to develop our higher plane of knowing and the techniques to access and use it.

Have you ever tried to make a statement about something worth saying, but no one listened? (You do know when you are ineffectual.) It is easy to believe, but rarely correct, that your ideas threaten people. When you believe strongly in what you say, people may argue with you, but they rarely ignore you. But when you are insecure about what you are saying, people simply accommodate you by ignoring you.

To start turning such behavior around, ask yourself on what issues you are willing to assert yourself—and which ones would you rather evade? Do you tacitly participate in social groups, in conferences, and in religious groups which you don't enjoy and may even disapprove of? Do you ever turn down social invitations without excuses because you don't want to attend? How easy it is to think that you would lose a friend if you did. Consider whether your friendships are truly satisfying or if they are just unsuccessful agreements. There are two apparent solutions, both of which require change. Either *you* change, or you change the agreement.

We are encouraged by our cultures, our families, and ethnic groups to maintain these dependent relationships, and we are offered security in return. I am not encouraging anyone to break laws or disregard the dictates of his culture. But if these are unwise and restrictive, change them. To remain dependent on others or beliefs that you do not accept only maintains your weakness. This is an unacceptable way to escape spiritual power. Stop giving energy to the things you do not believe in.

One student remembered a lifehood in Greece as an oracle who channeled information from the one God. The Delphi priests became annoyed—they wanted information from their many gods. When she refused, they drugged her food. In this weakened condition, she channeled the information the priests requested, knowing that her will had been overshadowed. Under the influence of drugs, she could not resist their pressure, so to maintain her integrity, she refused food, ultimately starving to death, believing that she had no other choice. The ideal response would have been a direct confrontation with the priests. The excuse she accepted, that she would have been killed, is not appropriate when we know that she starved to death anyway. Even the excuse of, "Why take a stand anyway because the priests would not change," is also inadequate. Acknowledging her strong beliefs in one God would not have saved her life, but her soul would not have suffered, and as I have repeatedly said, it is these situations which are the root of all our emotional and material problems.

Feelings of inadequacy are another almost universal problem.

I ask you to look realistically at these feelings—not at your behavior, but at your true capacities. Are you really inadequate? Approached this way, I have never found a person who actually felt inadequate. We don't choose that defense if we honestly feel inadequate; it would be too painful.

But why should one behave inadequately when one knows one isn't? The answer is simpler than the solution. When we feel inadequate, we don't express our opinions, we don't stand up to be counted, and we don't confront people and ideas that bother us. We don't threaten and we aren't threatened. In the process, we don't have to reevaluate our worth and we do not have to change. For example, the experiences of poverty and repeated failures are often, perhaps always, self-created and are rarely the truth. These are our ways of putting ourselves down and keeping ourselves in line.

Let me give you an example of how low self-esteem is used for protection. Once I questioned an Alcoholics Anonymous member if he was willing to give up his identification with being alcoholic. He pondered, then answered no. He said that his admission in Alcoholics Anonymous that he was an alcoholic had caused him to stop drinking. But I had not asked him if he was willing to give up alcohol—that is what AA does well. I asked him if he was willing to give up his need to deprecate himself with a negative self-image. I wanted him to consider whether he was tired of accepting himself as inferior, whether he was ready to see how an alcoholic self-image now shielded him from deeper struggle with himself. While AA helped him to overcome a difficult behavior, it only treated the symptom. It did not eliminate the problem.

Ask yourself if there is a part of you which purposely perpetuates low self-esteem, unworthiness, incapacity, and poverty. If your first spontaneous answer is yes, then without guilt or self-criticism ask if you are now willing to give this up, and to have it no more. You may discover that even contemplating giving it up literally leaves you "out on a limb" and frightened. No matter how bad these problems seem, they often feel more manageable than the unknown. They have protected you like an old friend.

If you have followed my thinking this far, you are getting a glimpse of a new problem for us humans: we don't know how to experience the power of God manifest in us. It is more comfortable to remain lowly humans than to become magnificent beings. It is true that we have few opportunities to experience being divine and human simultaneously in a world that offers this role only to the sages and the saints—not to us average mortals.

Other barriers to our experience of the entire emotional spectrum originate in the area of sexuality. Freud and others have elucidated multiple problems with our sense of maleness and femaleness. One's sexual identity is a source of self-worth, and the target of tremendous emotional energy. From a biological point of view, we know that neither sex is complete, and so we experience strong sexual drives. But on the soul and energy field level, the sexes don't differ and they are not innately incomplete. Actually, we have experienced being both male and female in different lifehoods with the ensuing expectations, opportunities, and restrictions.

The choice of our sex in a particular lifehood is strong, because it contains numerous motives, each somehow connected to our path to enlightenment; sometimes it reminds us of our unfinished business, sometimes it provides opportunities to solve problems in new ways, and sometimes it even helps us to escape.

When I find an individual consistently choosing the same sex, lifehood after lifehood, I know where the real work lies. It is a lifehood of the other sex. Macho men run from their gentle, tender urges just as delicate women run from their aggressive, assertive strength. Trying to solve these problems on a material man/woman level is unsuccessful.

A metaphysical interpretation of male-femaleness is very different. Energy in the right side of the body is said to represent the male; Jung used the word animus, Eastern philosophy, the yang. The left side of the body is believed to represent the female, the anima, or the yin. In a mystical sense, both of these refer to ways of processing perceptions and behaviors; they have no direct sexual connotation.

Strong electromagnetic energy on the yang side can occur in individuals of either sex who have physical and emotional skills to cope successfully with material reality—to make a living, to understand the physical universe, to take care of needs, and to behave competently in social settings. Strong energy on the left, the anima, or the yin side, shows the capacity for inner processing of stimuli from the world or the mystical—sensitive feelings, intuitive, imaginative, spiritual experiencing and understanding. Over the years I have tested the electromagnetic energy of many men and women, and these concepts are consistently correct.

Our culture has aligned maleness with skills in the physical world, the so-called "real" world, making a living, solving mechanical and financial problems, and judgments concerning this level of reality. Females, on the other hand, have been allowed, even encouraged, to process information in the more personal, intuitive, and mystical way. The sexual connotations are unfortunate, since both are important ways of perceiving, processing, and behaving—one on the mystical, intuitive level, the other on the physical, material one.

Regardless of the sex, if emotional energies are weak or absent in either side of the body, then the abilities associated with it are under stress. Contrariwise, if they are strong in either or both, those comparable perceptions are secure and operative. Unfortunately, many sexual unions are motivated by incompleteness at the metaphysical level where an ungrounded, dependent woman chooses a realistic, problem-solving mate, and the realistic, practical man chooses one who has mystical, intuitive qualities. Despite their needs, neither understands the other.

It is a fallacy to believe that by choosing a mate with characteristics that we do not possess, we somehow become complete. We may actually compound our basic problem as we seek to live through others. Ideally, one could choose a sexual partner as a model to help one grow out of one's limited perspective. Here our mate provides a stimulus to confront our limitations, to experience the emotion which blocks our growth, to personally change and become more complete. But in most instances, that is not the case. More people abdicate their evolutionary needs, becoming increasingly dependent on the other, and sometimes stoically comfortable. Or equally as often, one or both become angry at the other who has failed to make them feel complete by mere association.

But no one can make us over; only we can change and evolve. In the end, if one person moves toward becoming a more complete being and the other does not, the agreement no longer holds, the connection breaks up, or they persist in a stormy, unsatisfactory relationship. Of course, if both grow, the relationship of two evolving beings can be superb.

As we experience emotion, generally, we attach negative values to painful emotions like fear and anger, and positive ones to love and joy. But the value is not inherent in the emotional energy of itself. Rather, the value comes from the pleasure or the discomfort associated with the emotion and its resultant behaviors.

In our culture, fear and anger produce stress and anxiety about the potentially unacceptable behaviors which might result. Joy and love tend to produce relaxation and pleasure. Often, so-called negative and positive emotions play back and forth without clear-cut separation. Joy may border on fear of losing the happy condition. Love merges with anger when one is denied the object of one's love. It is also true that discordant energy is inevitable when one tries to control emotions.

Anger is universally the most maligned and potentially the most dangerous of all emotions—perilous because its fiery volatility can get out of control and become destructive. Anger is a sign that something is awry, that there is conflict.

Anger is also the power which motivates us to confront or redress the disorder. From a field concept, everything which threatens the integrity of the mind-field or soul creates anger. The energy field of a person experiencing anger is recorded in the spectrogram (Exhibit 16). This recording was taken from a man while he felt pain from an acute muscle spasm while being Rolfed. Note the heavy black line at number 7 (or 700 cycles per second) represents the energy of pain. He processed and expressed his agony with emotional outbursts of swearing and stomping his foot. This outburst is displayed in the auric color orange at 6 (or 600 cycles per second). The line at 13 or (1300 cycles per second) is white, stemming from the presence of small quantities of all color vibrations. Here white represents the mild altered state of consciousness he obtained from the energy of pain. (See Chapter X for other ways people process pain.)

Anger which manifests as dissatisfaction can be a prologue to change, but anger does wear many cloaks. It can be marvelous, like a shot in the arm that creates well-being, activating us to take action, to create, to free ourselves from real or imagined dangers. Normally, every time there is injury to the physical body or self, the energy of anger is stimulated, whether it is acknowledged or not. When the injury is to one's divine nature or ultimate truths, it carries a much more volatile emotional charge. Christ did not tarry on the Mount of Olives; he came down to express his anger at the money changers in the temple.

As described earlier, anger and fear serve to actually protect us from threats to physical life and to spiritual integrity. Anger may also function to protect us from experiencing the powerful emotions of divine love and ecstasy. But when we maintain a protective emotional posture, all dynamic feelings are weakened.

Psychology has exposed anger as the seat of all emotional problems, but it has been less successful at finding beneficial ways of dealing with it. Suggestions to "handle it," "control it," and even "transcend it" show, unfortunately, that our goal is to dispense rapidly with the unpleasantness of anger, rather than acknowledging it as a powerful teacher about our unfinished business from other lifehoods.

As we know, anger can and often does lead to destructive

behaviors. But neither is repression of anger ideal. It destroys the body, sabotages development, and if it escapes, creates violence. Nor is it enough to simply recognize our anger, unless we also understand our role in creating it in other lifehoods and perpetuating it in this one. I believe that the only acceptable method of eliminating strong residual anger is to discover its source in other lifehoods.

Transformational psychologists state that, "... the profound task of every individual in the journey of increasing consciousness is dealing with anger." They go beyond the historical discussions of repression and direct expression, to stressing the need to transfer the energy of anger to helpful, pleasant feelings or unconditional love. Such an emphasis upon transmuting negative emotions to more positive ones requires mystical capabilities. Many popular writers and conference speakers present methods for transforming anger to love by opening the heart chakra. Surely, love is the crowning human emotion that is often hidden and under-expressed. We must encourage the experience of our innate lovingness, and learn to transmute the energies of anger and fear into love and joy, which are more creative states.

Pir Vilayat Khan, a metaphysical teacher, stressed that, "... when the fire of anger gets transmuted into light, it is the same radiance but a different frequency, as a warm fire returning to a cold light." But transforming complex human emotions should not be likened to a simple, predictable chemical or physical change—no, a dynamic, living, human being is involved here. Theoretically, it should be possible to totally transform emotional energy. Actually, it does not work that way. Because transformed emotion still carries the field organization of its source, this energy is classically sublimated on a higher consciousness level. I am deeply concerned about promoting as ideal the transcendence of direct or displaced anger. It may be practically acceptable to society, but it is not ideal if we hold the conviction that evolution is our ultimate goal.

Actually, I have never seen emotional energy completely

transmuted. Even when emotional energy is no longer allied to its source, it is not eliminated. Also, I often find that when anger is transmuted into love, it is powerless, wishy-washy, neither pure nor evolving a kind of insipid love so characteristic of the New Age movement. They call their love unconditional, while I think it can be better described as bland and non-discriminating, with narcotic corollaries. It is not empowering. When persons transmute powerful anger, they become ungrounded, losing their orientation to material reality. The resulting love is an airy-fairy type of consciousness without the power to evolve either the individual or the world.

To reiterate, if emotions have to be altered by transforming them, then the person has not changed, the problem is not eliminated. Rather, a substitution has been made. It is far from ideal and should be considered a temporary detour which weakens emotional energy. On a more mundane level, we spend too much time trying to change or eliminate conditions that trigger anger rather than dealing with them at their source.

Since psychologists have not been able to offer an acceptable method of dealing with anger, it is time to look elsewhere. We must look to mystical experiences and other lifehoods as sources of residual anger to discover why people cling to anger and recreate it. Also, we must remember that anger is protective and is not the basic problem. Rather, it serves to keep the person dependent—in an inadequate state—certainly protecting him from knowing his profound emotions of divine love and the power of God. At the very depth of protective, mystical anger, one finds misplaced anger at God which I discuss extensively in Chapter XI, "Spirituality, the Ultimate Evolution."

When it is no longer fueled by prior life frustrations and neurotic needs, residual anger will abate. When the fire is not smouldering and the kindling is not dry, then anger can immediately and freely serve its paramount purpose to protect in this lifehood.

Have you ever used willpower to try to change an emotional

pattern? Have you ever experienced very intense emotions and had fear immediately overwhelm you? Have you ever had the impulse to jump, strike, kill, or destroy another person? I asked that question of one audience, expecting them to respond only to themselves. But two thirds of the group raised their hands, indicating that they had experienced such feelings. Probably, even those who did not respond have had the urge. I believe these violent thoughts are universal.

Some societies have hidden their angry urges behind apparently gentle, good-humored serenity. The Gebusi, living in the New Guinea rain forests, are an example. But behind their conviviality lurks a brutal paradox. The Gebusi murder each other at a rate that is among the highest ever reported—about four times the rate in the United States. Their pattern of peaceful living is punctuated by aggression which is unrestrained and frequently homicidal. Four out of five of the Gebusi killings are of someone branded as a sorcerer who allegedly caused the death of another who actually died of diseases or parasites. The study concluded that current theories of violence offer no satisfactory theories to explain why Gebusi, with their peaceful culture, murder for alleged witchcraft which they do not accept or practice. I believe that as the Gebusi seek an answer for the painful emotions of death, they intuit a mystical connection. Their murderous response both releases their hostile emotions and is mystically justified by blaming the destructive thoughts on another person.

Even the near-utopian Samoa, originally described by Margaret Mead as unencumbered by aggression, competition, or sexual repression, has since been found to be much more complex, and even violent. Rape is not an uncommon occurrence.

The Bushmen of the Kalahari Desert in Africa, dubbed "the harmless people" several decades ago because they were gregarious and peaceful, have recently been discovered to have a homicide rate nearly three times that in the United States, which is one of the highest in Western nations.

Similar patterns of goodwill and self-effacement are

combined with occasional flare-ups and even murders in Eskimo groups, in aboriginal Malaysians, and in the nomadic tribes of Tanzania.

Most of us believe that fear of death, the destruction of the body with loss of physical existence, is the ultimate fear. But as I worked with the past life recall of many clients, I found other information about fear and death. Life and death urges involve the person's will. Physical death is rarely simply the result of an accident, disease, or old age. The complex structures of personality and soul are involved here. There is always a deep personal choice about death, anything from a desire to escape to a passive acceptance, or even pleasure at its inevitability, or a determination to live and a refusal to die until one's time has come.

Some people would rather die than experience the source of emotions which would allow them to live fully. At this level, comfort comes from the fact that the soul knows it is forever. A new body is available with each reincarnation. Actually, the soul doesn't care whether you live or die—it cares only that you evolve.

Ordinary fear of physical death is not metaphysical; it is a material fear. Symbolically, it may become mystical if the person perceives death as leaving the known reality for the unknown. I could relate hundreds of clinical examples of other lifehoods where persons who recalled being killed, dying from human neglect, or even self-starvation, also experienced feelings of anger, release, and happiness. Some, with guilt, desired death as punishment. Many related that they chose to die. So, each of us knows how to die; we have died innumerable times before. Frequently, we repeat certain methods of dying, such as by violence, disease, or suicide; some quietly fade away, while others go out with dramatic flair.

To summarize, there are two major mystical sources of fear. One, the fear of the profound intensity of underlying emotions, is similar to material fears, but stronger. The second is the fear of feeling, knowing, and being responsible for one's divine self. This is the ultimate fear, for when the first fear abates, the second heightens. When mystical fears are not resolved, they are displaced as I have shown earlier, manifesting in death, or in sexual or social problems. You have experienced a mystical source of fear if you have ever daydreamed or had pleasant experiences with nothing particular happening, and suddenly became really frightened; or the deeper you went into meditation, the more fearful you became. To explain and minimize these fears, people say that they fear their dark side or the horrible things they did in other lifehoods—everything from murder to witchcraft. To be sure, we may discover these horrible and violent episodes, but when we probe these the fear does not dissipate. Generally, we discover instead that we have also done profoundly good things, not just bad ones. But it is actually easier to profess the bad, using it as an excuse to hide the real fear of spiritual power. Honestly engaging in the death-life struggle is a route toward inner peace, and only on the mystical level does it insure spiritual strength.

As infants, when our needs are fulfilled, there is pleasure and contentment, which we experience as love. It is no wonder that we associate these early love experiences with the humans who pleasurably satisfy our needs. How easy it is to locate our love feelings in another person rather than in our own happy state. Soon we learn that our love is contingent upon others since they can give it or take it away. In this sense, love can be bartered. But there is another aspect of love. While we hear a lot about unconditional love, love itself has no conditions; it is a field of energy with emotional components. Numerous things stimulate it. Whether it is conditional or unconditional depends on the stimulus, with what people associate with love feelings, and the conditions they place upon giving and receiving love.

While love and hate may shadow-box (similar to fear and anger), our deepest urge remains to experience love as a God-ordained human feeling. I call this "lovingness." Lovingness has no boundaries and no specific recipients. It is a state of being or a condition of the mind, and as such is not specifically associated with an object nor with the heart chakra; it is neither sexual nor spiritual, nor is it connected with a specific person. Lovingness is a quality of a coherent field that provides a happy awareness. In the laboratory, we found that unconditional lovingness carries a pink field—the vitality of red blended into the white of higher consciousness. Early on, all healthy, happy babies have pink auras.

Loving energy exists in the mind-field around the body during one's highest state of awareness where it is free from memories of earthly love encounters. It is in tune with divine experiences where love takes on universal proportions and is focused only on the person's highest concept of God. When persons first experience such profound love feelings, they often feel anxious about the freedom, for barriers do not exist; limitations and confinements are gone. Some feel exposed, even vulnerable.

To see where you stand, ask yourself the question, "Is it easier to experience a loving field or to create one?" Notice that this is different from asking if it is easier for you to give or to receive love. If you have ever appreciated a person for loving you, have you ever taken the next step which is to thank that person for providing you with the experience of your own lovingness?

To reiterate, there are two primary aspects of my model of emotions and mystical experiences. First, the most powerful source of all emotions resides at the soul level. If these emotions are not resolved at the source, a head of steam, anger or fear, is carried from lifehood to lifehood. These soul problems focus behavior in each ensuing life, providing patterns and emotional charges for material life experiences. Furthermore, when the source is unknown, people consistently fail to resolve them using techniques that focus on the material, everyday level of existence. Until we find the deeper sources, we will not solve our problems.

The second tenet is that all really traumatic earthly experiences become relegated to an altered state where common awareness is shut off. With trauma there is tremendous emotional energy, yet confusion about how to act. The energy catapults the person to an altered state where there is no awareness of selfhood or body and pain—a perfect escape. Talk therapy cannot easily access such trauma. Dreams, on the other hand, an expression of an altered state, can tap the source but unfortunately, the symbolic nature of dreams often leads to speculation at the material level and thus, to misinterpretation.

The better treatment is to directly open the mind-field by raising the physical vibrations, tapping expanded awareness, and imaging. This provides direct access to both past and present life material and mystical traumas.

Here is an example. I asked a very gifted psychic and minister if she remembered when she had discovered her unusual mystical capabilities. She said, "at birth," but she knew nothing about the details. As we opened her mind-field, we discovered that at birth, the physicians had placed her in a pan to die while caring for her seriously ill mother. Her will to live brought forth so much rage that she catapulted into an altered state, what we have called "out of body", where she was able to observe the proceedings without emotion or pain, and to physically survive. This rage was reactivated several months later when she was put up for adoption. These altered states became her primary reality. At these dramatic times she was able to perceive the world in an entirely magnificent way, with a purity beyond the ordinary reality that most of us live by. Here was the source of her deep spiritual knowing.

Those of you who have followed my discussion of emotions and mystical experience, and who are motivated to take the next step, are faced with a monumental question. "Are you ready to lay down your burdens?" While this may sound like a charge from a television evangelist, I am not referring to laying down your burdens at the feet of the Lord. Rather, are you ready to de-energize the personal problems that have preoccupied your thoughts and drained your energy for too long? Are you ready to open up to the real, spiritual problem?

Problem-solving at this level is always transforming and mystical. Hold these thoughts in mind as you make your dedication. By embracing mediocrity, we sell ourselves short of our infinite greatness. The deep level of the soul always wants to be free to manifest Godliness. Recall the evolutionary process described earlier, going from order to chaos and then back to a more refined order. Evolution is the reordering of life into a finer order. Unstable equilibrium is inevitable at times.

Grounding your awareness in everyday reality and in the electromagnetic vibrations of the Earth must come first in any attempt to tackle mystical problems. (Did you ever think that the sky begins at your feet? We think it's out there in the air rather than up there and down here simultaneously.) Again, the emotional blocks can only be resolved by returning to the mystical level for the deepest answers. But to fly there without a simultaneously firm orientation in the reality of the physical world is the ultimate escape. We only accomplish a flighty surcease or a life disconnected from self and the world.

There are different therapeutic approaches to activate specific layers of the psyche. For exercises to uncover the sources of emotional turmoil or the altered states hiding emotional energy, I refer you to my forthcoming book, *Mind Mastery Meditations*. Here you will find exercises for activating the physical field, opening the emotional field, accessing lifehoods and energizing the spiritual field.

Another key to staying grounded is to exercise regularly. In the chapter, "Healing: The Miracle of Life," I expand on the role of the connective tissue in transporting electromagnetic energy to every cell, molecule, and atom in the body, increasing cellular vibrations.

Allow yourself quiet times even in a busy schedule to get in touch with yourself, or plan time regularly for satisfying "diddling." Hobbies are fine if these are casually entertaining, where you get lost in the experience but not deeply emotionally involved. They should provide an opportunity to know and indulge yourself. Beware of hobbies that you approach as seriously as you approach your working life.

Prepare your body for the higher vibrations it will experience. A change in diet toward lighter, vegetarian, non-processed food is helpful. Actually, most people who reach this level have already changed their diets because their bodies no longer tolerate dead, processed foods, sugars, alcohol and drugs.

To meditate regularly for at least thirty minutes daily, I believe is essential—and not just quasi-meditation or daydreaming while occupied with something else. The total mind must be involved. Having a quiet, leisurely time is more important than the specific time of day. I do not, however, recommend a formal meditation plan. Be creative. Use a variety of methods depending on the day's need. If the body is tense, spend time on the physical field. If you feel emotional blocks, start on the path to find your child, observe what is going on, and find the unfinished emotional business.

If you discover a powerful lifehood with many messages for you, ask this image to return to you. Do not intellectually try to direct it. Your deeper mind knows the answers. Follow, observe, and don't get in your own way. Remember that you have control of your images. If you lose an important image, don't struggle to bring it back, merely command that it return and then wait, knowing that it will come. You created it and you can command it.

If you've found a profoundly radiant life or spiritual experience with little material structure, ask that it return to you rich with details. When it occurs, ask if you have ever had such an experience as a mortal being in this or other lifehoods. Don't think; accept the first answer. If the answer is yes, ask to have those images return to you purely. Frequently lifehoods open abruptly. As you enter these mystical levels, you, like others, often doubt whether these are real because we have learned to dichotomize the real and the imagined. Remember, what comes when you imagine or symbolize is your own personal message to yourself. Each image is your own, from your own sources.

When you are imagining on different levels, don't try to realistically or logically figure out complete answers from just a few clues. Look rather, for patterns of problems and emotions. The reason we try urgently to intellectually figure out the clues is that we want to quickly eliminate the problem. However, we can never succeed this way. The problem goes <u>only</u> <u>when</u> <u>we</u> <u>change</u>.

Place the new information in your memory banks and over time, fresh logic will occur. The mind does not give up its defenses or find its gems immediately. Although what you discover sometimes does not seem to fit, in time it probably will. Particularly with your early experiences, do not intellectually process what happens until later. Discover that expansion of consciousness must be negotiated; it cannot be forced.

These are all cues to help you become an active participant so that the mind can offer up its treasures. Have a great mystical trip. Join the rest of us in patient excitement and inevitably, some suffering—both are the nature of deep change.

Know that your first responsibility is not to others, but to yourself. As you hoist yourself to a state where you validate the divine potential of your being, you will elevate others simply by your presence. Your vibrations and you as a role model express more than anything you can say or do.

LIFEHOODS:
The Hidden Agenda

The word "lifehoods", is not just a word I coined for the old ideas about past lives. It presents a new philosophy of reincarnation created from very different concepts about humans and the Earth. The expression "past lives" emphasizes the physical existence of a life—a time-space construct. On the other hand, lifehoods, emphasizing the soul, which is a part of the mind-field, exist now and have no time reference.

To reiterate, lifehoods de-emphasize the space-time domain of the physical body and emphasize the metaphysical existence of the soul. Because it operates as a field, a lifehood carries information about the soul's experience in a material body at any time in history. Since the soul is never destroyed, as is each physical body it enlivens, information from lifehoods is always now, a part of each new life.

Stephen Hawking reminds us that the laws of science do not distinguish between past, present and future. Neither do higher states of consciousness. Likewise, the soul is not metaphysically past, for there is neither soul-time nor soul-space. Therefore, concepts like past-life regression, by whatever techniques, can make sense only when referenced to the current physical body's existence. Regression makes no logical sense when applied to the soul which carries the information about other lifehoods.

Karma, the series of beliefs passed down in Eastern philosophy from the Vedas, supplied answers about the reasons that humans reincarnate, and about the inevitable events a person must re-experience in the current life. These elaborate beliefs placed emphasis upon who you were, what you did and when you lived—all physical details of what they called "past lives." Quite different, the concept of lifehoods gives answers to what the person experienced, what he made of it, and what patterns and beliefs his soul carried with it into each reincarnation. These are the memories of soul experiences.

Lifehood information can either help or hinder our evolution; but in each new life this information powerfully influences the development of selfhood and behaviors. Even more, these memories are the emotional residue, the true psychological source, the deepest director of a human life—with an impact much greater than biologically-inherited traits or early childhood experiences.

The semantic use of the words "past life" and "lifehoods" depends upon who perceives the lifehood information. If another person, a therapist, psychic, or friend hears or reads the information or if the person relates his lifehood experience to another, he does so in Earth time—using concepts of past, present, and future. Here the words "past life" are meaningful. On the other hand, when a person re-experiences a lifehood, the past and the present are now and it is not a historical event.

Likewise, as people go up in consciousness and vibration to the levels where recall occurs, there is also no time but the present time. In field information, there is no past field information, there is only now field information. Past, present, and future can describe material happenings, but not mystical or metaphysical ones. To say it another way: we correctly use the words "past lives" when describing happenings that are time-locked. Lifehoods describe soul information, which always is <u>now</u>. I will use the words "past lives" when discussing ideas that are time oriented and "lifehoods" when not.

Explanations of past lives, reincarnation and karma have been with us from the beginning of history—formulated in ancient cultures where ways of thinking and knowledge about the nature of the universe were limited. Yet, these same out-dated concepts are the mainstay of our current literature. Apparently, current philosophies have neither questioned nor changed them, while many lay people believe these explanations are incomprehensible and undesirable for modern life. In the past, we had two choices; either we blindly accepted the standard explanations of reincarnation and karma, or we rejected the whole idea as irrational, unintelligent, flaky metaphysics. We need to dismantle these outmoded ideas, to bring forth a new paradigm which upgrades ancient ideas about past lives to lifehoods. The new ideas will be important to guide the masses of people of all ages who are and will be having these important mystical experiences. For as the spectrum of human consciousness broadens, with it invariably comes lifehood recall. People will need sound bases so that they will be able to accept, understand, and use this information for their own material growth and spiritual evolution.

I believe that as man evolves rapidly in the twentieth century, the concept of lifehoods will become a dominant, new, philosophical idea, important because it views human emotions, spirituality and the body in a way that focuses holistically on human empowerment. A recent survey from the National Opinion Research Center in Chicago reported that 29% of all Americans now believe in past lives. Even more astonishing is the comment in the *Journal of the American Medical Association* stating we now have " ... on record a large amount of data that cannot be ignored" which is "difficult to understand on any other grounds but reincarnation."

Today those people who find difficulty accepting lifehoods are those who have had no personal recall. Regardless of what I say or how powerfully the historical, religious, and philosophical literature confirms lifehoods, these will only influence our beliefs.

One can only know for certain when one has experienced the intense and spontaneous emotions, the information never before contacted, and the physical feelings as the lifehoods are being recalled; another confirmation occurs when one sees change taking place, and experiences the resulting peace and fullness.

My radical findings about lifehoods come from 25 years of clinical practice as a metaphysical counselor. I have opened the mind-fields of my clients so that they could remember their lifehoods and discover the emotional source of their immediate psychological problems. I believe that the emotions connected with lifehoods are forever the barriers to progress, and that remembering lifehoods is essential to the change which leads to higher evolution.

There are things that most people know in altered states of consciousness which they cannot recall in ordinary ones, such as lifehoods and spiritual experiences. Charles Tart reminds us of the importance of direct knowledge by experience. He believes that we have traded direct knowledge of things like the unity of life and connection to the divine, for abstract, intellectual thoughts and theories which are not very personally satisfying. Experiences with the soul and physical body constitute the most direct knowledge the individual can gain about himself. But the deepest knowledge comes in expanded awareness states, not in altered ones where recall is often strong but memory is limited.

Many years ago, I met a professor of mechanical physics from an Ivy League university during a scientific meeting. Over cocktails he inquired about my research in energy fields. Although he understood the scientific explanation, when I related these to consciousness and emotions he was intrigued, but lost. Some years later after he had retired in California, he asked me to work with him, saying that he wanted to remove his blocks to higher consciousness, while he adamantly denied that he believed in "that stuff." But as he persisted and denied less, I agreed to work with him.

To my surprise, as we worked he moved rapidly into an

expanded state of consciousness. He saw himself as a young man in Egypt, which he promptly denied, adding, "I don't want to touch that." Later, he remembered a tiny, baby boy abandoned to die in the harsh desert. Whatever he was experiencing was so emotionally loaded that his body trembled and he became fearful. He accused me of "zapping" him—which, of course, I hadn't or couldn't. I encouraged him to stop those images for a while because they were so painful.

Without encouragement, he started talking about Moses, immediately insisting that he was not Moses. He rationalized that his Moses imagery occurred because he loved "Porgy and Bess" which contained some reference to Moses. I confirmed that of course he was not Moses, but that there was something about Moses that he identified with and was trying to recall. A bit later, as he re-imaged the abandoned little boy near death in the desert, a regal woman found him. Like Moses, he was saved by a Pharaoh's daughter. This man's outbursts of emotion at being saved were intense and they frightened him; he denied them vehemently. Each time he tried not to remember, he remembered anyway, and each time a dam of emotions was released. But he could not understand nor integrate what he experienced on a rational level, despite the fact that his life had been saved. He grew up in the palace where he was loved, tenderly cared for, and appreciated. As a man, his life lacked luster. At this stage, he immediately denied this lifehood experience altogether, saying that he made it all up, which allowed him to return to a very quiet emotional state.

Later, I asked him to return to that memory and just tell me about it. Each time the sobs were uncontrollable, and each time, he denied its reality. Finally, after more work, I assured him that his imagination could have created that story, and if it did, he could just relate it to me again without the emotion of reliving it. But he never could. Each time when his life was saved, the same emotions arose spontaneously, with fear and shock as his body chilled. It was then that he left denial and finally believed in the notion of lifehoods.

This story clearly demonstrates that in one state of consciousness the subject experienced a life, yet when he moved back into a lower state he could no longer comprehend that he had had such an experience. Only at the end of our work when the two levels of consciousness blended in a continuum was he aware that he no longer needed to deny this lifehood experience.

Let us return here to the historical development of the concept of reincarnation; the idea of reincarnation developed simultaneously with religious ideas about divine power. It ranks among the oldest ideas entertained by successive cultures, and is one of the most frequently recurring themes in the literature of the world.

In the Orient and India, beliefs about reincarnation and karma were nurtured and developed. Krishna, the supposed Indian author of the *Bhagavad Gita*, first professed to believe in past lives and reincarnation. Today, Hindus encourage suffering in this lifehood so that their reward will be nirvana in the next. Some believe that the punishment for wrongdoing will be regression to existences as animals or insects in future lives.

The Buddhist faith, stemming from the old Indian philosophies, advanced reincarnation and karma as its two primary tenets, giving them the power of higher law. Like Jesus, the Buddha never recorded his beliefs, but his followers did in great detail. Tibetan Buddhism elaborated on concepts of death and rebirth by believing that the Dalai Lama reincarnated in a new life near the time of death of the previous Dalai Lama. In fact, all higher Buddhists are considered to be incarnations of previous lamas.

Confucius neither taught nor denied the reality of immortality and reincarnation. The Koran, the scripture of Islam, apparently affirmed the belief in reincarnation but did not propagate it as a primary teaching. The Koran states, "God generated beings and sent them back over and over again until they returned to him."

The strictly Orthodox branch of Hasidic Judaism teaches

reincarnation. The Talmud, however, expressed the necessity to cast a veil over the whole question of survival beyond the grave in an attempt to wean people from the idolatrous cults of the dead which preceded Judaism in the Near East. Reincarnation was associated with these.

Contrariwise, the Kabbala, a mystical system of interpreting the scriptures, was a strong current in Judaism that affected many forms of religious expression as well as Jewish history. Some believe the Kabbala is the traditional law. Others deem it above the law of Moses because of its mystical nature. Kabbalists believe that everyone carries the secret trace of transmigration in their souls in the lineaments of their foreheads and hands, and in the aura which radiates around their bodies. This power field extends beyond the limits of personal cell-selfs, even in ordinary people. The destiny of a person is connected not only to those things he himself creates and does, but also to what happened to his soul in previous incarnations.

The Kabbalistic teachings contain a wonderful field concept of the soul; soul sparks radiate from the individual like a spiritual aura around him when he returns to re-incarnate. For an advanced being, the whole world of mankind becomes a cosmic power field of his soul. The Kabbala presented the idea of attaining perfection through repeated rebirths, instead of rebirth being a form of punishment as taught by Plato. Kabbalistic beliefs were advanced by the Sephardic Jews in Spain in their *Book of Splendor*, also called the *Zohar*. For centuries, it reigned as an expression of all that was profound in the innermost recesses of the Jewish soul.

The Kabbala probably helped stimulate the Italian Renaissance and the German Reformation during a time when it was flourishing in the Jewish community. The Talmud and Torah were both strong then. But in the 19th century, Jewish scholars became hostile to Kabbalistic beliefs and aligned them with agnosticism and the skepticism of science. Today there are many Kabbalistic rabbis, but generally it is considered dangerous and out of reach for the average Jew because of its mystical nature.

Although today rabbis hold many life views, reincarnation is not openly taught in the four main branches of Judaism: Orthodox, Conservative, Reform, and Reconstructionist. Thus, Jewish people may have hazy beliefs about concepts involving the next life. There are some well-known Jewish scholars who believe that now is the eminently correct time for Jews to re-examine their religious heritage to see that rebirth was a dominant outlook in Judaism at one time. That vision may help to illuminate solutions to the problems of the modern world.

The mystical religions and philosophical doctrines of early Christian sects, combining Greek, Jewish and Oriental beliefs, embraced reincarnation. The Coptic copies of the original papyrus Gnostic texts documented this. But as early as 180 AD the Roman Church with all its power branded Gnosticism as heresy.

In the sixth century, a group of Christian bishops at the Council of Constantinople outlawed the teaching of reincarnation. Despite this edict, Christians continued to propagate the belief in reincarnation until it became so widespread that in the 13th century it almost overturned the Roman Catholic Church. The Inquisition in Spain, mounted primarily by the Catholic Church, had as a major aim rooting out beliefs in reincarnation. Over the centuries, the Church has generally substituted the word "rebirth" for "reincarnation" because of the heathen meanings associated with the latter. Interestingly, the same karmic concept of Hinduism, that is, a reward for good and a reproach for evil, was used by the early Christian church to control its members. Many eminent Christian theologians today accept these ancient ideas about reincarnation.

The great Greek thinker Pythagoras taught the doctrine of rebirth which he is believed to have brought from his studies in Egypt. Plato's philosophical thought, recorded in his *Phaedo*, expounded the highest Pythagorean doctrine. He felt strongly that we have lived before and will live again, and he wondered how it could be thought otherwise. He believed that innate ideas were inherited experiences from other lives. Reincarnation pervaded his philosophy with themes of life, death, and rebirth, which he unfolded in numerous myths. His writings had enormous influence on St. Paul and the early Christian church in Greece. Socrates and Aristotle, both students of Pythagoras and Plato, also professed the immortality of the soul and encouraged respect for this life because of its eternal nature. At a much later date, Tolstoy believed that if we remembered our past lives we would be wiser.

The arch-skeptic materialist Thomas Huxley theorized that if consciousness survived death there was no end to the possibilities of its development in future lives. Sir Julian Huxley dared to think that, under the scheme of rebirth, the incoming entity brings with him the footages of his own thoughts and actions from previous lives—he inherits from himself.

The preponderance of great Western intellectuals like Francis Bacon, Sir Walter Scott, Charles Dickens, Oscar Wilde, Rudyard Kipling, Ralph Waldo Emerson, Walt Whitman, Thomas Edison, and Luther Burbank all accepted reincarnation. The current Theosophical Movement, strong in the United States, England, and India, was probably most instrumental in regenerating interest in past lives and accompanying beliefs about karma.

Even with the strong evidence for reincarnation from religions and great thinkers, I personally found past life concepts stubborn obstacles. My scientific training led me to reason that if we are born into this life with new parents, a new genetic background, and a new brain to record this life's experiences, how is it possible to recall or even be remotely connected to a prior life? Added to that intellectual quandary, I had had no past life recall.

My first insight came from clinical evidence presented by Verny, a psychiatrist, in his book, *The Secret Life of the Unborn Child*, and from reports on hypnotic regression. Both indicated that the soul rarely entered the fetus at conception but generally it did so around the third month. If that were true, it stood to reason that the soul is separate from the union of cells at conception. As I pondered how a soul could enter an already-developing fetus, I had to conclude the soul could not exist in the form of tissue but that it must be an energy field of information.

The study of energy fields in my laboratory had encouraged me to believe that the highest level of the mind is located in the auric field. This led me to further speculate that the soul must enter the fetus as a field, directly into the mind-field. Therefore, the brain which records this life's experiences would have no direct knowledge of the soul's lifehoods.

My changing beliefs about lifehoods were still purely intellectual; still I had had no past life recall. As a rational being I had grave doubts about what I considered superstition and misconception from "ancient wisdoms." But I recognized that we humans need to explain life happenings and so we will do so from our state of awareness and with the information available at the time.

So philosophies of reincarnation had been guided by limited models containing a motley collection of metaphors, each generating its own way of thinking and compatible answers. Although most of the world's people believe in reincarnation, many Westerners are repelled by the idea. My final acceptance came from my own lifehood experiences and those of hundreds of my students—so powerful were they, that my doubts vanished. I encourage you not to discredit the value of reincarnation because of previous faulty explanations.

The following discussion will, I hope, open new avenues for you. I am sure that it will not change devout followers of Theosophy or yoga or some psychics, and it will fall on deaf ears among those who use belief in karma as a crutch. But for those truly seeking enlightenment, these ideas may find intuitive acceptance, even filling gaps between intellectual believing and experiential knowing.

Ideas about action at a distance, or action through a field are difficult to grasp. When we want to cause something to happen we lift or press it, push or pull it, or manipulate it in some other way. This we understand. Of course, we accept radio and television waves or signals, even if we don't understand them. The modern physics concept of a field states that it is a continuous medium of transmission and information storage. Into this field are transmitted radio and television signals from which we receive and decode sound and picture. Likewise, the vibrations of the past are always in this universal field. The whole of the past of a soul is always in its energy field whether it is in spirit or human form. From this we realize that what happened a thousand years ago in physical time is not one thousand units apart from the present—it is now here, in the present time. Now although the soul is immortal, it has taken a mortal course in its evolutionary process. So to know about the soul's immortal struggles we must uncover the mortal lives it nourished, that is, its lifehoods.

Some people who accept past lives with vague details do so intuitively, not by mere faith, but as some ill-defined aspect of consciousness. These people often recognize their soul's oldness—many times it has existed in a human form. Aurobindo, the great Indian philosopher, believed that when one becomes enlightened the most immediate experience is that of always having been and of being forever.

Other people want scientific validation that the material body existed in time and space, as confirmation of the information they recall. Studies by Ian Stevenson of 2,000 reincarnation-type recalls from ten cultures note that children of Burma, India, Sri Lanka, and Thailand easily remember past lives when they begin to speak. He validated 204 Indian children's reports of recent past lives. There are many other such attempts, one being the study of Bridey Murphy's numerous lives. I take no issue with such reports because I believe that reincarnation is a fourth dimension concept and therefore, time-space proofs are irrelevant.

One common factor in all reincarnation doctrines is the existence of a soul, the source of life, reaching for perfection and divinity. I believe that we reincarnate so that we can evolve to the highest level of human capacity, manifesting the divine and human nature simultaneously. If the soul could do this in spirit form, there would be no reason to return in human form.

Early karmic concepts veered away from mystical religious explanations in favor of material, scientific ones. Later, physical laws were applied to karmic reasoning to enhance its credibility. Today, this logic must be critically rejected. Quantum physics tells us that even the laws of physics, these supposedly unalterable truths, are only relative. The natural laws of the universe exist only in the limited situations described by material reality and certainly should not be used as arguments for the reincarnation of the soul. Actually, in the reductionist world view of material science, there is no place for mysticism, religion, or lifehoods.

Ken Wilbur, a popular metaphysical psychologist, warns against trying to carry mysticism on the shoulders of physics. He believes that the material realm is not the most fundamental; it is the least fundamental with less "reality" than life, mind, or spirit. Physics in this sense is a study of the realm of least being. Yet, cosmic determinism called "Infinite Laws" is a frequently used term to describe the soul's reincarnation in human form. To me, it seems strange that such rigid determinism could be associated with a fluid concept like lifehoods. Surely, we cannot determine the truth about reincarnation using such distorted thinking.

We should accept that mystical truths do not need the "proof" of science, nor will proof come from material science. Karma has been described as the acceptable, logical explanation of rebirth because it is based on laws, even called divine laws, to make the explanation more impregnable to question. This is a subtle trap that we humans fall into. If we are really afraid of something, put a divine label on it, and we all leave it alone. Reincarnation, in fact, is divine; karmic laws used to explain it are not. Actually, so-called divine laws are usually moral dictates which are neither divine nor universal; and more often than not, a "divine law" is simply a rational belief that has not been exposed as such.

Let us evaluate some karmic laws. Principles of conservation of energy declaring that energy is transformed but never lost were borrowed and distorted by karma enthusiasts and called the "Law of Parsimony." Madame Blavatsky in the 19th century held that karmic law does not create anything, but it adjusts everything. On the other hand, most current thinkers believe that the world changes by interaction, even chaotic interaction, and not by deterministic adjustment.

The "Law of Service" has been coined to describe a reason for reincarnation—we return to the world to carry out our predestined service work. It is true that all lives have cycles, as a soul must have cycles of reincarnation in order to evolve. As humans become more evolved, they have a corresponding awareness of the state of the Earth, the humans upon it, and they have more divine vibrations which they will manifest in service. Service here is an outgrowth of our change, but not the reason for reincarnation. When we come into our divine levels of lovingness, we will serve. It is not true that we will experience divine vibrations simply as a result of performing service. The former concept is fluid, while the other is rigid and static.

To summarize, I believe that the concept of laws is so tremendously final that it does not encourage the human mind to change. Further, all laws are relative; they are not universal. Pythagoras taught that although the material world was subject to laws, "... there is another higher state of being in which the soul would rise above the laws of the lower world." What we have called the laws of reincarnation, the ultimate laws, I believe will not hold up in light of the facts and intellectual scrutiny.

Karma, the companion doctrine of reincarnation, professes tight cause-and-effect relationships between lifehoods and the soul. Remember, cause-and-effect laws relate to the time-space aspects of the physical world, which is not the world of lifehoods and souls. Furthermore, science tells us that two things may coexist and even be related, but one may not cause the other. For example, two lives may manifest similarities because it is always the same soul existing in them. This does not necessarily indicate any cause-and-effect relationship.

These cause-and-effect cycles of karma were also encouraged

by religious beliefs. Biblical references of "an eye for an eye" and "as you sow, so shall you reap" are examples.

Many writings about karma say that the same enemies continue to appear in each lifetime until we learn that the only way to destroy an enemy is to make a friend of him, as if the "enemy" is the recurring problem to be solved, not "us" and the fact that we keep attracting such people. Actually, until we have straightened out ourselves, the cycle will continue and we will attract people whom we interpret as the same enemy. Simply making friends with this "enemy" is a childlike, impossible solution, and further, makes the "enemy problem" a predestined one that is bigger than we are. I believe that we choose many circumstances in each lifehood, and no matter how bad these may be, they carry a dramatic reminder of our unfinished business—that here we have handled things badly and need to change. Only then will the "enemies" fade away.

Here is an example of a client who uncovered experiences where she was killed by Mongols in northern China while she was a temple priestess. She had been stabbed to death because her spiritual radiance stopped the Mongols from raiding the village. She relived three other powerful lives in which she also came to a violent end, by the sword, by hanging, and by bludgeoning—all at the hands of "enemies." This unfinished business persisted for three lifetimes until startlingly, she discovered that she had been a spiritual leader each time who had abandoned her spiritual power on the threat of death. She learned that had she maintained her power, instead of killing her, her "enemies" would have become her followers. She began to change when she emotionally declared that she would never again allow the fear of death to strip her of her spiritual strengths.

Karmic laws state that we return to work out our social/sexual problems with the same human beings. Therefore, we will marry the same mate, we will have the same parents, siblings or friends reincarnated. Indian philosophy indicates that we reincarnate to work out our personality problems and to change our behavioral traits, and that to understand our humanness we must experience a life of all five races. I view these reasons as superficial, and based on ego, personality, and the self level of the psyche, not in the soul level where there is truly sufficient scope to demand many reincarnations. I believe instead that we return to evolve as humans and to become divine. Actually, this superficial reasoning about personality and self is convenient; it allows us to release pent-up energy while not requiring us to change deeply.

Karma also decrees that every decision has its deterministic consequence. We return to a new life because we did something in the past that we must repay in the present, to wipe the slate clean. This concept of predestination, a direct outgrowth of cause-and-effect karma, constitutes the primary reason why many people reject reincarnation today. However, an enlightened interpretation of an orderly world declares that decisions are not preordained, but are arrived at by choice, even if the process is not rationally understood. Our choices may lead to repeating unsuccessful attempts to work on the problems from other lifetimes. There will also be "repetitions" in the sense that one will find common threads, such as interest in the arts or music or sensitivities to nature. These are manifestations of skills one has gained.

Some explain reincarnation with the belief that humans must experience all human weaknesses; all types of earthly relations and responsibilities, every desire, affliction, and passion; every form of temptation and conflict in order to understand humanity. This seems absurd. The limitation of this logic is the premise that reincarnation occurs so that we accumulate experiences. Actually, no experience guarantees learning, and certainly not constructive learning. Therefore, a person who deeply experiences and evaluates, and learns on the higher mystical levels, does not need as many experiences as one who is constantly butting his head against the same walls, failing to change or gain insight. To evolve means that each experience in each life gives us more and better insights. I am sure that some souls neither discover nor use insights as effectively as others. Likewise, the selection of where we will reincarnate and at what time in societal development places us in different arenas for experience. For each individual, there are some growth experiences that are superior to others. These contain more challenges—often more stress—and present both the greatest opportunity to remain dormant and potentially the greatest stimulus to change and to evolve.

Often it is said that old souls are not required to reincarnate as many times as newer ones. If we accept that the function of reincarnation is to evolve, then the number of reincarnations is immaterial. Rather, the only criteria for advanced souls is the quality of evolution, the level of perfection reached.

The function of lifehoods is not to learn tolerance. In fact, you can't learn tolerance. That is an attitude that comes with security about oneself and others. If we handle such big problems, then the little ones are gone. When man learns to experience divine love, he loves himself as a divine manifestation, making unloving behaviors impossible.

As I have said repeatedly, I object to people spending so much energy trying to solve soul problems on a personality level. Yes, we can learn from all new opportunities, both positive and negative ones. There are simple lessons and there are profound ones. As a person who has advanced to the level of energy field concepts, who sees the world as one unit, who has touched spiritual enlightenment, I have little tolerance for empty, superficial answers that produce nothing. The causes that affect me spiritually at the deepest level of myself are non-deterministic. Our soul evolves in an open system. And psycho-physical development alone does not produce soul evolution; it accompanies it.

During my lifehoods I have killed five people, and I have not returned in this one to pay a debt. I have no motivation to do good because I have killed. I suffered desperately in those lives for these huge mistakes and returned to know it and to change. The lessons we can learn from lifehoods are very deep and abiding lessons—not the superficial ones of karmic reasoning. To work on minor behavioral traits as a way to evolve relegates man's higher knowing, his destiny, and his goal of perfection to the realm of inconsequential things.

Although the philosophy of karma purports to deal equally with the body and the soul, most of the writings dwell upon the material body, not the metaphysical aspects. The very reference to the so-called "layers of the aura," calling these "bodies," places emphasis on material things. Never have I seen any reference to a field energy having layers—there are vibrations, but these don't have the linear structure of layers. The aura layers seen by many people are actually the visual perceptual organizations of information, not irrefutable facts. Smoke does not layer just as light does not appear as a spectrum until refracted by a lens, water, or a crystal prism. Then, the layering results from the interactive process. Describing astral, physical, etheric, and spiritual bodies as layers created in the auric field is a misnomer. Any qualified difference in these vibrations, at best, will become a blend.

The concept of auric bodies comes from the *Secret Doctrine of Madame Blavatsky*, published early in this century. She faced a quarrel between the profane and the esoteric sciences. To distinguish the astral essence from the physical body composed of tissues, she posited mystical *bodies* in the auric field, using the concept of bodies metaphorically. These metaphors have been literalized and elaborate psychic constructs have been fashioned around them.

I would like to discuss here one remaining standard concept that is common to reincarnational beliefs, that of Akashic Records. This is a metaphysical metaphor for the belief that everything that has ever happened in the world is available in some recorded form. Generally we think of records as written or otherwise recorded histories or legends. Actually, I believe that direct information of all the great thoughts and profound happenings in the world from all civilization is available in the form of organized energy fields. Probably, someday we will be able to recover directly such things as the Gettysburg Address, Christ's Sermon on the Mount, and teachings of the Apostles—the profound events of each civilization. In fact, those individuals who have reached higher evolutionary levels can tap into and decode these fields as they "read" their own soul's history. Our new histories will be written from this reference. I object to the idea of Akashic Records only when it is used as a deterministic source of the reincarnations of the lifehoods of people.

Of course, there is the perennial question of Job: "Why do the wicked prosper and the righteous suffer?" The reincarnationists, believing in the doctrines of karma, have a ready answer: people come in to this life to receive their punishment or their reward. I strongly believe that we make our own choices and that these choices are not based upon suffering or non-suffering, goodness or wickedness. We base our choice on what we come in to do, on where we are on our evolutionary ladder, on what situations we believe will assist us in removing obstacles, and not always directly or easily. For example, impossibly difficult situations of crippling or poverty or prejudice may seem to deter evolution, but on the other hand, they create such a great stimulus that they may actually assist the individual in removing all other barriers, barriers that may be more difficult to the soul than the physically crippling ones.

It is true; if one probes lifehoods, one may find recurrences of maimed bodies. My interpretation is that both are connected to a deeper, unresolved problem. During the lifehood in which the maiming occurred, the person's role must be probed, not just what happened, because the handicap in this life is a reminder of unfinished business of previous lifehoods. The problem will not be solved until the individual looks beyond the physical or sensory imperfections.

In this vein, the Bible offers the well-known story of the disciple John's question, after Jesus healed a man who was born blind: "Rabbi, who sinned, this man or his parents, that he was born blind?" Jesus answered, "It was not that this man sinned or his parents, it's that the works of God might be made manifest in him." (John 9:2-3.)

Remember, when handicaps occur, these are opportunities for heightened development and refinement of other senses, as well as for profound transactions with the deeper self.

The doctrine of predestination, that by divine decree souls are born to be saved or lost, is the worst sin some theologies have inflicted upon the world. Most people who accept karma believe that somehow we will be punished for our sins. I believe that neither God nor karma punishes us. Our moral knowledge does an adequate job. Many people have weakened the bonds of material consciousness, but have not yet given up religious dogma that was designed to keep them loyal, but not necessarily spiritual. I contend, however, that even if we don't have all the answers, we should not lock ourselves into half-truths about reincarnation, nor should we embrace any unclear, misleading beliefs that limit our evolutionary growth.

To me, karmic thinking about man's experiences is like fool's gold. It is appealing—it enamors us for a time, but there is no truth there. It is not gold, but only an imposter. We cling to these untenable theories because we fear being out on a limb, or we simply don't want to change. I prefer the writings of the Kabbala which describe reincarnation as a great privilege; I reject the concept of punishment or misery to pay back debts for previous misdoings. In the final analysis, lifehoods provide an opportunity for soul work, not for personality struggles.

We, as physical beings, are not God, we are humans trying to live through the full range of our souls' potentialities to manifest divine vibrations. What the soul carries with it between lifehoods, consciousness and awareness, are points of orientation for the new venture.

How do we know about lifehoods other than by blind faith? In the past, most evidence came through psychic past-life readers. Remember, past life information is carried in the human energy field, and as such it is available to anyone who is capable of perceptually tapping into it.

Some mystics are particularly skilled in tracing personality trends throughout lifehoods in order to understand current, ordinary reality problems. Some are predisposed to read in the fields only "acceptable" information designed to remove life stress. Their skills are appropriate for those who wish to work on isolated problems. At best, psychic readings comfort the mind for a time, but they also can become unnecessary crutches. At the deepest level we want truth, particularly when it doesn't hurt. What is limiting about past life readings, even by those who are clear channels, is that the information they find concerns the material, time-space, physical aspects of life—the least important ones. They retrieve information about who you were and what you did. This information is then often filtered and translated through the ideas of karma. Their reports are already laden with interpretation. Furthermore, the most compelling reason for recovering lifehood information is to discover our interpretations and misjudgments, and to change them. It is not to gain material information.

George Meek believes that past life readings have very little validity, yet he believes that past life records are a reality. "Everything that ever happened, every thought ever held, every word ever spoken is permanently embedded in the fabric of the cosmos ... on a master recording tape—but very few souls on Earth today can easily and accurately tap into this material and get the precise and accurate read-out of data."

Olga Worral, one of the honored mystic teachers, commented that as she traveled abroad, she was shocked to find what was happening to people as the result of false teachings about reincarnation. She met dozens of St. Pauls, St. Johns, and Mothers of Christ. These phony past life readings were causing a breakdown in many families; they were leading to immoral behaviors stemming from information these people were given about their "soul-mates."

Each individual must discover and relive his own lifehoods. No one else can do it for us. In every session where I help open the mind-field, I see lifehood information, but I never announce it to the person. I only confirm and then assist the person in putting the information into perspective.

Many instances of past-life recall are reported during near-death experiences. It seems that psychic information from a deep source is available for review. During a traumatic experience, a person goes into an altered state where the information remains hidden. In near-death experiences, the person again reaches a deep altered state where this cloistered information, particularly lifehood information, is readily available. I find, however, that near-death experiences happen so rapidly and are so truncated that only small parts of the experience are ever recalled. Fortunately, there are other ways that one can become aware of lifehoods.

Another indication of the existence of lifehoods is that infant precocity and genius have not been explained by heredity. The statement, "geniuses are born and not made" allows that past lives may account for special talents in music, art, or dance—all material skills. These talented people are extremely sensitive and mystical, and were attuned to the arts and movement in other lives—but not always to the specific gift that they currently demonstrate.

Speaking in tongues, or zenoglossy, is rarely reported during lifehood recovery, probably because lifehood recall takes place in now-time, not in past-time; current thought has to be expressed in one's present language. However, Dr. Ian Stevenson, at the University of Virginia, found that among more than 2,000 cases around the world of children with past life recall, many exhibit zenoglossy (*Omni*, January, 1988). When adults recall a lifehood, sometimes there occurs a childlike babble resembling the primitive language invented by children for other children, but this is different than "speaking in tongues."

In my practice, I have found only two adults who spoke in a true foreign tongue. One woman spoke the lilting rhythm of the Nubian language of the people of the upper Nile in southern Egypt. I recognized the rhythmic quality of this language, for I had traveled through the Nubian tribes, south of the Aswan Lake. I directed her, when she broke into the "tongue," to let her thoughts flow into and through the English language. She did this without losing the tonal or phrasing qualities of the Nubian, and she re-experienced her life as a Nubian princess who was captured to become one of Pharaoh's mistresses.

You may know that there are some religious groups in this country whose ceremonies are structured around "speaking in tongues"—each person with a different tongue. I believe this is a way of experiencing lifehoods on a level where emotions are released, but the meanings of that lifehood remain hidden—again, a perfect way to escape responsibility.

The most prevalent method for obtaining early childhood information is hypnotic regression. There is understandable confusion in people's minds about regression. I believe the word "regression" itself should be used only to describe a technique for uncovering the current life information that is subconscious, memory of which is recorded in the brain. This is space-time locked information and can be recovered rapidly by regression that requires backward steps in time memory.

Regression methods should not be applied to lifehoods where the information is metaphysical, held in the mind-field. As such, it is out of time-space and so is not available by regression. Mind-field awareness is superconscious, not subconscious. Remember, mind-field information is now, not in the past. This probably explains why not all hypnotists uncover lifehoods. Those who do are breaking barriers to mind-field memory, but not by regression. Hypnotherapists generally work on subconscious material stored in the brain. They do not as readily access super-consciousness material in the mind-field.

Hypnotherapists do not understand why some people slip into lifehoods and others do not; they report that when lifehoods appear, the regression is an unusual one. I believe that this may occur during hypnosis when a person automatically catapults into the altered state, which is where lifehoods are recovered. We do know that, when a high enough vibration exists in the mind-field, lifehoods are available, independent of the technique one uses.

True regression primarily opens the neural memory of this life, but not the mind-field memory of lifehoods. Classical hypnosis creates low vibrations in the body similar to those in the brain. Lifehoods tap into the high vibrations of the field. Dr. Brian Weiss has extensively reported recovering past-lives by means of hypnosis. He found that past-life therapy was a quick, vivid, and relatively inexpensive therapeutic technique for dealing with emotional and physical problems in this current lifehood (*Omni*, March, 1994). Hypnosis, as Dr. Weiss used it, activates a state of focused concentration which is different from the emphasis of classical regression hypnosis.

Dr. Weiss and I obtained somewhat different patterns of brain waves during lifehood recall. I believe this occurred because his therapy accessed information primarily geared to the material world of personality and body. He reported that his patients exhibited an entire smorgasbord of brain waves. My lifehood work focuses primarily upon the mystical, spiritual aspects of lifehoods which I find to be the ultimate source of this lifehood's problems. Not only do people get better, but they evolve. The brain waves accompanying this level of lifehood are alpha, with a dramatic increase in the frequency and quantity of the energy field. This field aspect, I believe, is the determining factor in the level of lifehood recall, that is, whether one retrieves soul information or personality/body information.

Psychologist Wambach analyzed 800 hypnotically-induced past-life experiences. Although she did not state that these "proved" past lives, she did comment that it became more and more difficult to explain past-life recall as fantasy. Her study involved the physical aspects of previous lives, such as location, dates, and so forth. These lives were scattered in time and place and were not primarily the lives of famous people.

Numerous authors have reported that the traditional Chinese medical use of acupuncture needles seems to unblock nerve channels to release past-life information. Apparently, placing needles around the third eye, the psychic meridian points on the right and left shoulders, or on the galactic points of the ears, encourages the person to experience scenes, memories, and vignettes of their past-lives. Acupuncture circumvents brain activity as it taps directly into the energy field.

Sometimes, after the long and arduous training of physical, spiritual, and mental development, one frequently has the experience of higher, inner initiation. Intuitive psychic facilities are awakened. This allows for direct investigation of every detail of lifehoods, which sometimes requires weeks or even months. The memories that emerge are elegantly detailed, complete with facts, thoughts and emotions. At this level, the person changes beyond recognition because the evolutionary process is hyper-accelerated. Wisdom begins to replace knowledge, and reincarnation is no longer just an appealing idea; it is a fact.

Many people experience fantasy lives which seem to be stimulated by recent books, movies, or by famous fables. But if probed more deeply, these fantasy lives can provide some amazingly correct information about the subject's real lifehood. It seems that couching the material in fantasy releases some of the energy, without requiring the subject to own it totally. The information, however, is important because it can lead to new awareness. The caution, of course, is not to take these fantasy lives too literally.

There are, however, some very clear criteria for differentiating between symbolic and real lifehoods. Fantasy experiences flow freely, lucidly, and intellectually, without vibrational changes in the body. With real life recall there are hesitations, blocks, physical symptoms or sensations, and spontaneous emotional charges; and the affect may be animated or stumbling and flat. A fantasy is narrated and elaborated like a story, quite removed from self. In actual lifehoods, the memory of each statement is a surprise for the person, who exclaims, "Amazing!" or "Unbelievable! And yet I know it's truth!"

Here is an example. A very upbeat, creative, outgoing, socially and professionally successful builder suddenly experienced a slump after he had finished a major project. As I worked with him, his images were elaborate, copious, and beautiful. I suspected that reality was just the opposite. He saw himself as a desert potentate with a huge caravan, animals, harem, and fine clothes and possessions. He was taking his entourage on a yearly trek into the depths of the desert to commune with the divine. This was a colorful and happy pageant which became more elaborate as the narration continued. I asked him to respond quickly to my next question: "Is this a real life?" His answer, to his surprise, was no. I told him that the deeper structures of his mind were trying to tell us something. I explained that if he had had a similar real life that fostered this fantasy, memory of that life would come to him slowly if he did not try to create it, but just allowed the memory to surface.

It came falteringly. He saw a young man dressed in ragged sacks, emaciated and stooped, but compelled to discover his destiny. He was walking toward a vast, arid desert. It took a long time to reach a place distant enough that he could not be traced. Here, he lay beside the sparse, stunted growth of the desert in the daytime, and climbed a small hill to be warmer at night. Each day, he returned to the desert floor to await insight while he warmed himself and took nourishment by chewing roots. As he recalled this experience, his speech was hesitant with spontaneous bursts of emotion about the hardships, but he revealed no additional content.

One day he found a long stick which he saw as his staff, divinely given to him. His emotional state deteriorated until, in his weakened condition, he became delusional. At times, he would snap out of it into his everyday, lighthearted patter only to realize that the sudden depression in his current life was the same. Eventually, he placed his staff over his body, dedicated his soul to God, and he purposely gave up his life.

When his awareness returned to his current life, he was very touched by these experiences. He commented that this was surely his life—he had felt it deeply. He wanted to pursue what in that life or prior ones had caused him to deny his spiritual nature. We made the appointment, but he never returned. We both knew that he was not willing to take the next step—what could have been a glorious step, but one which would have demanded that he change to honor his soul's need for spiritual power. Perhaps someday he will be ready.

Children's reports about past lives are probably the purest, because they don't yet know that "reality isn't that way." Ages two to four are the most fluid; at those ages, children have only limited information from which to build an intellectual case for reincarnation. They produce names and places with a great deal of affect. Their images are so clear and vivid that they seem surprised that we cannot see them. If these early recalls are not blocked, children use them in fantasy play, denying their validity only as these begin to blend with the experiences of this life. Stevenson, at the University of Virginia Medical School, sought records to verify the reality of children's statements about past lives. He found that 90% of the past-life recall of children who had reincarnated rapidly was in fact verified by records.

Why can't we remember past lives easily? First, remember that the information is not recorded in the brain; only experiences of this life are stored there. Lifehood information is stored in the field. Early in life, the field is our primary memory bank, not the brain, because obviously a child has had few experiences to record in the brain. Also, the importance of mystical information wanes as we become more dependent upon our biological senses—we become more materially conscious. And finally, our culture says that mystical knowledge is not real, so we lose contact with it, though we never forget. Additionally, there is a personal motivation to forget the soul's struggles and to be freed from deep emotions—to repress our soul's unfinished business.

Again, I would like to stress that my techniques for lifehood recovery do not focus on relieving social pressure or solving isolated problems. They are geared toward ultimate evolution—to assist the soul in its growth toward divinity. During my work with individuals of all faiths, both sexes, a wide age range, different races and ethnic groups, and different stages of advancement, I find a common problem. The problem is not a subconscious one, but a superconscious one. Each person has had difficulty experiencing divine feelings or images of God.

At times of great stress or insurmountable problems, all people turn to God. If their questions are not answered, or at least not in the way that they wished, they experience doubt, anger, and frustration. They continue their problem with God, feeling guilty and unworthy. Eventually, these feelings become associated with their parents. If this problem is not solved, no soul can reach its destiny to become one with God, nor can it manifest a divine energy. This is the ultimate problem. It can never be successfully sublimated or circumvented. It can only be eliminated by recovering the first and all subsequent experiences where problems with God or divine power became manifest. Finally, with this information, one has the opportunity to change—again beyond recognition. The burden is released. Enhanced wisdom, creativity, higher beingness, and enlightenment are the end results.

Many people tell me that they don't want to delve into past lives and learn painful things. They don't want to regress. Quickly, I tell them they will not regress or go into a trance nor will they lose consciousness. They will only go up in vibrations, expand, while still maintaining their sense of reality as the mind-field opens. At this stage, one assumes an active-passive state by allowing the information to interact with thought—to create images, to produce all manner of body sensations, and to bring forth truth.

We never judge the specific information until we see that it has settled into a pattern. These patterns are both facilitators and inhibitors. They can be evaded, but not eliminated. We can examine our role in creating these patterns—what were the judgments we made and are still holding, and what determination prompted our decision to never, ever recall these experiences again. Despite that resolve, you have been trying ever since to discover your divinity, and to satisfy your need for spiritual experiences. You have been running from the very thing you have been longing for.

Ideally, you should be able to move randomly, and at will, among any number of lifehoods so that you can understand your accomplishments as well as your unfinished business. All these disparate aspects of your soul can be integrated into your current personality. I also want you to take hold of your own power and to know that you have the skill and divine guidance to evolve more rapidly without outside help. If you have patience, you can indeed discover the patterns of any life as well as the decisions and the beliefs that are still with you today.

I conclude with this offering of lyric prose which came to me one day:

The strongest human beliefs arise from the profoundly invisible reality of God.

No man can become self-realized without belief in his immortal soul. The fulfilling of human destiny depends upon what we have become aware of and what our soul has done with it.

And yet, forgetfulness dims our early remembrances of this life, and a body veil of secrecy seems to hide other life experiences as if to insure that this life remains the soul's primary concern.

The truism—to know thyself will set you free—is unattainable until awareness of the unfinished business of childhood expands to include the uncompleted work of lifehoods.

Then as man's level of awareness—his consciousness—is fed with these inner knowings, he can command the full spectrum of his existences. Only then can he realize truth—and his soul be freed to exercise his will as the "Divine Will of God."

As Leo Tolstoy wrote: "Our life is but one of the dreams of that more real life, and so it is endless until the last one, the very real life, the life of God."

CHAPTER X

HEALING:
The Miracle Of Life

"If the head and body are to be well, you need to begin by curing the soul."

—Plato, *Dialogues*

I extol a social consciousness which acknowledges that life choices can be debilitating and lead to illness; and I applaud a consciousness which chooses to eliminate illness rather than resort to common scapegoating like: "I caught my disease from other people," or "the work-place contamination made me ill."

Both society and individuals must take action to decontaminate our living spaces. But the motivation for health must come from deep convictions that it isn't alright to be ill, from a personal perspective of suffering, expense, immobility, and loss of contribution. It isn't okay to be an emotional burden or a financial drain on loved ones or society. And it is not acceptable to contaminate the environment with bacteria, viruses, and the anti-coherent vibrational fields of illness.

In other words, your being ill hurts you and everyone else—because wherever there is illness it distorts the energy field in which we live. Whether I can catch your bacteria or virus, or you mine, is perhaps less important than the fact that disease, wherever it is, presents an anti-coherent, disturbed field within the electromagnetic pool of our mutual lives. Every one of us must be responsible for all disease and dysfunction.

First, this requires that we replace old, worn-out ideas about illness. We should tolerate illness which fosters constructive change, that is, healing the body and/or the soul. And we should be increasingly vigilant of illnesses or treatments that do not hold both goals in mind.

Furthermore, freedom from disease is not enough. A broad perspective of illness demands a widespread, comprehensive and diligent attack upon human filth, industrial contamination, poverty, and personally irresponsible and destructive habits which lower human resistance. We must attack all human conditions known to lower human resistance and those that stimulate diseases. This mandates that people, individually and collectively, assume responsibility and participate fully. Individuals and groups should not have the freedom to do otherwise. Negligence seems strange when freedom from illness with vital health is within the capacity of the world community if we declare that illness is no longer acceptable.

We are tackling global infectious illness through world institutions and conferences. There is growing legislation in this country to provide for the aging ill, handicapped and addicted. Some insurance companies are contemplating health policies with lower premiums for good health, although there is no widespread public acceptance as yet. But I hear only a whisper instead of a shout demanding that each person assume responsibility for his health. Social welfare consciousness that we are our brother's keeper is an inadequate approach to improving world health.

The treatment of illness is coming full circle. Medicine and healing, which started out together and then separated, are tentatively acknowledging each other's value. Actually, the bulk of orthodox medicine is still empirical, as is esoteric healing. Western medicine began with Hippocrates and the Island of Cos, where he studied with the Aesculipian healers. Healing was tied to the religious beliefs of the time. Healing rituals actually preceded formal religion. Before Judeo-Christian belief in one God, healing was attributed to many gods and goddesses. All societies had major healing gods who were invoked to intervene in illness. Healers held an elevated role and were worshipped in early cultures, similar to physicians today. As Greek medicine became more involved with alchemy, the connection between healing and the gods began to unravel, setting the stage for chemical treatment of illness.

Although specifics of early healing practices are not known, they are believed to have come from India by way of Tibet, where these "top of the world" peoples were more isolated and could protect their medical secrets from marauding bands. A Buddhist monarch is reported to have sent 80,000 medical missionaries to Greece, China and Egypt. Perhaps this explains why these countries have a very common medical tradition. India is reported to have developed the first surgery, followed closely by Egypt.

Moses' seraph, represented by three pairs of wings with a serpent coiled on a staff, believed to indicate the highest order of celestial beings, supposedly gave him the power to heal his people in the wilderness. The universal healing symbol remains some form of an asp—a small viper or serpent—crossed and coiled around a staff. These symbols have been described as the Ida and Pingala or the male and female life energies. Near the top of the staff, representing the spine, are the spread wings symbolizing the latent healing power and knowledge contained in the physical body. All races and societies have used them as symbols of the healer. The Greek god Mercury was depicted carrying this ancient staff to herald the medical profession. Understandably, it was adopted by the American Medical Association.

Occult or esoteric healing continued to develop around the divine power of regeneration believed to emanate from the chakra vortices of the body. When the power flowed upward from these areas, the person's aura became white and the sacred lotus flower at the crown chakra was said to open, bringing divine insight. Magical healing elements were developed, symbolized and passed on to each advancing culture.

Healers in ancient Greek healing temples, and later in Egypt, stimulated a dream consciousness state in patients to initiate the curative process. In Europe from the 11th to the 18th century, the ability to heal was attributed to royalty who were reported to lay-on hands. Philip I of France and Olaf of Norway were particularly respected as successful healers. In the 18th century, Mesmer advanced his sweeping new ideas of mind intervention with his renowned healing. His techniques and ideas were brought to America with Phineas P. Quimby, who developed a technique called the Science of Health and Happiness. Mary Baker Eddy, one of his patients, later founded Christian Science.

During the 19th century there was an upsurge in the spiritualist movement in France, which had originated in African shamanism. These spiritual-healing beliefs were also taken to South America by early colonizers to become the strong Espiritiste movement which now sponsors large healing hospitals where psychic diagnosis, healing, and surgery parallel, and are acknowledged by, orthodox medicine.

The early physicians and scientists were mystics, astrologers, alchemists, religious and spiritual leaders. Gradually, as alchemy and herbal treatment took over, medicine lost its magical and spiritual connections.

Yet even with the advanced information from anatomy and physiology in the late 19th and early 20th centuries, the physician was generally still a healer, taking time to understand his patients and be concerned about their general welfare. But the human element in treatment, stressing the importance of the transaction between physician and patient, gradually weakened as medical schools upgraded standards and focused upon using advanced technology for diagnosis. Research into the electrical nature of the body advanced early in this century until a choice was made to focus primarily on the chemistry of physiological processes.

As disease became more impersonal, so did treatment. The treatments of choice became shots, pills and surgery, all disease and illness-oriented rather than geared to the person and his healing response. Physicians seemed to use more and more powerful and potentially dangerous substances for supposed good, all the while ignoring and negating man's healing energies.

The use of drugs gathered momentum in medicine during the 19th century, but the discovery of penicillin in the 20th century declared the science of biochemistry the source of medicine. In a short time, life was defined as a purely chemical phenomenon. Earlier treatment concepts that did not fit this pattern were abandoned. While this biochemical fix handled infectious diseases easily, degenerative health problems such as heart attacks, arteriosclerosis, cancer, stroke, arthritis, hypertension and ulcers, the major enemies of life, were less amenable to chemical treatment.

In contrast, occult and psychic healers were trained by other healers. They were selected and initiated into secret orders in which unwritten information was guarded and protected with the belief that it belonged to the chosen ones of a higher consciousness. Yet, there has always been a large number of persons who, without formal training, have discovered their power to channel energy and initiate healing. Their only source of explanation for these healing events was the ancient occult literature, heavily steeped in superstition, metaphysical deductions, and myths. This apparently satisfied the unscientific, but also caused them to be relegated to a less acceptable second class. Generally, in modern times, only when scientific medicine failed to cure complex diseases did patients seek out healers as a last resort. Fortunately for them and for health care, there was sufficient success when all else failed, to bring older healing methods back to the attention of the so-called enlightened world.

It was also true that modern healers who worked intuitively, like the ancient healers, were more scientifically oriented and sought better explanations for their cures. Likewise, professional individuals trained in medicine and science, who recognized their mystical and visionary tendencies, began to study the source and course of illness by studying energy rather than chemistry. From these beginnings, research on human energy fields began to appear during the 1970s and 1980s in some of the outstanding research laboratories throughout the world.

With this historical perspective, it is easy to understand that medical development resulted in a tunnel vision which lost sight of the dynamics of life. Medicine has followed the path of biochemistry to discover life and health and has not revised its direction in light of new evidence.

During this century, physics has moved further away from a mechanical model toward a more organic view of life, while biology and physiology have generally migrated in the opposite direction by attempting to explain tissue behaviors almost entirely in a reductionist way by genetics and DNA. Their work did provide some information about these component parts of a biosystem, but with it was lost the true notion of the "organism" as a fundamental entity that generates its own healing and regenerates tissues to conform to its biologically intrinsic order. (Truelinger.)

W. Ross Adey, an eminent neurophysiologist, has noted that, "Over the past twenty years a series of observations has pointed with increasing certainty to an essential organization of living matter, physical in nature at a far finer level than the structural and functional image defined by the chemistry of structures." Physicists have commented similarly.

> In a little more than a century our biological vista has moved from organs to tissues, to cells, and most recently to molecules that are the exquisite fabric of living systems. There is now a new frontier, more difficult to understand, but of vastly greater significance. It is at the atomic level that the physical processes, rather than the chemical reactions in the fabric of molecules, appear to

shape the transfer of energy and the flow of signals
in living systems (Trullinger.)

Chemical theories contend that biological life as we know it has a purely chemical source. This centuries-old model is frequently described as bankrupt, yielding scores of impossible problems and contradictions about life's secrets. Electrical theories, on the other hand, insist that there is some electromagnetic energy associated with all life's processes. The view that life is an electrical force is gaining recognition. Answers are coming from nuclear, not mechanical, physics.

We have learned that the body remembers a chemical in its field long after the chemical molecules have disappeared. The disturbed field is believed to cause many debilitating aging diseases, most of which have unknown etiology. We have learned also that all chemistry is based upon and controlled by electrical charges and their distribution. Command of these electrical stimulations controls the biochemistry of the cell and the body. This has encouraged the practice of homeopathy, the treatment of field disturbances with chemical fields.

Since the early 1800s, homeopathy was practiced in Europe, India, Pakistan and Sri Lanka for treating illness. Only recently has it become more popular in this country as we became alarmed at the many long-term toxic reactions to current drugs. At the Research Institute of Glasgow, one drop of a chemical substance was diluted 99 times until no molecule of the original substance could be expected to be present. Yet the diluted substance affected the cells in the same way as the original chemical. Clinical evidence of homeopathic effectiveness was the only convincing evidence until 1963. At that time, a double-blind study at the Research Institute of Glasgow showed that homeopathic remedies were significantly more effective than placebos in treating allergy.

The *Brain-Mind Bulletin*, December 29, 1986, stated,

Most medical preparations act on the physiological
or   tissue   level.   Homeopathic   preparations
reportedly act on a cellular level in accordance with

a pharmacologic law: a weak stimulus excites life processes in the protoplasm, a moderate stimulus impedes these. a moderately strong stimulus depresses them, and a very strong stimulus stops or destroys protoplasm.

About homeopathic solutions it was said that,

By serial dilution the substance tends to spread out evenly in the solvent. The higher the dilution, the greater the resonance or potency. There is more `elbow room' in which the medicine molecule can resonate. As it resonates, it generates ultra-low frequency electromagnetic wave emanations. The greater the resonance, the greater the intensity of the frequency generated. Beyond the 30th dilution, it is unlikely that any of the original molecules are contained in the drop extracted. In theory, the original molecules, acting as templates, have imprinted their characteristics on the polywater molecules.

The prestigious British science journal *Nature* published a paper by a French allergist, Benveniste, of the University of Paris, South, in which it commented about "observations for which there is no physical basis." The editors called the results so startling "because they strike at the roots of two centuries of observation and rationalization of physical phenomena." Basically, the article shows that it is possible to dilute a water solution of an antibody indefinitely without losing its biological activity. Researchers in five other laboratories in four countries have confirmed Benveniste's results. I believe that within the next few years we will be able to scientifically demonstrate that homeopathic chemical fields resonate with the human field, to explain these remarkable findings.

In like fashion, herbal medicines may indirectly trigger the same healing mechanisms common to specific therapies or drugs, or have a direct placebo effect through the vibrational field of the herbs.

Quite beyond the electrical source of molecular life is the pattern of the organization of the body's electrical field. Subatomic physics failed to give full account of the organizational features, but quantum physics showed that macro answers cannot come from collective atomic molecular activity. Now a new perspective emerges: things are controlled not only from below upward, by atomic and molecular action, the micro-source of fields, but also from above downward from mental, emotional properties or fields.

The existence of energy systems and streams of energy were professed some 4,000 years ago in Oriental medicine. Disease and debilitation were seen as malfunctioning energy fields. Treatment by acupuncture and herbs was designed either to release dammed-up energy in organs and meridians (energy tracks) or to stimulate deficient organs and meridians.

Orthopedist Robert Becker's studies and mine give the most extensive evidence that healing occurs through changes in the electromagnetic field. At the cellular level of molecular circuits, there are endless electro-windings as well as a microtubular array of collagen, that is, connective tissue, the support structure of all tissue. At every level throughout the body, from cell, to molecule, to atom, there are structural evidences of the intrinsic electromagnetism of life. The whole body oscillates It has even been speculated that the non-resistive superconductive circuits at the molecular level intimately connect life on a global basis.

This growing emphasis from biomagnetic field studies on the electrical nature of life has given birth to the new Energy Field medical specialty. Similarly, because of interest in shamanism and religious healing rites based on energy field beliefs, there are the new specialties of medical anthropology and spiritual ethnology.

Throughout these chapters, I have presented the human energy field as the mind-field. The characteristics of body tissue and the nature of transactions with outside fields determine its dynamic, non-random organization which fits the classical mathematical chaos pattern. The mind-field is our first and primary contact with the world. Transactions of the field change it and all participating fields. Although the human field may have unknown energies, or even scaler waves, we know that it is composed also of both alternating and magnetic currents of the electromagnetic spectrum. As described in the previous chapter, the magnetic current appears to be the facilitator—the interlock of organism-universe interaction. Magnetism which exists in the body is the primary energy of the Earth, of volcanoes and of batteries.

A living field is much more sophisticated with electrical energies than the electrical energy of inert fields. It is believed to radiate from small to smaller units: cells, molecules, atoms and particles. The density of tissue helps determine the frequency and pattern of energy released. Dense tissues, like bone and cartilage, present a slower moving, lower frequency, with more sluggish energy, while lighter tissue such as nerves and glands, produces a faster, higher, more dynamic frequency.

Dense fields probably absorb more from other fields. We might speculate that the more fluid the field, the more interaction. Remember that living things with their more elaborate fields do select transactions on the mind level rather; they do not simply react. Furthermore, the living field with its complexity responds more readily to elaborate fields than to simple, isolated ones. For example, if one were in Machu Pichu in person, one's field would react more than if one saw a picture or held a rock from Machu Pichu.

Otologists were greatly surprised to find that the ear, supposedly a primary instrument of sound reception, also transmits a frequency. All parts of the body, as well as the ear, are both radio transmitters and receivers. When we say that a body remembers its experience, probably it is the field that remembers best; and the more fluid the field, the more information is available. This leads us to ask about how field transactions take place. In general, fields are known to be attracted to like fields that they resonate with; they are repulsed by those with unlike characteristics.

We find that the human field or aura hangs around the body probably because of the positive electrical charge on the skin and the negative charge of the field. Every ingress and egress to and from body tissue is apparently through thousands of acupuncture points on the skin's surface. Oriental medicine charted these major points and modern science measured and found them to be lower in electrical resistance, acting like a couplet between the inside and outside of the body. These electrical meridians, not physically locatable but electronically verifiable, seem to be channels for the flow of this energy. Our research in the Mu Room demonstrated the extensive flow of this energy in all the body's connective tissue as well.

When instruments in the Mu Room lowered the electricity in the air to a near ambient state, aura readers could accurately see past the skin to the inside of the body. They excitedly observed the ripples of energy in the minute connective tissue around cells and between tissues. They described flowing, waving, fishnet-like structures we know as human connective tissue with its many different forms such as fascia, ligament, cartilage, as well as the scaffolding for all cells. Its yellow and white composition we knew provided different mechanical capabilities such as elasticity, tensile and shearing strength. But we had never before envisioned connective tissue as an anatomical, electromagnetic circulating system.

Adey reported that cells are separated by narrow fluid channels that are especially important in cell to cell communication. He believes that these fluid "gutters" are the preferred pathways for energy field migration because of their electrical impedance which is lower than that of cell membranes.

Theorists of complex systems believe that biological membranes, where the edge of chaos is found, serve as the space transition between field and tissue. This is the place where "... information gets its foot in the door—where order and chaos meet." (Lewin.)

Let's return our attention to the electromagnetic current.

Although electrical and magnetic components are inseparable, one can have greater intensity than the other, giving the current different capacities. The predominant electrical energy of nerve and muscle is an alternating current with rapid positive and negative deflection back and forth as evident in EEG, ECG and EMG graphs. The magnetic current lower in frequency with less deflections shifts slowly between a positive and negative pole. In the body, the iron in the hemoglobin may be its primary source. Both aspects of electromagnetic systems are intrinsic to the body field, allowing a flow of electrons.

In laboratory tests we found that an increase in magnetic energy preceded a change in consciousness, emotion, or any dramatic change in the electrical energy—as though it acted as a harbinger or facilitator. We know from physics that weak energy facilitates energy interaction. Becker found that at the location of an injury, the magnetic energy increased and flowed from the center of the body outward. This agrees with our observation that the magnetic flux precedes changes in alternating current activity.

A simple test for "good" or "bad" field interaction is demonstrated with applied kinesiological manual testing of the muscle strength of the arm when a single food, herb or medication is placed in one's field or held in one's hand. If the muscles test strong to downward pressures on the arm, the field interaction is positive and that substance is not harmful to the person. If the muscles become weakened and the arm cannot resist pressure, the field interaction is poor and the substance should be avoided. For example, the fields of poisonous, caustic cleaning substances, alcohol, coffee, and sugar weaken everyone's field reaction. The strength of the field can be determined by the same method if the person being tested simply thinks about a specific food or substance. Actually, the tester can get the same results if he thinks of a substance or food while pressing down on the testee's arm and asking him to respond to the tester's thought.

Concepts of energy field transaction introduce a new perspective on illness and healing. The body slides into a chaotic reaction precipitating illness and by readjusting, heals itself. Medication, surgery, rituals, supplements and foods only facilitate the healing process. The best description of healing refers to the activation of the body's energies toward dynamic equilibrium, growth and evolution.

Perhaps the best measure of health is an organism which is constantly self-healing. Here, healing implies an elimination of the disturbance and maintenance of the body's integrity. Whether conventional or other methods are used, in order to heal, the person must actively "will" to recover. For best results, all health procedures must take into account beliefs that inhibit or facilitate positive attitudes toward cure.

Because medical diagnosis is based on description and classification of symptoms and pathological states, the mind and emotions have been given less recognition. Spiritual and psychic healers, on the other hand, place primary emphasis upon healing the soul when it gets off track. They attempt to reach into the painful and misdirected areas of the soul to gently awaken the healing response. They believe that the source of all illness is forgetting who we are. The healing process helps us to remember that we are divine and perfect beings. They maintain that outer healing saves the biological life, while inner healing focuses on belief systems as the contaminating source.

Electromedical researchers believe that each disease or functional disturbance has its own energy field which must be reversed before healing can take place. Probably illness is a disturbance first in the energy field and healing is the restoration of that field to health.

Soon we should be able to show unequivocally that field disturbance precedes all tissue changes. When tissue is diseased, the problem is already far advanced. Even pain occurs in the field before it is felt in the body. Energy field evaluations to detect potential health problems should be the health exam of choice. Allopathic medical tests should follow when indicated. Such an assessment will disclose potential health problems perhaps weeks, months, or even years before symptoms or tissue changes occur, and will therefore predict health more accurately.

Do you realize that there is no valid measure of health today? Health is assumed if there is no pathology or dysfunction. Yet we have all heard reports of individuals who were declared healthy following a complete medical exam; then suddenly they were stricken with a massive heart attack. The seed of the electrical disturbance that was not detected in the EKG will be evident in the energy field exam. These comments reiterate that the static models of illness and healing that have guided treatments thus far are not so much incorrect as they are incomplete.

Health, then, should be viewed as the perfection and maintenance of a dynamic energy field which is flowing, coherent, and strong, giving it the capacity to vibrationally interact. In his many writings, Burr stressed the electrical phenomena accompanying all growth and life. He reminded us that the myriad of body cells, except those in the brain, grow old and die to be replaced by new cells. The electrical phenomenon remains the only constant as new cells are created and organized in the pattern of the cells they replace.

The new electromagnetic model of illness and health is like this: material tissue ages, gets sick and diseased. It repairs itself, but eventually entropy takes over and causes deterioration and disintegration. This is not true of the human field where, by the introduction of new energy, the field improves, or even becomes more refined. The field is affected before we breathe, eat, or ingest substances, making it the first line of disturbance, defense, and regeneration. Regeneration comes from re-energizing the field, and hence the tissue.

Fitness, a positive affirmation of a healthy state, is first characterized by a dynamic complex field allowing a person to react to situations in numerous adaptive and evolutionary ways. A fit field is critically self-organized so that it gravitates to the edge of chaos, its favored position for maximizing and sustaining its fitness (Lewin.) Stated another way, to be healthy an organism must exhibit dynamic flexibility in all of its systems and tissues.

Recently I saw a vivid example of the old, static concept of health. A courageous, insightful woman physician called me to the hospital to see her patient suffering from a potentially fatal heart attack. She did so at the displeasure of the intensive care unit staff. I found the patient's energy field to be concentrated in the upper body, weak and anti-coherent. Her feet were cold and her face revealed acute stress. I laid-on-hands primarily to ground her field and to make her more comfortable, for I knew not how to help her cardiac condition. Intuitively, my hands went to her feet. Within minutes her feet warmed and she seemed to be experiencing less stress. In 30 minutes, the cardiac monitoring equipment showed a stronger, steady condition as she went off to a peaceful sleep. The supervising nurse who had been observing was amazed because this patient had not rallied during 12 hours of intensive drug treatment. By morning she was much improved. It was then that I taught her how to experience the flow of electromagnetic energy throughout her body and to consciously manipulate it with breathing exercises. She progressively recovered in the months that followed. With cardiac medication and her energy field work, she is still alive in her late 80s.

Another example is a 65-year-old asthmatic woman with bronchial congestion from the flu. She had been in bed for several days prior to directing a small, intense, working conference. At the end of a long evening she collapsed with paroxysmal breathing, weakness, tachycardia, and a feeling that she was dying. A nurse companion reported her pulse became too weak to palpate. While awaiting paramedics, I stabilized her random, anti-coherent field. The energy was concentrated in the upper body, streaming out over the top of her head, and absent in the lower body. As the field became more coherent, the cardiovascular and respiratory symptoms diminished. By the time emergency help came, she was resting quietly and needed no hospitalization.

Lastly, a woman physician with months of cardiac dysrhythmia, who could not be stabilized with medication, was scheduled for a pacemaker. Knowing of her impending surgery, I visited her at her home. Since there was no emergency, I did not lay-on-hands, but I taught her to use breathing to consciously redirect her energy field from a moderate chaotic condition to a more coherent one. With one week's breathing practice, the symptoms of dysrhythmia were sufficiently improved that her cardiologist cancelled the pacemaker surgery. Several months later she was allowed to travel by air to professional meetings. During a trip to China she visited the Great Wall at an elevation of 8,000 feet.

Such happenings are not the result of magic. It seems logical that when the entire field is weak, anti-coherent, and incomplete throughout the body, all the electrical systems controlling breathing and the heart will eventually come into sync with this anti-coherent field, producing these symptoms. Furthering these beliefs was the fact that by using a cross plot analysis comparison of two different simultaneous recordings, the dysrhythmic heart showed the same anti-coherent pattern as the anti-coherent field. Conversely, a healthy heart and field are both coherent. By improving the field coherency, anti-coherency in the breathing and heart come under automatic control.

Let me review information about normal healing. Injured dense tissue, like bones and ligaments, heals more slowly than less dense soft tissue. We attribute this to the slower blood and lymphatic circulation in dense tissue which delays the removal of the local acidity produced by injury. Also, the electromagnetic flow through this tissue is diminished, and slower than in softer tissue. On the positive side, the magnetic part of the electromagnetic spectrum is facilitated. This is the energy which we find to be associated with healing.

During the first few days of regeneration, hyper-acidity from tissue death is carried away by the circulation—regrowth requires a more neutral environment. Becker explains the regeneration process by cell dedifferentiation followed by redifferentiation. Dedifferentiation of cells, for example, means that a blood cell can lose its unique capacity to generate a blood cell and can be redifferentiated or transposed into a muscle cell, a nerve cell, or a connective tissue cell. He believes that the magnetic energy flowing outward from the site of injury stimulates this. Unspecialized or dedifferentiated cells accumulate around the injury, later to become differentiated into osteoblasts (bone creators), neuroblasts (nerve creators), and fibroblasts (creating patching or scar tissue). These are the body's built-in growth cells which it uses to heal itself. Becker states that for regrowth of these cells to occur, apparently about 30% of the normal nerve tissue must be intact to serve as a catalyst. Yet I am finding instances where the energy field takes over and operates like the nervous system when it is defective.

The template pattern for regrowth is provided by the field. The DNA is known to carry genetic information about cellular development, but it has not been found to create the form of living substance, i.e. arms, legs, or noses. Remember, material tissue can be destroyed but a field, with its holistic properties, cannot be. If bits were cut out of a field, it would only become smaller. As a hologram it carries information which guides development and regeneration. For this reason some leading researchers have hypothesized that we humans should be able to regenerate not just tissue but limbs and organs as we learn to stimulate the appropriate electrical aspects of the body, perhaps when our consciousness is more evolved.

All healing is a movement toward wholeness with cells regenerating along their original healthy plan. Therefore, the regrowth of complex body areas comes from regrowth of several differentiated cells along each cell's original growth pattern. Becker, in his extensive studies of animal regeneration, noted that the ability to regenerate declines as an organism moves up the evolutionary scale where the cerebral cortex commands the lower neural centers.

Singukin measured the electrical field around plants as they healed, finding a current flowing outward from the leaf wound for a few days—negative at first, and later changing to a positive charge as tissues multiplied. He called this the "energy of injury." Becker, using surface electrical measurements, found the same phenomenon in human limb amputation. I have discovered that the energy at the injured site, normally stronger in the electrical component, becomes dominantly magnetic, as do the healer's hands when performing a treatment. I have therefore entitled the phenomenon the "energy of healing."

How does the field information system work in healing? Is the field essential or is it just a relay station? We believe that the activity of the immune system from chemical secretions of the thymus, spleen, lymph nodes, bone marrow, tonsils and pineal gland is the first line of defense in healing. Neuropeptides, protein amino-acid cells attached to the outside of all nerves, glands, muscle and bone cells, seem to be the first communication lines of cellular distress. It is the premier information system for all cells. Candace Pert, while at the National Institutes of Health, reported that when neuropeptides connected to brain cells are stimulated, remote neuropeptides on cells in distant body areas responded faster than the nervous or circulatory systems could transmit the information. An energy field relay is the only logical explanation.

Immune cells have been thought to affect other cells simply by lying adjacent to them. Now we know that they have a remote telepathic communication capacity. In other words, there is a communication system attached to each cell which is in touch with remote cells, not just by direct contact or regular circuits, but by almost simultaneous transmission through the energy field.

Pert further states that while every cell has some receptors and combinations of different receptors, one cell might have as many as 60, while another might have relatively few. These informational substances get titillated or vibrationally activated to change shape, often floating and attaching to another molecule, or sliding laterally around the cell membrane, or even cascading while still in contact with the internal events of the cell. Apparently it is at the cell's surface where interface and interactions take place among systems. Pert describes the action as "exquisite specificity."

Today we know that there are some peptides that are sensitive to receiving information from body chemicals and drugs. Sensitivity to a vast array of other information is hypothesized. We have known about classical information substances, acetylcholine, adrenaline, norephinephrine. Now it seems that 95% of all information substances, and hormones except sex hormones, are neuropeptides causing action from outside the cell. Apparently, sex hormones chemically affect the cell inside. Neuropeptides are called behaviorally active because there are similar receptors in the brain. Although not yet clearly defined, one function appears to be that of creating emotions. These informational substances seem to integrate the whole body with a high proportion of action coming from a distance—and sometimes a rather long distance.

Many body workers insist that all cells have emotional memory. While the fact that cells are replaced during life points to new explanations of tissue memory, the scientific facts about neuropeptides will probably replace the old ideas that the sole source of emotion is the limbic system of the brain. Pert believes that subconsciousness is deep down in the peptides of every cell, not just, as Freud taught, in the lower brain structures.

To summarize, I have presented three aspects of a new energy field model of healing. Robert O. Becker's work on the cellular, biological aspects of cells shows that with injury or disease, repair cells are instructed to go to the injured site to initiate the healing process. He notes that the increase of the low frequency magnetic field encourages repair cells to redifferentiate and grow. At the site of the damage, peptides are released, often part of the clotting reaction, from damaged cells or, are already circulating in the area. The local peptides sense that repair cells are there and start the regrowth process in a very organized and controlled fashion.

Information from my research with the more complex higher frequency aspects of the electromagnetic field demonstrates that the mind-field is the source for instruction of the lower magnetic healing process. This can overshadow, hasten, assist and resist the built-in cellular healing process.

Pert's work I believe is the direct interface between the mind-field and the bio-healing response. The neuropeptide communication system, a field telemetry system, "talks" most rapidly directly from cell to cell and from remote to local areas eliciting total cooperation. I believe also that this exquisite communication system not only integrates the lower bio process, but it has the exclusive communication lines between the mind-field and the senses, to instruct the healing process of the body as a whole, and local tissue in particular. These three integrated processes I view as the healing response.

Probably, laying-on-of-hands, touching and manipulating encourages the release of peptides locally. Although Pert has carefully described the local information transfer, she did not discuss emotions and attitudes as factors affecting healing. I believe this influence is carried to local tissues by way of the field—a system that can be accessed from distant or local levels. In other words, the neuropeptide is the receiver and encoder; while the source of information can come slowly through the liquid system, it is rapid through the electromagnetic field. The energy field system is non-linear because it has no central clearing house or hierarchy like that of the brain to the body or a cell to a cell.

Rossi believes that "neuropeptides ... are a previously unrecognized form of information transduction between mind and body that may be the basis of many hypnotherapeutic, psychosocial, and even placebo effects. These may be more pervasive, flexible and unconscious than the central and peripheral nervous system ones."

Theoretically, such information can bypass intermediate processes and have direct input at distant locations from the source. Thus, neuropeptides seem to be a major dense system for integrating the whole body structure, to provide a direct interface with the body energy fields and those of the cosmos. The human field is an information system operating not like nerves and telephone wires, but like light and television systems.

It is clear that patterns of thought and emotions trigger

specific illness. Likewise, other thoughts and emotions create the appropriate energy for healing. In cancer, psychological trauma may be a stronger precipitating factor than a genetic one. Acute stress and strong emotional states such as depression and anxiety often suppress activity of T-cells, natural healer cells, and other immune system elements.

Early work on psychosoma stimulated by Hans Selye pointed to emotions and the activity of the hypothalamus of the brain as the mediating mechanism of illness. I find evidence of a deeper source, probably centered in the emotional organization of the field. These new biological models are even paralleled by ancient philosophical ones. Hippocrates stated, "Disease is not an entity but a fluctuating condition of the patient's body, a battle between the substances of disease and the natural, self-healing tendency of the body."

Brendan O'Regan of the Institute of Noetic Science studied records of spontaneous healing and placebo effects which provided information for his new healing concept. He viewed the healing process as a healing response, recognizing that the body knows automatically how to heal itself. He likened the healing response to a functional system of seemingly disconnected happenings acting together in a specific direction. The healing system, he believed, accounts for self-diagnosis, self-repair, and regeneration as it serves as an interface between the immune and nervous systems.

When we finally fathom the healing system's structure, I believe it will resemble a communication system between mind and matter. Such deductions lead us inevitably to the energy field as the means of communication between the internal biological healing process and the instigating source in the mind.

Spontaneous remission occurs in all kinds of illnesses. Some patients with tumors also had an infection during the illness which activated a healing response. When the fever subsided, the tumor slowly disappeared. O'Regan hypothesized that a blood-borne factor will be found to account for this. I believe that more probably changes occurred in the mind-field that released a coherent flow of energy which reestablished a normal field instead of a tumorous one, again reiterating that healing is a restoration of harmony in the energy field.

Physicians and researchers are realizing that the placebo or nocebo component is present in all therapeutic interactions. If one believes surgery will cure the problem, a placebo phenomenon occurs, or if one doubts the therapist's capability or the treatment, a nocebo one takes place. Even diagnostic procedures alone can induce a placebo effect. Words seem to trigger a patient's recovery or demise. Attitudes and conversations of the surgeon when the person is supposedly unconscious are clearly remembered on the subconscious level, and as shown with comatose patients, may be the primary placebo or nocebo effect. O'Regan stated, "The placebo effect is a poorly understood process where psychological factors such as beliefs and expectations trigger a healthy healing response that can be as powerful as any conventional therapy, be it drugs, surgery, or psychotherapy, for a wide range of medical and psychological problems."

However, the nonspecific factors of the placebo's healing response cannot be explained by the current chemical model of health and disease. An electromagnetic model is required.

O'Regan found that sugar pills, which should have had no effects upon healing, had two distinct effects based on the information supplied with the pills. When subjects were told that the sugar pills were drugs that would heal them, there was a positive placebo effect. When told that these pills would not heal them, there was an opposite, negative, or nocebo effect. He alluded to a study demonstrating the placebo effect of surgery for angina pectoris and another study showing that 30% of a control group given a placebo, knowing that chemotherapy caused hair loss, lost their hair. He speculated that the healing response might be dormant until a person is confronted with stress, trauma, disease or illness of some kind. This is in agreement with Norman Cousins' statement that healing and belief systems work together—the healing system being the way the body mobilizes all of its resources. The belief system is often the activator of the healing system.

All of us are aware of the research about the contaminated environment with the disastrous fumes we breathe, chemicals we absorb from foods and water, and the electromagnetic radiation with which our fields resonate. The man-made vibrations are potent and everywhere, from microwaves, computer and video terminals, X-rays, and ELF signals from the satellite receiver dishes and high tension wires. Even chemical fumes from industry, household solvents and cleaning fluids carry a destructive field. Geomagnetic forces seem to increase the incidence of cancer. W. Ross Adey showed possible links between electromagnetic field exposure and cancer by way of static electrical broadcasts from cell to cell, assisting cancer cells in confusing normal cell functioning.

Whenever there is an electromagnetic frequency pattern in the environmental field which falls within the pattern of the human field, resonance occurs, immediately affecting cell structure, probably by way of neuropeptides. The environmental field may be immediately destructive, disorganizing the human field with all manner of predictable results, or it may be milder and continuous with an insidious effect over time.

Delgado's research in Spain disclosed that chick embryos became abnormal when they were in close proximity to video terminals. In this country, women who worked at video terminals produced deformed babies twice as often as other women. Miscarriages were three times greater, and stillbirths six times more prevalent. Animals showed stress reactions around video vibrations. Probably the new diseases of the future will result from field interaction with contaminated environmental fields.

The body is particularly susceptible to environmental electromagnetism. Life is electromagnetic at the atomic, cellular, molecular, and systemic level. Life exists and is molded by its environmental fields. As we discovered in the Mu Room, behavior and consciousness are changed by interaction between environmental and human fields.

Broad consideration of the healing principle implicates societies, humans, individuals, as well as body tissues in the process. Each is a part of the illness-wellness syndrome. Since I have discussed this in other chapters, here I will consider only the illness or health of the physical body, still reiterating that what one believes about health is what one's health becomes.

Belief systems that are firmly ingrained culturally take on the power of absolute law. They not only create many field disturbances, but they also determine how these disturbances are manifest. Here are some dramatic examples. Only recently have we understood the physiological mechanisms of voodoo death. In those parts of the world where tribes still cause death by voodoo ceremonies, anthropologists have for years witnessed, but could not explain, the phenomenon. These cultures believe that if a person is condemned to death by a voodoo ritual, he will die. This has been borne out for centuries, so that all members of the society are deeply programmed with this belief.

After the elders or shamans sentence the person to death, a time is then set for the death ritual. The victim is informed so that conditioning will take place during the interim. On the appointed day, the community gathers for a large ritual ceremony with costumes, dancing, music, drums and fire, and often violent acts, though not toward the condemned. Each of these rituals stimulates the body, its field and physiology, as well as its mental processes. Ideally, the sympathetic nervous system should respond with hyperactivity and vitality. But because of the profound death programming, this automatic response is reversed and stimulates the parasympathetic nervous system, and with it, lowers metabolism, blood pressure, heart rate and breathing until the condemned person dies.

Doctors complicate matters by expounding their beliefs that patients should not hold out false hope. It is supposedly dishonest of the doctor to believe one thing while the patient believes another. The problem is that during an illness, patients readily accept the doctor's beliefs. I raise the question, what hope is false? Hope is hope. We have evidence that so-called impossible things have happened. The deepest hope or the lack of it, or even ambivalence, dwells in the mind. In serious illnesses the soul has a choice, and that choice is easiest when the hope is shared by doctor and patient. But the hope is broader than life; it is hope for the soul's best solution. The healer's job is to provide a stimulus and sufficient energy for this soul to heal if it chooses; if not, the energy can be used to complete personal preparation, "crossing over" to life in another form.

Both repressed and conscious mind-field information from other lifehoods can directly create this-life health problems. These are broad psychosomatic disturbances if emotions are repressed, or they are highly specific disturbances similar to what was experienced in prior traumatic episodes. The mind-field has access to the soul's memory and delivers instructions to the body tissues. As an example, one person contracted a major case of shingles before learning that she was stabbed to death in another life. The problem was diagnosed by her internist, who was amazed to notice that the shingles healed rapidly without treatment when the lifehood was recovered and the dynamics understood.

The source of asthma was found in the field of a physician who in one lifehood died of an allergic reaction to cats, causing paroxysmal asphyxiation while he was cloistered in a healing temple in Egypt. An auto-immune reaction of acute skin rash on the hands occurred with another person connected with recovery of a lifetime as a hands-on healer. Loss of memory, fuzzy thinking and amnesia occurred as another person lived a life of a mystical, spiritual epileptic.

Lifehood information carried in the field also helps determine tissue sensitivity and proclivities to various illnesses. One is already programmed from other lifehoods to compound the genetic and experiential determinants in this lifehood. Such information can be triggered into action by current life situations, showing up exactly as it did time and time before. Many people know that they are hypersensitive to anti-coherent physical and emotional fields. What they do not know is that they are affected in two ways: directly, by the anti-coherent field reaction, and indirectly, by how the information pushes their current emotional buttons.

Whatever conditions affect the human energy field will positively or negatively influence the body's healing capacity. The idea that the healing response is reserved for healing disease and tissue trauma must be expanded to include that the healing response also heals inroads (the field) to the body's function before clinical or laboratory tests show affected tissue. Healing the field is as important as healing more advanced tissue pathologies. I repeat my belief that whenever tissue loses its normal capabilities there is first a disturbance in the energy field. The field is the location of the primary interface. It first contacts other fields and serves as the direct body ingress.

If the healing response is automatic, accessing the chemical- and energy-field levels of information, then what goes wrong when healing does not occur? Following my discussion that life is an electromagnetic fact, it seems logical to believe that the primary breakdown in the body's healing response is in the electromagnetic system. Specifically, the problem is in the flow of electromagnetic energy, its strength and range of vibrations, as well as its coherency. To say it another way, when consciousness or awareness is cut off from an area, stagnation occurs, creating a functional health problem. Or, when anti-coherency or lack of energy exists in areas of the body, pathology and degeneration occur. Electromagnetic hyperactivity, likewise, overstimulates tissues.

Probably all diseases are connected with a break in the flow or a disturbance in the energy field; this is functionally transferred to the organ system with ultimately destructive consequences. By the time organ systems are involved, degenerative changes are already occurring. In the future we should be able to diagnose field disturbances by an aurascope and to treat them months or years before they upset physical tissue. Cancer may be one disease that can be arrested by such early diagnosis and field treatment.

An eminent hematologist recently told me about his new findings regarding metastatic diseases. Both cancer and thrombosis are metastatic in nature, where bits of tissue or blood clots move into the circulatory system and block its flow. Apparently it is this metastatic characteristic of cancer that causes death, and not the tumor *per se*. His research disclosed that both cancer and thrombosis are associated with a faster blood clotting time. He further alluded to anaphylactic shock, or acute allergic reactions from such things as bee stings, causing an immediate capillary paralysis of the circulation and possible death without warning. He reiterated that the anaphylactic shock occurred sometimes before the injection needle touched the body. Obviously, the initial shock was registered in the field first—followed by a shock to the circulation. We discussed my observation that increased flow in the energy field occurring when healers lay-on-hands might improve blood circulation, delaying clotting time.

As energy field blocks are removed and energy flows, the neuropeptide information chains are apparently activated to facilitate normal healing responses. Thus it seems obvious that energy fields have an immediate, direct effect upon the healing response as well as a long term one. When all conditions are ideal, the healing response will take over and restore health without external help. When this does not occur or is slowed, the best and most natural treatments are those which directly impact the mind-field. I believe every debility and dysfunction begins, continues, and stops first in the mind-field.

Well-documented spiritual and attitudinal practices can cause temporary improvements in the field. Prayer may immediately submerge unsatisfactory belief systems. Meditation and imagery can quickly manipulate and stabilize the field. But unless these permanently change the field to make it more coherent, so that the energy flows unimpeded, the disease will persist, recur, or take another form. The ideal antidote is to live a life that by its very nature is constantly self-healing.

The miracles of healing throughout the ages have never been explained scientifically. But two requisites seem essential for these miracles—the power of divine thought and its associated emotion, love. Some persons call on God to heal them; others open themselves to love. I know these to be the same, releasing in or through the person the power to heal. In that sense we are all healers of ourselves and others. For many of us these powers are but under-developed.

Testimonies by those who were apparently cured by prayer and documented cases from Lourdes and other religious spas are legion. Recently three leading cardiologists stated that doctors should pray for their patients. They personally believed their prayer assisted their patients' recovery. What they apparently overlooked was the highly coherent vibrations these doctors provided to their patients.

A professor of medicine at the University of California, San Francisco, and staff cardiologist at San Francisco General Hospital, conducted a ten-month double blind study of 393 patients at the Coronary Care Unit. Two comparable groups were randomly selected: 192 patients were prayed for by outside groups, and 201 patients had no prayer intervention. They found that the prayed-for subjects suffered fewer complications. Only three required antibiotics, as compared with 16 of the control group. Only six suffered pulmonary edema, compared with 18 of the not-prayed-for group. None of the prayed-for group required tubular drainage. Twelve of the controls did.

Self-healing, which has been called unorthodox in the past, is becoming more popular today. Some physicians limit their practice to patients who will cooperate fully by following their health regimes, even as far as giving up tobacco, alcohol, and losing weight.

I have created what I call "Mind Mastery Meditations,"* which are self-help healing procedures to improve the energy field. These can be applied to broad categories of illnesses: paralysis, hypo- and hyper-dysfunction, immune deficiency, and to cardiac and orthopedic disorders.

Public curing ceremonies, healing rituals, healing myths and cultural rites have been used as primary healing modes throughout history. Their efficacy is not easily evaluated because of limited systematic records, diagnosis, or information about the longevity, mortality, morbidity or survival rates from a disease. If the criterion of consumer satisfaction was used, these healings probably rank higher than those in our Western medical practice.

There is today a growing interest in shamanic healing practices and non-Western medicine by the World Health Organization, and the Agency for International Development. They are seriously considering incorporating this form of alternative medicine into world health plans for areas where health costs prohibit the use of Western medical procedures. I believe that shamanic group healings with their use of sound and rhythm to reorganize the human energy field have sufficient value to be included in standard medicine as well.

Contrary to the tenets of Western medicine, shamans believe that illness and disease come from incorrect relationships between man and his environment, the mystical and physical worlds, and fellow beings. Illness is thought to be as much a condition of the community and social system as of the individual. Therefore, curing rituals do not clearly separate and distinguish between religion, myths and medicine. The healer practitioners work on many levels to restore harmony to nature and society. They are not restricted to a specialty practice. These non-Western energy-field methods probably have less direct effect upon bacteria, virus and parasites, but they provide more stimulation to the healing response.

*MIND MASTERY MEDITATIONS, Malibu Publishing Publications, Fall, 1996. P.O. Box 4234, Malibu, California 90264, (310) 457-4694, www.malibupublishing.com.

All healing rituals and ceremonies stimulate mystical levels of consciousness. In fact, they are directed toward the spiritual or mystical aspects of illness and healing rather than the disease or its physiological components. When shamans diagnose, they focus on consciousness problems, not the pathological entity.

There has never been adequate explanation to account for these apparently miraculous shamanistic cures, other than the placebo effect. Anthropologists have attributed them to psychosocial support and changes in status and security of the person within the group. But from my observations of many healing rituals in the primitive cultures of Africa and the Pacific Islands, I believe there are more specific and profound explanations. All major ceremonies are accompanied by drums, chanting, rhythmic music, and dance. These carry dramatic sensory stimulation and symbolism. Participants seem to know that whatever happens requires a progressive build-up, a continuation and termination. Such ceremonies last anywhere from hours to several days. Often many people participate, including the healer, the family members, and the community at large. The sounds are low and rhythmic, regular and slow in the beginning. The movements are continuous, downward, stomping movements, sometimes staccato and sometimes undulating, all grounding the electromagnetic frequencies. The monotonous, repetitive sounds encourage a trance-like consciousness in which the sensations from the material world lessen and mystical awareness grows. A powerful group energy-field is created, low in frequency, which seems to sedate the ordinary senses and heighten the extra-sensory ones. This initial phase is followed by a gradual heightening of sound, a quickening of movement, and an increase in pitch and frequency of the drums and chants. These high frequency, high amplitude vibrations move the consciousness higher and higher into the spiritual realm, often with tetanic contractions, rigidity, great physiological stimulation, and emotional excitement. Such hyperactivity may result in physical exhaustion and collapse.

In these states the group field is expanded to include the full frequency spectrum, and it is so strong that the field transaction with the ill person is profound. Everything is alive and accessible. Because this healing field is maintained for so long, the healing response is not only powerfully stimulated, it is also nurtured. Disease fields have their own unique patterns which perpetuate themselves, so short treatments of the field are less effective.

We know that overdoses of drugs and chemicals and even herbs often create unforeseeable long-term repercussions. But overdoses in the energy-field are probably self-terminating by stopping the field transaction. An energy field not only transacts, it selects and it also terminates interaction with a barrier field response.

The meaning of these rituals to the group and individual cannot be underestimated. One component of illness seems to be isolation and alienation, fostering a sense of abandonment. Actually, a major part of healing is a re-identification, or a rebonding with people. Energy-field healing centers of the future must take into account such group healing rituals. Here, individuals will be encouraged to create self-healing rituals using sound, color and movement which have deep meaning for each person.

The practice of wearing copper, crystals, semi-precious stones or amulets comes from early herbal medicine and shamanism. These may be effective if the person believes that they have magical powers to heal. Crystals held by healers may focus and make more coherent the healer's energy, but there is no evidence that any of these alone has any measurable effect as a healing tool.

The elusive relationship between doctor or healer and patient is an emotion-laden connection which carries many messages. We are aware of the importance of gestures, touch and words to relieve anxiety, provide hope and stimulate healing. Less well accepted is the direct field-to-field, patient-healer interaction which provides immediate, pure information that is not consciously offered. When both modes tell the same story, an impact is assured. When these differ, the patient feels confused and ambivalent.

Many authors have reported clinical evidence of the healing effects from hands-on healing. Elmer Green with a Menninger Clinic team found that healers produce bursts of electromagnetic energy when they direct their efforts. The surge from meditator-healers surpassed that from non-healer meditators. Some healing surges were as much as 1,000 times greater than those recorded during emotional responses. Also, they were negatively polarized like the auric field.

My research has taken a different approach, geared to the scientific recording of the energy patterns of individuals and the energy transfer between healer and healee. I tried to understand the phenomena of energy healing by simultaneously recording the auras of both healer and healee during a hands-on session. From hundreds of recordings the following information surfaced.

At the onset, both fields are distinctly different in amplitude, frequency spectra, and patterning. The healer's field is stronger, containing a wider band of frequencies; it often displays a unique frequency pattern when healing. Healers creating the strongest vital field carry the complete spectrum of colors. They are also very successful at shifting their field to affect many illnesses (Exhibit 10).

Our data show that the auric field turns red when there is pain. It also becomes red during strenuous extended physical exercise, and during emotional pain red combines with orange when anger accompanies the pain. The escape from pain comes through an altered consciousness, with white vibrations in the aura. These do not replace the red, but minimize its intensity (Exhibits 21 and 22).

Painful diarrhea also displays a dynamic red field combined with a wide green spectrum frequently representing a transitional state (Exhibit 23). Healers who remove pain display an intense blue-violet-white field which eliminates the patient's red pain vibration (Exhibit 8).

Blue constricts blood vessels, removing swelling and therefore the throbbing of traumatic injury. Blue-violet calms muscle spasms and tensions and lowers the hyperactive state. Pain either decreases or goes away, and the person experiences relaxation, calmness, feelings of comfort, peace and tranquility. Muscle soreness, common after extended exercise, is lessened. Insomniacs and restless babies are lulled to sleep. Blue and violet also calm agitated emotional states and anger, and may ease depression by moving the person into a higher consciousness state. Let me caution, however, that for treating emotional states, there is no one sure color vibration.

Healers specializing in tissue regeneration carry a complete color spectrum with an elaborate red spectrum sometimes resembling the double helix of the genetic code. Emilie Conrad, is the only healer who presented this unique red spectrum. She is also one of the few proven tissue regenerators (Exhibit 8).

There are times when no transaction takes place between the healer and healee—both fields remain separate, with no field interaction or change in the ill one's symptoms. For some reason these fields did not resonate. If a healing transaction occurs, the healee's field changes remarkably toward a complete, strong, coherent one, often becoming identical with the healer's. The healer stops work when this occurs (Exhibit 10, Healee).

Because these laboratory findings are objective, testable happenings, the healing relationship should not be described as simply a placebo, which refers to an end result without understanding the phenomenon. Healer-healee interactions are understandable. The direct, powerful field effects are not illusory; they are to be expected.

Healers can quickly and safely remove anesthetic from patients following surgery. Anesthetic is known to be stored in tissues, taking some time to dissipate through regular circulation channels, thus slowing the healing process. Probably more accurately, the field which permeates all tissue initially holds the anesthetic. To remove it, the healer increases the field flow of energy in the viscera where circulation pools as she allures the anesthetic field to the body's surface where she literally attaches it to the field of her hand and removes it from the patient.

Beginning healers frequently experience numbness in the hands and arms. With heavy anesthetic they may experience a mild anesthesia themselves until they learn to direct the anesthetic up their arms and out the elbows. As the anesthetic is removed after 15 to 20 minutes, the patient rapidly becomes aware of his surroundings, color returns to his face, circulation improves and breathing deepens. Others in the room may smell a strong anesthetic odor.

Hands-on and healing by one's presence emphasize the transaction between two people, each with an intent—one to become well and the other to serve as a catalyst. I believe the best healer does not attempt to heal; that belongs to the healee. But rather, the healer intends to present a positive, enlightened presence to manifest a strong, radiant, complete field to nourish and encourage the ill field to change. Ideally, the transaction should reinforce the healing response with the desire to heal oneself. This means that the patient must tap into personal strengths rather than weaknesses. (Anyone who has ever spent dreary days in the ill fields of some conventional hospitals, with rushing doctors and tired nurses who punch the clock, dole out treatment schedules, and provide for bodily wants, yearns for friends, home and a healing environment.) The healer must provide a model of vibrant life. Who and what he is, is as important as his ability to "run energy," select vibrational spectrums, and direct it to the ill areas. Such is a powerful charge.

Healers are often labeled as spiritual, psychic, or energy healers, as though these were different approaches. One says he asks for divine intervention; another calls on guides and mystical powers; and the third, quite rationally, senses the ill field, notes its strengths and weaknesses, and consciously screens and sets a course of action.

A beautifully spiritual Jewish healer used meditation to cleanse herself before healing. Her frequent image of Jesus. while it seemed to hold great meaning, perturbed her because of her religious background. At first she adamantly rejected the Christ symbol. At one stage she sought professional help to understand. Finally she received the key: the Christ was a powerful symbol of love which could rule over death. With acceptance of the power of love, her capacities as a healer bloomed. At times when she entered a room, healing took place.

A psychologist, David McClelland, discovered a phenomenon now called "Mother Teresa's effect." When Harvard University students watched a British Broadcasting Corporation documentary of this remarkable nun, their immune systems produced more immunogloblin A, an antibody which fights colds. He concluded that despite some students' dislike of the film, the filth of the surroundings or Mother Teresa's techniques, the strength of her "tender, loving care" boosted their immune systems.

Actually, spiritual, mystic, and energy processes are not different. They refer to the different ways that the healer prepares himself, and to how he explains his results. In actuality, every fine healer uses all of these modes. Each expands his level of awareness into the mystical, raises his vibrations to the level where he can communicate with divine vibrations, experience lovingness and sense the healee's vibrations as he creates a vibratory field. During healing, the awareness state is not an everyday one; creating this state sometimes takes time. Therefore, it is understandable that some healers develop elaborate rituals to get themselves prepared; but probably these do not directly determine the results of the healing.

Some healers pray for divine guidance and ask that nothing from their field except the positive energy be allowed to enter the healee. These healers do not understand that nothing from their field can enter another unless the other allows it to do so—unless his field resonates with the healer's. Therefore, the healer had best concentrate on radiating the purest and the highest vibrations, rather than dwelling upon such personal rituals.

The emotionally appealing humbleness of saying that one is only a channel, a conduit, or an inert circuit is also not helpful in a healing relationship. If your presence assists healing, you are more than a mechanical circuit; you are an important link; you are divine energies manifest. While you can be humble in view of the profound changes which take place, you are dynamically a part of what happens. To acknowledge it strengthens you. To be "merely a channel" weakens you.

Many healers diagnose disease by screening the body with both their hands and their mind. This can create a problem if it locks the healer into the old disease concept approach. In most instances, except possibly injury, the problem is first a field- and secondarily a tissue-disturbance. The overall field must be changed if there is to be more than just a change in symptoms. Likewise, the field carries both general and specific information about the illness. Some trained healers feel heat or cold in the area of pain, interpreting heat to mean inflammation and cold to be stagnation or lack of circulation. Prickly feelings are interpreted as regrowth. Others see forms in the energy field—blocks, breaks, colors and shapes. Over time, healers learn to associate these with symptoms and diagnoses. These are elaborately described in Barbara Brennan's book, *Hands of Light* and Rosalyn Bruyere's book, *Wheels of Light*.

The capacity to look into the body and see with the penetration of a microscope is wondrous, but may also seduce a healer into becoming involved with the material, spatial aspect of illness. This emphasizes the disease element rather than its source or the goal, health. There are healers who lightly record all these sensory impressions, not working on any one in particular, but allowing their attention to culminate in the wisdom of knowing. This makes beginning healers insecure, but it offers the greatest security for the highly evolved.

Many healers develop techniques for treating specific illnesses that are particularly successful. When I open the mind-field of such healers, I frequently find their motivation coming from other lifehoods. A very successful nutritionist wondered why she was so compelled to work with AIDS patients and why she agonized so deeply when they took a turn for the worse. During our work she found her answer. In the early 16th century, she had been a leper in Europe, imprisoned to keep her away from people. Leprosy was the most socially stigmatized and misunderstood disease of that time. Unfortunately, AIDS is today. She escaped the prison to live as an outcast in a remote cave. At night she stole food; by day she sold it in the markets, posing veiled as an old woman. She existed for many years in the midst of people, yet totally isolated and without identity. It was the emotion of this miserably sad life without hope that was reactivated by any worsening conditions in her AIDS patients.

We have observed that many whose life's work is healing are considerably overweight and frequently in poor health. You may wonder why this occurs, and why they do not heal themselves. There is a common belief that in healing one gives of one's own energy, which creates systemic problems in the lymphatic and circulatory systems. To remain in altered states for long periods of time without grounding oneself in the lower Earth vibrations does create real field problems, and disturbances in the alkaline-acid balance in the blood.

But I believe these are not the only sources of poor health among healers. The cause lies deeper. Perhaps the motivation to help others comes from a genetic weakness that led to a long history of illnesses. Possibly, many healers are not emotionally secure. Like many of us, they have not conquered their soul's problems. But unlike average people, their poor health stands out to be criticized. The profoundly satisfying experience which comes to the healer when assisting another does give superficial comfort, peace, and belief in oneself which should ideally facilitate one's evolution. But these experiences can be used to delay the search for one's own deep unfinished business. These healers do have a disturbed physiology and they also heal, two factors which coexist but are not related in a cause and effect manner. I find that when satisfaction from healing relationships becomes a defense to block the deeper emotional needs of feeling worthy, the systemic problems are inevitable. We may praise healers who are compelled to heal. On the other hand, compulsion may come from personal insecurity rather than from heightened social awareness. The most effective healing occurs when one is so full and rich with divine energy that it will manifest wherever one is; it is not so much healing as it is sharing the abundance.

There are as many effective healing techniques as there are practitioners. Some heal remotely by thought. Our inability to understand distant healers makes us think that they are even more remarkable than contact healers. But remember, one's energy can be controlled by thought. If one successfully projects energy via a thought-field, one can transmit energy over great distances with specific intent. First, the healer must believe that he has the power to do so. For the healing transaction, the healer with a strong field, focused through intent, will provide a coherent, powerful energy-field. If there is a healee with a different, hyperactive or deficient, anti-coherent or diseased field, who at some level wishes assistance, there can be a positive connection. Without a positive field transaction, the healing response does not occur. There must also be sufficient transaction time for the healee's field to change. Likewise, there is a termination time when the two fields have become unified, when no more interaction can take place. At this point, the two fields move apart. For the healer, this is a time of lowering the field pressure and leaving the healee's field to process its energy without help.

Lastly, the healer should assist the healee to consciously recognize a feeling state, and to return to that euphoric sensation that all is well and that the body is healing. With quite ill people, I encourage them to revisualize the healer-healee experience and feel the fresh energy pouring into them. Here, they learn to process the environmental electromagnetism. And finally, each healer should as soon as possible teach the person to move energy into his own field. (See *Mind Mastery Meditations*.)

I have not discussed the new energy field computer diagnostic equipment and generators, the Oriental medicine field diagnostic techniques, Chi Gong or Yoga which may demonstrate effectiveness in healing. Before I commend them, I await electromagnetic testing to discover what about the field provides keys to disease which are purportedly sampled or cured by these instruments and techniques.

For 30 years I have sought a chemical-field model of health that reached to the cellular source of disease, one that would provide the missing link to the mind-field model to complete a holistic electromagnetic-chemical picture of health. People repeatedly asked me how changes in the mind-field affect specific diseases, or more definitively, how energy fields directly alter enzymes, free radicals, T-cells, or body proteins—all somehow connected with diseases. While these substances are known to have electrical charges through their atoms, a neat global connection eluded us. I thought it was faulty logic to seek correlation between things that didn't belong together, like field patterns and specific chemicals. If cause and effect existed, these would emerge through some complex chemical patterning. But none existed.

Homeopathic research has shown that chemical fields are more potent than the dissolved chemicals. But homeopathy, although based on a field concept, was still allied to the old medical model of disease in that a homeopathic remedy was merely substituted for a chemical drug to cure a specific malfunction. Also, electrically charged particles are at the core of blood chemistry, but again blood substances were always measured as deviations from a mean, as though each item had its unique imprint on disease.

So, with excitement I discovered the Life Balances Health Program developed by John Kitkoski, a genius biochemist. For 25 years he has researched the patterns of minerals, vitamins and blood proteins in a new way (Smith). Kitkoski researched and cured animal disease by balancing blood chemistry before he successfully applied his methods to humans. His organization, Life Balances in Spokane, Washington, has prepared physicians' manuals and training sessions to carry out their stunning procedures.

Both Kitkoski's models and mine exist to improve the body's ability to adapt—health—and to cure disease over time by removing the cause. This program is not fast, but it is sure. Both involve people in their treatment so that they become accountable for their own health. By working with these treatments simultaneously, one can incorporate the conditions of a more stable and dense cellular electrical field with the non-material, rapidly changing electromagnetic field.

Kitkoski uses a simple framework of the acid-alkaline balance in the blood, along with the deeper, intricate patterns and proportions of blood substances which enable cells to function properly. He reminds us that the life and health of all cells result from an interaction with the fluid systems (particularly the blood) which carry the nutrients and facilitating substances to the cell membranes. Here, the conditions of blood, the cell membrane, and molecules allow for osmotic interchange of inner and outer cell substances. Metabolic chemicals are forced out of the cells while fresh supplies enter. Remember, the cell membrane of connective tissue with its piezoelectric capacity has the capacity to carry electrical charges.

The emphasis on acid-alkaline blood balance came from Kitkoski's discovery that when the balance was disturbed, the blood could not absorb minerals and vitamins, regardless of the food or supplements ingested. The balance was upset by eating habits; toxic contaminants in air, food and water; and chemicals from drugs—tobacco as well as consciousness-altering substances. These enter the blood stream and become lodged in the cells, disturbing cell function.

The common belief among body workers that tissue remembers is confirmed by the fact that the mind-field flows throughout the body and toxic poisons are harbored in the more dense form of the cells. If either field condition is less than optimum, the cellular effectiveness breaks down and disease and malfunction occur.

The form of disease or malfunction is directly related to the areas weakened by disuse and injury and to the genetic susceptibility of each person. "Any symptom can be traced back to some tilt in the blood." (Smith). Kitkoski believes that illness is not due to simple mineral or vitamin deficiencies, but to the complex ratio that enables metabolic processes to work.

The treatment for reestablishing the acid-alkaline balance is electrically synergizing of acid substances with their positive charges and alkaline ones with their negative charges. Inside each cell these positive and negative charges create a small battery providing the energy for cellular life. The specific Life Balancing procedures are as exquisite as the model. In water or milk, one takes special electrolytes with balanced positive and negative ions of the same dilution as the blood. Based upon a blood test, one drinks ionized mineral drops in acid fruit juices. Other mineral substances might be recommended, based upon a computerized analysis of changes in blood chemistry.

Acidity is required for blood mineral absorption. Kitkoski found that drinking fluid containing all the necessary electrolytes is the best way to maintain the fluid electrical balance so that the cellular exchange improves and starts to heal itself by dumping toxic substances which have lodged in the cell. In turn, cells generally and completely detoxify themselves. This is quite different from detoxification using a homeopathic substance for each specific chemical, mold, fungus or gas. During treatment, symptoms may be exaggerated temporarily as is generally the case with any detox program. The level of discomfort is determined by the relative extent of the imbalance, the cellular condition, and the individual response.

I have been asked how acid-alkaline detox differs from diets, colonics or chelation. First, these are geared to minimizing symptoms or temporarily clearing out some of the gastrointestinal or blood toxicities. These are not based upon altering the cellular function so that it detoxes itself. Therefore, these treatments take less time but give only temporary results. They do not eliminate the cause. Colonics may offer some relief from congestion, but there is no evidence that major toxic substances remain in the intestinal wall. Neither does improved diet insure acid-alkaline balance and better cell function. Nor does blood chelation or filtering create a balanced blood picture—at best, it only temporarily removes some blood contaminants.

I am particularly enthusiastic about Kitkoski's program because it works. I know as a participant and from the progress I have observed in others.

Today, most people living in North America have an alkaline blood condition. The earth, water, snow, air, plants and even lower forms of animal life are more alkaline than they were before. Vegetables grown in this environment have less balanced electrical systems. Amphibians, fish, alligators, salamanders, and even birds have been found to have reproductive problems from the estrogenizing chemicals in the environment, all of which are alkalinizing.

We in consciousness research have found that as persons' electromagnetic frequencies go up, as they evolve, many become ungrounded. This means that their field loses its lower frequencies or the acid-reacting positive ions, which are replaced with more alkaline negative ions. Furthermore, these people gravitate to lighter vegetarian foods with higher mineral content, some of which are more alkaline. Women particularly seem to fall into this vicious cycle; they have higher electromagnetic frequencies; they are often ungrounded; they eat fruit and vegetable diets with less acid-producing substances; and they have lower hemoglobin, less energy and weaker immune systems. Kitkoski and his associates are particularly sensitive to these destructive biochemical conditions in women.

Although Life Balances does not focus on specific diseases,

the improved cellular condition cures them. Additionally, less significant but annoying conditions such as rough dry skin, minor rashes, chronic candida, nail fungus, recurring muscular aches and complaints, chronic sinusitis, throat irritations, gastrointestinal disturbances and hypersensitivity miraculously lessen or disappear. The problem was a general cellular electromagnetic imbalance caused by a stressed chemistry and consciousness.

We have known that cells throughout life regularly replace themselves—some take months, others longer. However, we have not understood why new cells don't operate perfectly but tend to inherit the problems of the old ones. Old injured back cells seem to perpetuate new injured back cells. I believe the template for this maladaptability or cell chaos existed in the imbalanced electromagnetic and biochemical blood fields of old cells. Therefore, new cells adapted and succumbed in the same sick way. These new models show that this doesn't have to continue.

Both systems have built-in techniques for health maintenance—ones that remove the guesswork. Emphasis is upon enlightened, ongoing choices. Consciousness workshops, meditation, and new information are ineffectual without changing deep belief systems—the causes. One cannot plan an adequate diet without considering the needs of his unique biochemical system. And there are no standard daily required supplements for all individuals.

I believe that my electromagnetic mind-field model and Kitkoski's chemical-field model should steer the future direction of nutrition, treatment of diseases, and health practices. The reorganizing of the emotional aspects of the mind-field and the reordering of the biochemical field of the blood, combined with improved life practices and the cleansing of the environment are the only truly holistic approaches that can insure health. By raising the body's healing response, all diseases and problems associated with aging are directly attacked. Both Life Balancing and electromagnetic field evolution work could be used in conjunction with homeopathic or allopathic treatments until these are no longer necessary. And as both encourage the mind and the cellular tissue to learn to heal itself, the healing response is conditioned to help withstand social and chemical contaminants in an improved way.

I encourage you not to separate your illness from your body. Do not think that emotions have nothing to do with it, or that your spiritual development is an isolated aspect of your life. During illness, these components are somehow out of balance; but in health, there is a perfect blend, a oneness you feel and live. Electrodynamic field interaction is the premier holistic view of life.

Yes, the body has an etheric double. It extends beyond its boundaries into the universe as a field. If that etheric double is closed, so are our experiences. We just replay the same old tape. If it is in turmoil, the tissue will suffer, down to its atoms and cells. The body will revolt. Illness is that insurgence.

Healing celebrates the miracle of life rather than the avoidance of death. Illness can teach us about life, that health is not an end; it is a means that enables us to serve our divine life purpose. I honor the healing powers of self and others, as I hope you will yours. My own abilities were first apparent, even if unexplained, when as a young physical therapist, my "permanently" paralyzed patients recovered. My first information about unorthodox healing came from the healers who worked in my laboratory, who taught me, and who healed me of a potentially "terminal" illness. Until I found the phenomena that started to explain these healings, I, too, called them miracles. And then I learned from using my own loving, healing energies that the miracle lay within.

My one prevailing message in this book comes from a demonstrable model, a view of humans in a new and oh, so glorious light. We are beings with divine power which at its crowning best is the giver and maintainer of life.

CHAPTER XI

SPIRITUAL ENLIGHTENMENT: The Evolutionary Goal

By profession I am a scientist, a physiological researcher of human energy fields—trained as a rational thinker to doubt all that cannot be scientifically proven. You may wonder, with this background, why I undertake a treatise on spiritual enlightenment when I am neither an orthodox religious leader nor a philosopher in the academic sense. For me, this is the better way, for my thoughts have been limited by neither religious dogma nor philosophical constructs.

Today, many eminent scientists are expressing strong spiritual insights with the surety of conviction that comes only from deep personal experiences. Some have redirected their lives. Others have come to spirituality from their knowledge of the infinite grandeur of nature and the cosmos. Robert Jastrow, Director of the Goddard Institute for Space Studies, said that, "For the scientist who has lived by his faith in the power of reason, the story ends like a bad dream. He has scaled the mountains of ignorance and he is about to conquer the highest peak. As he pulls himself over the final rock, he is greeted by a band of theologians

276

who have been sitting there for centuries." Religion had traditionally maintained a stance divorcing reason from faith; science separated emotion from reason; and herein lies both errors. The scientist repressed his emotions, the priest his reason, and both their mystical natures.

It is true that these two ways of pursuing knowledge about the world had staked off separate domains in the past. But now it is time for a dialogue between scientists and theologians because we know that objective reality does not exclude the transcendent reality of spiritual experiences. Current research on the laws of nature, from the microscopic physical phenomena—quantum physics, to the macroscopic order of the material universe—cosmology, implies an abstract interpretation of creation rather than a material one.

Even the previous inability of science to explain the miracles in the Bible is now dwindling in importance. The stand-off lessened as we began to recognize that the true criterion of spirituality cannot be found in the physical nature of the universe, but rather in the essence of the spiritual, mystical experience of humans. What a glorious time, now that scientific thinking and divine awareness can hold hands again as partners.

My route to spiritual understanding came not from religious education nor from scientific deduction, but from my own experience of carefully observing my own evolutionary quest over many years. I also learned from my work as a spiritual therapist with many hundreds of people already advanced in their process who entrusted me to assist them in discovering their soul's unfinished business.

As I discussed in the last chapter, I did not use past-life regression nor did I subscribe to popular cause-and-effect karma thinking. Instead, I used meditation and imagery to make coherent the person's energy field and to open the mind-field. In other chapters I have established the scientific basis for my concept of the mind-field. We uncovered other lives, but our goal was not to fathom the ego or the physical problems of the current lifetime. Rather, we were after the patterns of behavior and problems that resulted from deep spiritual experiences. These patterns are the sole causes of continuing personality problems in the current life. My goal is to empower each person to reach his ultimately attainable level. This is spiritual empowerment.

As a university professor, I focused on intellectual empowerment, helping students to learn facts and to think. As a physical therapist, I assisted patients to redevelop lost capacities and gain new skills. Now, I help people to claim their own spiritual power.

When I work with individuals or conduct workshops, I ask the following questions:

1. Do you have intellectual power? Are you intellectually developed? Can you think deeply and coherently on many subjects?

2. Are you physically vital, robust, and powerful for your age and sex? Are you secure in your ability to do ordinary work and to respond to emergencies?

3. Are you emotionally spontaneous, dynamic, and sure? Do you express this in your life?

4. Lastly, are you spiritually developed and sustained? (Not, what do you believe, but do you live and manifest spirituality throughout your life?)

I believe the answer to the last question is particularly important; it provides the context for all the other answers. The answer I receive most often from my clients is, "I don't really know." Others answer by describing spiritual beliefs learned from mainstream religious systems. Some, who have no religious affiliation, describe spiritual experiences derived from nature, such as sunsets, a particular tree, the ocean, or from classical music. Very, very few, however, ever relate a profound personal experience with a divine figure or God. This is understandable, because in our culture if we talk to God we are called religious, while if God talks to us or if we see God, we are considered insane. Yet I know the longing for spiritual experience exists in all humans, for without it there is an unconscious sense that knowledge of the physical self and the material world is simply unsatisfying and insufficient. I accept the truism: When one represses emotion, one's body hurts; when one represses consciousness, one's mind aches; when one represses spirituality, one's soul suffers.

There are worldwide signs of spiritual awakening perhaps stimulated from the horror of religious wars, famine, and catastrophic climate changes. Contemplative people, dissatisfied with life and work despite economic plenty, have turned to religion, frequently without surcease. Even yuppies who became professionally successful and accumulated an abundance of material possessions, are disillusioned about their futures. More and more, people turn to meditation.

For a while, higher states of consciousness seemed like a sufficient reward—now, they are not. For as people reached these states, they realized that they were not spiritually free. Many of the early psychedelic drug-users who were seeking enlightenment have recognized that, despite the euphoria of their experiences, their lives remained unchanged.

Mainline churches report decreased attendance and diminishing financial support, both at a time when more and more people are on spiritual quests. Apparently the church does not adequately serve parishioners' needs. Charismatic radio and television Christian ministries seem to grow. Even a recent Gallup Poll found that 33% of the population studied admitted to a personal spiritual experience. Actually, I believe that that number is much higher because few of us are comfortable acknowledging deep personal experiences.

As the atmosphere becomes contaminated by both extremely low and high frequency signals, all physical phenomena seem to be accelerated. As electromagnetic field vibrations rise, there are concomitant biological changes. New medical syndromes with metaphysical-sounding names are being reported. Several physicians state that their practice has changed from psychosomatic medicine to spiritual medicine.

Even the cosmic vibrations seem to be quickening as the Earth evolves. Some believe that the universal mind, or the morphogenic field, has risen a notch. Nothing works correctly anymore, one's life, politics, the weather, money, and institutions, all reflect the breakdown in the old scheme of things.

Human unrest is reflected in the field of psychology as it attempts to cope with human complaints. The steadily growing humanistic psychology movement with its emphasis on human growth and self-actualization, admits that its methods are still too limited. The new approach, transpersonal psychology, acknowledges that spiritual and transcendent needs are intrinsic to human nature and that satisfying these needs is the right of every individual. Consciousness was on the cutting edge of psychotherapy in the 60s and 70s. Today it is spirituality.

To summarize our discussion thus far, it seems that humankind is now experiencing a rebirth—the goal is to live a more peaceful, happy and fulfilled life in harmony with the vibrations of the divine. This requires a readiness to understand our own deep spiritual nature. The problem is that the models we have held about the mind-body and the spirit are weak, impotent intellectual constructs that underestimate the human potential. They are not spiritually anchored; and they are inadequate for the future.

The most enduring and widely read book, the Bible, is man's eternal dialogue with God. It relates the history of man's experiences with one, supreme God. Primary among the many reasons for reading the Bible is to discover ways in which God imparts truth, laws, signs, and wisdom to humans—how God communicates with collective humanity. The Bible relates the collective history of humanity; past life information carries the history of each soul's experience with God.

Many times during lifehood recall, themes emerged that

mirrored Biblical stories about the individual's relationship to God. At first I surmised that the similarity existed because these people knew the Bible stories. But strangely, many were not Bible readers and had not been active in religion. The surprising detail of their recall, however, led me to realize the universal nature of human spiritual experiences. It is at this level that humans can experience their uniqueness <u>and</u> their ability to participate with the cosmosphere and ionosphere. This is not rational in the ordinary sense; it is mystical.

Let me review for you the different relationships between man and God as described in the Bible. The first record of "bonding" between a supreme God and a human occurred with Abraham. Remember, Abraham was a simple shepherd in Mesopotamia. He lived at the base of the Euphrates River and traded with the caravans. As a Hebrew, he believed in the one God, while other groups around him embraced many gods. According to the Bible, God communicated directly with Abraham, giving him specific orders to leave his native land with a band of Hebrews to found a new nation in the land God had chosen, Canaan. He promised to guide and shield Abraham from harm during his epic journey. This was the first biblical record of the classic human experience of forging the most important of all bonds: that between a human and the divine.

It is written that to Abraham, God became a fearful and loyal friend. He was a personal, living God. Abraham made a covenant with God. When He spoke to him, Abraham obeyed his commands. The story of God dropping in for a fine meal which Sarah, Abraham's wife, was preparing, to give her the news that she, an old, wizened woman, would conceive and bear a son, emphasizes the relationship between these early Hebrews and their God, a rapport which allowed God to materialize for dinner with a skeptical old lady who laughed at Him.

The Biblical story of Jacob expressed how in his communication with God, he argued and fought God. To Jacob, God was frequently his adversary until, in later years, he accepted

God's teachings and became "The Lion of God."

Remember Joseph, Jacob's son, who was sold into bondage by his brothers? He saw angels on the stairway to heaven and heard God promise, "I will protect you wherever you go." Later, as a man in Egypt, Joseph's relationship with God took on a mystical nature in which God told him about things to come and how he could survive and prosper during famines and pestilence. Although Joseph carried out God's commands, the bonding seemed to be more co-creative than that of his ancestors.

Biblical records indicate that God gave Moses a divine mission: "Lead forth my people out of Egypt." This was not a unified nation but a rabble of a group, fearful of the future but glad to be free. Moses is said to have had personal misgivings about his journey because he thought that his followers would not believe he had received his instruction directly from God. It seems that he needed divine assurance, which the Bible says he received in the form of miracles. These reports depict God as a great protector when people followed his dictates, but as a wrathful God who judged and punished them for their transgressions. He was depicted as a powerful judge, the source of the law, the Ten Commandments, and a judge who could hand out sentences of punishment.

The rabbi Jesus, called the Christ or the Son of God, brought a still different idea about God; a loving and protecting father who cherished equally all humans as his children regardless of their beliefs and practices. Jesus' relationship with God was as a devout son who carried out His teachings directly by manifesting God's power in miracles. Jesus was said to radiate a divine light.

Certain great events in history, the parting of the Red Sea, the ark of the covenant, and the flood, are said to be God's way of revealing Himself to humans. Similar is the concept that God makes His will known through the inspired insights of great men whom we call prophets.

The value of these stories is limited in terms of effecting deep life changes. Perhaps a more valuable belief is that God is revealed everywhere and at all times to those equipped to discover Him. Perception of the spiritual world is relative to the light the person sheds on it. If the person has no light, then he cannot perceive the spiritual. The prophets have this light which gives them the clarity to interpret messages from God. Cataclysmic events on earth often reveal God because they so greatly shock even those vibrating at the lowest levels.

As humans develop in their awareness and expand their vibratory complexity, they will no longer need the ordeals of cataclysms nor the wisdom of the prophets; they will become the prophets. As humans grow in their capacity to be God-like, they will experience divine energies not only in themselves, but everywhere.

Today, many are still attached to concepts of God based on religious teachings and personal needs. Whereas the Biblical leaders derived their ideas of God from direct personal experience, our beliefs about God today are more remote.

A recent American poll indicated that 95% of those surveyed "believed in God." Yet when asked to define what they meant by "God," many spoke vaguely about heaven that they could not define. It is always "out there" somewhere in the atmosphere. Yet people reach out and pray to this being, entity, or vibration that is located out there somewhere. It is rare that an individual perceives that God is in himself. Our beliefs are basically intellectual and serve to satisfy our emotional needs. However, belief in God is one thing; knowing God is another.

I recall the story of Carl Jung, the eminent psychiatrist, who was interviewed in his later years by a young cub reporter. He asked Jung if he had believed in God when he was a young man. Jung said that yes, he had believed. But, queried the reporter, now that you're an old man, do you still believe in God? Jung responded slowly, "No, I do not believe; I know, for I have experienced God."

Reading Biblical stories about humankind's struggle to discover the divine may assist us on our path as we await signs that we have contacted God; but for a deep emotional understanding, we must experience God directly. These direct, personal experiences are mystical in nature. Remember, descriptions in the New Testament indicated that Jesus taught mystically, by parables. Ezekiel, the prophet, as he moved toward his direct knowledge of God, described visions of animals, which were emotional symbols. Soon, his animals took on wheels, moving the emotion into human feelings. Later, he heard sounds. As his vibrations and emotions grew, he struggled until he reached that stage where he had direct contact with God. When he recognized that he was receiving God's messages, his profound shock and humility caused him to fall to the ground.

Theologians who continually debate whether some Biblical happenings were miracles and therefore God-ordained do so to question religious beliefs. But I do believe that they miss the essence of spirituality—man's profound personal experience of knowing. Those who criticize miracles as illusory fail to realize that the matter and meaning created by the mind are all illusionary. Illusion is a function of the mind and is as real as any "facts." So spiritually, the mind's highest experience is also an illusion, but so profound that its effect in the lives of humans is inestimable.

The great sages have said, "Every human being is nothing but God." Likewise, the popular concept of "I Am" has been accepted by many religious leaders. Actually, I have found almost no one who is considered sane who experiences the great "I Am". Rather, most people respond that they are much too limited and unworthy. They hold these limitations deeply in their minds.

When people ask me if it's all right to think of God as a material being like man, my answer is yes, that is the way we understand many of the Judeo-Christian ideas. I believe that we can imagine the entity of God in human form. As the Bible states, we are made in God's image, but we do not imagine God as a blood, bone, and tissue being, but as a metaphysical being, or an energy, a vibration or a light.

Most of us believe that God reveals Himself in certain great acts in history. Some, such as the rending of the heavens at Christ's crucifixion with the splitting of the rock, have been attributed to divine energies. The inspired insights of the prophets have been interpreted as God's revelations. Whether these actually are methods God uses to reveal Himself, they are undeniably how we understand God's revelations.

Similarly, many people experience God in nature because they believe that God created and controls it. Remember, it is <u>we</u> who see God in nature because of the emotional charge our senses receive. In these instances, we have projected our experiences outward into the beauty of the world, but not inward to ourselves. Our experience of God is then stimulated by the harmony, beauty and grandeur of nature. Unfortunately, what we experience we project back out there, thinking that God and nature are the same thing. However, a profound mystical experience with God in an instant shatters the illusion that our subjective and our objective wills are the only reality. In this mystical state, a new awakening dominates the entire scene, including our own life.

I read and hear that God is everywhere. Some ask me when science will prove it. Wisely, science has not tried to prove God's existence as an entity or vibration. Probably the closest we will ever come to understanding God made manifest will be by knowing more about man himself. In my laboratory, we found that when a person's energy field reached the highest, most complex vibrations, from imaging or meditation, that person had spiritual experiences, regardless of their beliefs. Even though the imagery was culturally-linked, each person identified his experience with a divine essence that was beyond any specific religious belief system.

From my experience, I believe that all children know about God. Birth and early childhood experiences and illnesses, when relived, contain deep spiritual feelings. Children also sense the spiritual attainment of adults.

This reminds me of a story my father told about me when I was a six-year-old. My family had just moved from Indiana to

Florida because I had a thyroid problem and needed the iodine of the ocean. Apparently, I had great spiritual urges and asked to go to church. The closest was a fundamentalist church where I attended Sunday School. I wanted to be baptized after my parents told me that I had not been as an infant. When the day for children's baptism came, we girls were all dressed up in our white, lacy dresses and, with our parents, sat in the front pew. In the middle of the sermon preceding the immersion, I got up and stomped angrily down the aisle and out of the church, announcing loudly, "If you think that ugly man is going to baptize me, you are wrong." Yes, I was paddled, but I knew that that preacher and I did not have the same feeling about God.

The Bible stories depict God working through real, fallible humans like ourselves, in a co-creative process. Yet the old concept of spiritual leaders was that people must realize that the hope of man was not in himself, but in God. This implied that God is outside man, a concept that is happily being refuted because it is hazardous to our evolution. Human behavior does not change when we experience the power of God separate from ourselves. With this kind of experience, we do God's work in its profound sense.

Quite new in Western thought is the grandest of all thoughts—I am God manifest, I have become God-like. And yet it has existed in the minds of men, Ken Wilber found, since the time of the early Upanishads—that the personal equals the omnipresent, or the eternal self. Mystics of all centuries have recognized this truth. The *Bhagavad Gita*, the ancient Hindu scripture, says that if you understand your own mind completely, you are not just a human being, you yourself are God. The old sages likewise viewed humans as God made manifest. So the current "new" philosophical concept that "I am God manifest" is not really new; what is new is the understanding that I am neither competing with nor separated from God. With this understanding, abject humility cannot exist.

I concur with the statement of contemporary theologians,

"God is indeed within man." But I do not believe that man can perceive his "God-like" qualities until his field reaches higher vibrations and attains a greater degree of coherency. No matter how hard we try to receive spiritual guidance, we cannot until our fields are attuned to that vibrational system. Does this mean that God is a vibration? No, God is man's experience and the structure he gives to his experience. Obviously, this is not the same for all people because their fields differ, colored by their cultural beliefs.

I believe that at my deepest level, I carry divine images which, when brought to the level of experience, manifest God's energy. My acts are no longer totally willful, and it is impossible for me to behave destructively. I have already chosen to move to the vibrational level of the soul, which is divine. This refutes the common belief that, in the sight of God, man is humble and basically bad because of his humanness, and therefore unable to manifest Godliness.

Writings on Egyptian papyri offer similar wisdom. "... and the kingdom of heaven is within you, and whosoever knoweth himself shall find it, and having found it ye shall know yourself that you are sons and heirs of the Father, the Almighty, and shall know yourself that ye are in God and God is in you."

Transpersonal psychology acknowledges the reality of experience; and it seeks to explore the unfinished business of spiritual experiences, that is, personal experiences of divine feelings. Like consciousness, spiritual experiences vary in intensity, running the entire spectrum from strong to dilute. They are accompanied by a wide range of sensory phenomena. Primary among these is a blinding, brilliant white light, more intense than anything the eye has ever seen. To some, this is an experience of total radiance; to others, it is like a light at the end of a tunnel preceding death. Some see it as a star or sun. Occasionally, the light appears as an aura around a God-like figure from the Bible. Light is the oldest and most pervasive metaphor in spiritual experience. In the New Testament when Jesus took Peter, John, and James into the mountains, it was recorded that "his face did shine as the sun, his raiments as white as light."

Recently, the Polish physicist Slawinski recorded the flash of light that occurs at death. Apparently, death is a transition from one vibrational state to a higher one. He describes the "death flash" as 10 to 1,000 times stronger than the light radiation emanating from the body when it is alive. The rapidity of physiological death apparently determines the rate of dissemination of the light. There is less radiance at death following a slow, lingering illness than after a sudden, traumatic, or instant death. I believe the day is near when we will understand death as a profound change in vibration which releases this "flash of life."

Recently, I saw two flashes of light accompanying a traumatic death of a woman and her unborn child. I had seen a violent head-on auto collision during broad daylight on a sunny day, where one car had catapulted into the air after hitting a center divider, then collided with an oncoming truck at the cab level. I hastened to bring spiritual energy to a badly mutilated young woman who was partly through the windshield, while others administered acupressure to stimulate her heart and save her life. In my higher state of consciousness, I saw a flash of light so bright that it looked like a camera flashbulb nearby. I thought she had died, but the accupressurists said no. Some minutes later, a second flash occurred, even brighter than the first. This happened simultaneously with the cessation of breathing and heartbeat. We discovered later that she was eight months pregnant. The first flash probably was that of her unborn child, and the second her own. The suddenness of each of these deaths must have created the intense flash of light.

I have learned by observing deaths in other lifehoods that, at the onset of non-traumatic death, the experience into transitional consciousness is beautiful beyond description. Death itself is peaceful, idyllic, and evolutionary. It is only during pre-death or near-death experiences that images of tunnels with lights at the end, and beckoning relatives who had crossed over appear. This is also the time when there is either peace or a tragic struggle. I have found that those who are extremely fearful of death receive traumatic pre-death experiences from other lifehoods when they experience near-death episodes in this life.

Near-death experiences occur independently of religiosity or religious affiliations. Yet after recovering from such experiences, people report increased spiritual awareness that remains throughout their lives. The change is sometimes so great that they become healers or religious leaders, leaving behind the personal life they knew.

Increased physical energy is a universal characteristic of divine experiences. Waves of energy create body jerks, shakes, and undulations as a flood of sensation seems to carry the person upward into an altered state. Intense heat is common and sometimes frightening. When a person deeply and quietly prays, his field often reaches its highest living vibration and becomes more coherent with all energy focused in the same direction, and in sync. This is a state of immense power.

Verbal information is also reported during divine states. The person perceives messages of wisdom coming from God. This is generally a "charge" such as those received by Abraham, Moses and Joseph—a destiny. This information is never concerned with the material world or everyday problems. There are instructions "to trust in one's own divine guidance" and to accept the divine power.

In the most profound spiritual experiences, the person moves to a state of oneness with divine vibrations, where the identity experiences no separation between the human and divine fields. The two fields function as one, where "all is all" and everything is perfect. From that moment on, the person is changed and can never again deny his spiritual nature. As a result, conscious knowing and wisdom have broader, more profound dimensions that are not anchored in the reality of things, ideas, and physical existence; instead they are anchored in the spiritual.

If we have never had such direct spiritual yearnings or these profound experiences, what stimulates our spiritual quests?

Ultimately, all thinking people eventually ask: who am I and why am I here? Intuitively, we know that the personality we have developed, the selves we identify with, the jobs we hold, are only superficially "me." The deep part of ourselves we don't even know. If we do happen to get a glimpse, we quickly cover it with culturally encouraged denial. Most of us have relegated these questions to old age when there is time for life's evaluation.

But something has changed. People in their twenties and thirties, even those with strong work ethics and materialistic goals are beginning to ask these questions. More people are discovering that the major job in life is attending to their own evolution. In every aspect, this is deeply spiritual. We have made strides in the physical, intellectual, and emotional improvement of our lot, but we have done precious little to manifest divine energy in our own lives, our institutions, and our relationships.

Surely by now we comprehend that relieving human suffering and pain provides comfort, but not deep happiness. I believe that peace and joy come only when we are about our evolutionary work; the insights we gain from this work change us so that we behave differently. More and more we begin to accept the spiritual aspect of our nature. This is not a simple nor an easy change; it is a profound transition which alters our concepts of ourselves as humans, and our beliefs about our potentials and the relationship of the soul to our daily existence. Our mission on Earth, then, is to grow spiritually so that we manifest the divine, not just personally, but in a way that influences other people, nature and institutions.

These ideas are generally believable and are not new to most readers. Why then, if we accept these, are we not deeply spiritual? And why, as we reach for enlightenment, do we become more afraid, conjuring up all manner of reasons to forget the struggle and give up spiritual searching? Why do so many get "stuck"? The problem is always fear of the intense emotions that occur at the mystical level. We do not want to go through physical, vibrational shocks in order to perceive the light which brings with it experiences so real and profound that we cannot easily comprehend or accept them. And most of all, we don't really want the great power of divine vibrations to be at our command.

Another way of describing our blocks is to say that we don't want to change our priorities, nor our beliefs about ourselves and God. Although they may be underdeveloped, our ideas are familiar and comfortable, and make no demands upon our behavior. In short, we don't know how to be divine and human simultaneously. With spiritual maturity, life's primary directives come from the soul level, not from the material or intellectual level. In general, the course is uncharted; we have existed for so long emphasizing the human body-personality that we have little soul-self knowledge of our needs and weaknesses. I grow increasingly intolerant of the trite supposedly transcendent concept: "We are perfect; we don't need to change." We all know that we neither feel nor manifest perfection in either our own or others' eyes. Such a "pie in the sky," uninspired statement may please the ungrounded dreamers, but not the masses of humanity.

What are the specific reasons that we are spiritually stuck? During my many years as a metaphysical counselor, I have concluded that each emotional block is connected with an overwhelming experience that the soul had with God and divine vibrations. These were all in some way traumatic—sometimes causing physical suffering, and always emotionally foreign, challenging our accepted notions about what it is to be human.

I have found five different spiritual experiences that commonly are not integrated. Sometimes we choose to misuse our capabilities, but more often we deny and turn away from them. Or we may choose to dilute our spiritual power with a bland "goodness." Denying spiritual power is a primary defense. Cultural dictates sometimes encourage denial; at other times they only serve to complicate the trauma.

One of the five commonly unintegrated experiences is experiencing a God-like energy. The exact image that appears is not as important as the emotional nature of the experience, which seems to be universal. Often great religious leaders appear: Jesus,

Mohammed, or Mother Mary. In these cases the imagery seems to be related to cultural patterns that have been associated with spirituality. If these images are vivid and emotional, they tend to be viewed as unreal and imagined, a fine way to deny the profound image. These experiences are often referred to as illusions. But again, many great thinkers remind us that most mental actions are illusionary, even if they stem from supposedly "real stimuli."

Frequently, people react to the experiences by saying, "I'm losing my mind," or asking if they are sane. I always answer, if you can co-experience mystical reality and material reality—if you know the difference, yet can integrate and use the force of this awareness—then you are not merely sane, you are super-sane. I don't really think that there is a soul that exists in the world today that does not know at its deepest level about divine things. These feelings seem to be "built into" humans. When you touch such knowing, it is as emotional as going home to a place that has always been yours, a place that you know fully but only glimpse occasionally. But if the mystical and material realities are not connected, the memory wanes rapidly and doubt follows.

The second usually non-integrated experience is one in which the person recalls a past lifehood as a mystic possessing simultaneous comprehension of the past, present and future. Often they have access to knowing all manner of things beyond the capacity of their five senses. These people are generally singled out for either punishment or honor. Physical torture, even to the point of death, is frequently their fate if they dare to be spiritually different.

The third type of unintegrated scenario involves a person who has been a spiritual healer with the psychic power to perform miracle healing and to alter material substances. Sometimes as they relive these vibrations, they recover these capacities. These come quickly and are disconcerting. If the past healings have the qualities of miracles, the person's deep emotional beliefs about himself are shaken. With this emotional release, he recognizes divine power, but often very slowly. Even if the thought is intellectually comfortable, emotionally, it usually isn't. It rocks one's personality and identity. Being, manifesting and knowing that he possesses divine power no longer allows a person to pass off such miracles with comments such as "I am only a channel of God." You are, in a sense, God's vibrations made manifest, if you own them.

The fourth unintegrated experience can occur in any of these lifehood situations. If the person has been leading a good life and serving a divine purpose, and then finds himself in deep emotional and physical troubles as a result of natural catastrophes, wars, punishment, or starvation—things that threaten his life—he calls upon God's help. If he feels that he has exhausted his resources, then in a weak, dependent state he pleads with the "father" as the last resort. Frequently, he does not receive help on the level of his request, and he dies depressed and angry at God for forsaking him—just as Jesus called out from the cross, "Oh, Father, why hast thou forsaken me?" When it comes to this lifehood, most people are not willing to acknowledge their rage at God's abandonment of them. Certainly, our religious teachings don't encourage us to do this. But if in that life or in the present one, we express our anger at God, we can receive guidance. Only then can we recognize how our miscast anger at God has denied us access to our divine power, and then without guilt we can see how our humanness has played such a devastating trick on us. We not only comprehend God's message, but our emotional power comes storming back, sufficient to handle any physical problem. Even more significantly, this regained spiritual power eliminates human torture because our light causes attackers to fall back.

The last non-integrated experience is spiritual in origin, but generally occurs without spiritual awareness. If the person taps into the full spiritual vibrations which he has experienced in the past, his body heats up to such a degree that it causes intense physical discomfort. Kundalini power may then rise up the spine, blasting him into an altered state. If the Kundalini starts to rise but is thwarted by emotional blocks, acute pain can result. The

Kundalini shock to the nervous system is well-known in meditation circles by those who have practiced kundalini yoga without supervision and for the wrong purpose. So much sensory bombardment often activates a protective response, keeping consciousness locked into the material world. Generally, there is little spiritual insight to be gained from these experiences.

In these situations the person must lower his vibrations in order to physically recover before entering the spiritual experience again, and this time, very slowly. Frequently, it takes months for the body to become attuned to vibrations that are high enough for the person to pursue these memories in detail. This probably accounts for the time and patience so necessary for deep spiritual experiences.

Implicit in all of these variations is the challenge to change. Neurotic defenses such as "I am unworthy," or "I have low self-esteem," are threatened. New, overwhelming urges come— urges to be forever this new spiritual person, to live it, know it, profess it, to have such feelings always, not merely as an overlay but as a warm, nourishing and dominant part of us.

When people do successfully integrate their spiritual experiences, they usually do it in a very uneven way. People move toward them and away and back again; they run away because it's all so overwhelming, and then back again because their souls demand it—a push-pull situation like a moth to a flame. These vacillations create frustration. Many want to jump in all at once and, as they say, "get it over with." But there is nothing to get over except resistance. After that, the path continues forever.

The major insight I gained from several of my own past lifehoods was that although I was somewhat spiritually developed, when my life was on the line and the chips were down, the urge to maintain physical life came storming through and I gave up my divine power in an attempt to live. While it is true that we must maintain the physical body if we are to spiritually evolve in this lifetime, the logical question follows: Why do we have to come back at all in this human form? Can't we evolve in spirit form? I have no ready answers, only impressions. Apparently, our task is to be both human and divine at the same time, which requires physical existence. Spiritual growth probably can occur when the soul is outside a physical body, but to achieve complete spiritual maturity, it appears that taking on a human form is necessary. Otherwise, there would be no reason for reincarnation.

Sometimes a person's life is so changed by spiritual enlightenment that he no longer fits into his culture. This is traumatic. Cultural rejection is the most damaging. When people who are motivated exclusively by ordinary reality have a strong spiritual experience, they develop grave doubts about their cherished assumptions about life.

When a critical number of the world's population reaches a state of spiritual vibrations, our institutions will change. Institutions are created to facilitate, regulate, and guide human behavior. During spiritual experiences, guidance comes from a higher source. As a result, some behaviors will vanish, not by abstinence or will power, but because one's motivation has changed.

Finally, fear of spiritual power is universal. This also seems strange because material power, money, prestige, leadership status, and rewards are coveted by most people. Yet, when it seems that spiritual power is available, people begin to describe it as a heavy burden; the sense that they will be required to carry responsibilities and obligations that they don't want. This means giving up some things that seem superficially desirable for others that can't yet be totally known.

I hear so many people say that when they pray, asking for divine guidance or solutions to problems, they get no answers. Others ask devoutly what they should do with their lives, what is their higher destiny? I have discovered that people do earnestly solicit spiritual help, but accept help only when it corresponds to how they have structured their lives, and who they think they are, so they can remain the same. Answers that don't fit this structure are not considered plausible answers. Furthermore, when prayer comes from ordinary material levels of consciousness, the vibrations are characteristically low and the person cannot perceive the divine information available to him. He cannot communicate with the divine unless he is tuned to that same wavelength.

If we could be God-like and not human-like, or *vice versa*, we wouldn't experience much stress. Or if we could totally separate out or completely integrate our divine and human natures, we would also be more comfortable. Actually, most of what we create around us is designed to maintain our human identity. Most of our official, compulsory institutions are devoted to human concerns. (Remember, institutions for spiritual direction are volunteer in nature.)

All metaphysical, mystical experiences I have described add credibility to the idea of a soul and past lives. I have publicly expressed my acceptance that the soul is indestructible. I agree with the teachings of Plato, Aristotle, and the major religions: the soul can produce its own energy, can move objects or barriers, and it precedes and exists after the material body.

There are many practical problems when one dedicates oneself to a deep spiritual path. By its nature it is a solitary journey where loneliness abides. We have unavoidable urges to be validated, but whom do we tell about the experiences we believe only *we* are having? For instance, suppose you are an average schoolteacher or an engineer, and you've had an enlightened experience of walking with Christ. It was so profound and so real that you were shaken up. What are you going to do about that? You don't understand at all; it's got to be weird. Generally, you have three options. You take it to your minister. But unless he or she is pretty enlightened, you know what your minister will do. Ministers pray with you. Praying is a step in the right direction. But it doesn't help you understand the experience, only to accept it with faith. Or you go to a psychologist who tries to explain it using the physical model of reality, but it cannot be explained that way. Or it may cross your mind to talk to a physician, but most would probably recommend a sedative or a pill. Maybe you think of a psychiatrist—they work with these unusual experiences—but somehow you know this is a real and sane one, and cannot be explained by a psychopathic model. In short, these highly respected professionals are not trained in mystical matters. Some can intuitively help by listening, while others become fearful of their own strong, spiritual urges.

In vogue today, when you are spiritually stuck, is to turn to a psychic reader to predict your future and to tell you about your past. Their predictions provide what most seekers want—some security about the future or some rational reason for why they're stuck. Very clever readers can present information about the client's current life amazingly well by reading the mind-field. The questions they answer are generally superficial, on the personality-ego level, not on the soul level. But what is more important, their answers about past lives tell you who you were and what you did, rather than what you experienced, the decisions you made, and how you established patterns of behavior which are today your unfinished business. Unless you bring forth your own lifehoods with the vividness of primary recall along with the associated emotions, you cannot truly know your soul's work. You are caught in a web of trying to figure it out intellectually and logically.

When he was at Esalen Institute, Stanislav Groff, a pioneer psychiatrist in the study of altered states, established the Spiritual Emergency Network. This network service, now connected with the Institute for Transpersonal Psychology in Menlo Park, California, provides trained counselors, who by telephone, help people frightened and confused by unusual experiences.

There is hope, however, in a new breed of transpersonal counselors who will understand and who know the way. Support groups are helpful if there is an experienced, wise, mystical leader comfortable with his own spiritual nature and wise with his interpretations.

Those of you who find my words compatible with your intuitive sense, if not your practices, may find that you hold some deeply ingrained religious and cultural beliefs that are creating additional barriers. There is a belief that God is the Father Almighty, that He personally makes everything happen, and that we, His children, are passive recipients of His love (when things go right) and His wrath (when they don't). This is an extension of karmic belief, of paying for all our bad deeds and profiting from our good ones.

I have no difficulty with the father/child concept; it is one of dependency. I reject the idea that all that happens to us should be excused as God's will. I do not believe that God wills us harm or suffering. The divine part of our soul is indeed a rigid taskmaster, and when we stray from the path of spiritual evolution, it reminds us with unhappiness and with physical and emotional illness. Rather than punishment, this is an indication that we are not on course. From all misfortunes should come profound learning. Those of you who know me personally know that I have been blind, so that I might see, and physically paralyzed so that I might turn inward for instruction. Both misfortunes were ever so profitable.

The metaphysical literature contains many references to entities, both good and bad, as though these were physical beings capable of doing destructive or constructive things to us without our participation. Anti-God, possessions and evil entities are their names.

Never in my many years as a mystic have I seen or experienced a demonic entity or vibration that in any form threatened me. True, I have felt some chaotic fields, morphogenic ones in places, and anti-coherent ones around people in my travels into so-called "haunted houses," and in Haiti and Africa where black magic and voodoo are performed. In Brazil, I made friends with the Espiritista healers who believe in spirit possessions, and I watched them work—even participated in their ceremonies. I assisted in the freeing of a house in the West Indies from thought forms; the house had been declared possessed.

Yes, I have made contact with souls that have crossed over

and are in spirit form. I have the capacity to read the ancient history of a place from the vibratory energy that remains years or centuries later. But I have never been attacked or bombarded, or even upset by what is called a diabolical entity or a negative energy. I have found these to be merely an organized energy or thought form. If one decodes these thought forms, and for some reason has similar thoughts, one's field resonates and one is affected. If one doesn't resonate, one can perceive the thoughts without effect.

To acknowledge diabolical entities that possess power in and of themselves without the person's participation, I believe is inaccurate and destructive. It is destructive because it allows one to project anger at God and the fear of one's own power onto some entity, which further masks the problem. It assures protection from uncovering one's unfinished business, because one is looking in the wrong place—out there, away from self, attached to some make-believe entity—making the unfinished business difficult to find while allowing for all manner of imagined threats. Satanic and demonic forces are only operative—effective as a field of thought—if people resonate with them, react to them, and act upon them. So the real threat lies within us.

I vividly recalled a lifehood as a young priest in France in the 16th century. He was sent to his first parish church not knowing that the congregation was split by some believers in black magic. One day the black magic group appeared at mass to heckle him and break up the service. Suddenly, a rage came over him which caused him to strike out with his arm, knocking down the hecklers some fifteen feet away. The men bolted in fear while the worshippers seemed paralyzed by the priest's power. He talked with them about how power could be used creatively in the service of God or negatively against God. He described how black magic is truly anger at God, used to defeat all that represents Godliness, and unless people join them or become weak with fear, black magic is powerless. In fact, black magic is weak if compared with the strength of power used in the service of God.

Professional interest in Multiple Personality Disorder (MPD), possession and "walk-in" has grown spectacularly in the past years since a mystic unfortunately introduced the idea of another soul taking the place of the existing one to explain sudden changes in personality. She called them "walk-ins." I go on record as rejecting mechanical concepts such as a foreign entity cohabiting a person, a possession, or a "walk-in." These concepts are erroneous because it is the soul that brings life to the body and when the soul leaves, death occurs. If this were not true, at death when one soul transcends, another would be waiting in the wings to take over, and death of the body would be a thing of the past. Personality changes, shifts, or multiple expressions do happen; but multiple personalities do not.

The idea of "possessions" is given credence by research. Eighty-five to 90% of all so-called multiples apparently have a childhood background of physical and emotional abuse with a history of criticism, inconsistency, abandonment, and betrayal by adults. These factors apparently coexist with personality shifts or splits, but this does not justify the thinking that some outside force intervened. Multiples display two or more consciousnesses which seem to battle for control. A break in selfhood—the person as known to the person—seems to occur.

I would like to present a different explanation for these psychological aberrations. First, we are all "multiples" in the broad sense, with behaviors that we cannot explain. But these behaviors are not the result of separate entities. Ideally, we experience the total integration of a rich, flowing, evolved, complex personality. But in cases of MPD there are sudden shifts in personality without integration. It seems strange to me that lifehoods have not been studied as a possible explanation for the gamut of behavioral and physiological differences in those we label "multiples," "possessed" or "walk-ins."

My questions about MPD stemmed from one client who experienced grave personality stress. Over time, as he moved beyond repression, he had major conflicts like those of MPDs.

Finally, he was able to recover in detail three lives as priests, and one as a scientist, and a mystic healer in China, Italy, France, and India. His beliefs in each of these lifehoods conflicted with his current life beliefs. Then he suffered stress from the need to change, to integrate the best of each into an elaborate expanded personality. But he did accomplish this. Now he has skills, even information, from all these sources integrated into his present personality. But more importantly, he is aware that it is the same soul carrying all these many personality characteristics in a complex human being, and that these are all him now.

Many researchers still contend that the distinct shift from one ego state to another is proof that the minds and bodies of those with MPDs are invaded. In reality, what the shift does is allow the person to express the unfinished business of other lifehoods—which clashes with current life experiences—without having sufficient conscious recognition to change.

We need to be reminded that our habitual stream of consciousness is not the only consciousness which exists in the organism. Therefore, it does not follow that other consciousnesses are induced from outside "possessions" and "walk-ins." These consciousnesses are a part of the experience of one soul that has existed in other lifehood bodies; they are carried by that soul into this current life. This is possible because the information is carried in the mind, not in the brain.

Probably the most dangerous belief is that the MPDs' behavior is caused by the invasion of the minds and bodies of entities and other souls. That simply is not correct. Furthermore this belief dictates the treatment and the expected and actual outcomes, and it can lead to disastrous results. I suggest that simple integration of so-called separate personalities is a superficial goal and that psychologists will keep hanging on to the "strangeness" they attribute to this syndrome because they don't understand the problem.

I hasten to add that there is value in bringing attention to failures to integrate apparent multiple personalities or parts of the same personality. This demands that we evaluate the complex signals that the mind issues to the brain. It behooves us to clear up our deficient ideas about soul-life and reincarnation with thorough investigations into lifehoods. The impact on psychological diagnoses and treatment will be great.

Why are the numbers of MPDs apparently mounting exponentially, so that it is no longer considered a rare disorder? We have discovered that the memories of lifehoods common to all children are repressed by cultural pressures by about age five. This is the same age as onset of childhood MPD. With adult MPD, the current relaxation of cultural beliefs about mystical things allows these repressions to loosen sufficiently for multiple consciousness to emerge, but not enough to encourage spontaneous personality integration.

I believe that if studies were made of cultures which accept the concepts of lifehoods and encourage this kind of knowing, we would not find any MPD. Also, I believe that as more and more people remember lifehoods and have the ego strength to integrate these, we will recognize the falsity of "possession" beliefs. What excites me most is that we will be able to treat personality complexity not only at the surface integration level, but also on a deeper mystical plane. The latter is essential to the evolutionary process and to spiritual enlightenment.

DiMele, a New York psychologist, has said: "Suddenly, multiples are here like messengers of the gods to skip us eons ahead of our acceptable understanding of brain and body." May I add: more than the brain and body, but mind and soul and lifehoods.

The fact that the brain wave may be different at different times is sometimes used to justify the belief that two or more souls could possess the same body. But brain waves also are a part of the material, structural pattern which is carried in past life memory—by the same soul, which now has a different personality and a different physical body. In fact, I am sure that it is impossible for two souls or entities to inhabit the same body at one time. Again, as a person brings to conscious awareness and owns past lifehood experiences as his, the so-called "possessions" are no more. "Possessions" are only unorganized and hidden parts of the same soul.

These are the same criticisms I levy against the idea of "walk-ins," the miserably inaccurate answer to sudden changes in personality explained by psychics and latched onto by psychologists and psychiatrists for lack of a better label for mystical problems. The concepts of "possessions" or "walk-ins" are cop-outs for not owning and integrating spiritual experiences, whether these be gross or great.

More and more people are perplexed about possessions, and more therapists are trying to treat them with an outmoded model. Religious groups are considering or even practicing exorcisms to drive out the "devil." In one sense, possession is a psychopathic phenomenon, not the devil's work; but in a more enlightened vein, the source and direction are distinctly mystical and spiritual.

When it comes to treatment, therapists must encourage the patient to experience the "entity possession" in a safe psychotherapeutic situation as was done during the treatments at Epidaris. The therapist must accept the mystical reality of entities, but have no fear of them or the behavioral aberrations they create.

At the beginning, the therapist must refrain from indicating that the person's mind has created the entity, but must warmly understand the trauma the person experiences while strongly assuring him that he knows the way to remove the entity. He must be able to convince the person that his strength and mystical know-how will protect them both—that they can cope with anything. Short, hourly treatments don't work in the beginning, because the patient rapidly needs to be free of the dependent victim state. Each session should move the person up in consciousness using imagery to find his child, or perhaps walking on an imaginary path while describing what he sees.

As the imagery progresses, if the person trusts the therapist, he will find his "entities." These come in many forms and have numerous behaviors: a diabolical human; an ugly space monstrosity; animals with huge teeth and claws; spiders invading the world, or snakes coiled and striking; ghastly, hideous noises that will not stop; verbal castigations, vile words and thoughts against self; threats to never tell a soul and never think of God. These schizophrenic delusions do provide information for the therapist to set the stage for the game. Actually, the "possessed" have some consistency in their experiences, and they have created enough coherent thought to be closer to reality in their life than many with acute psychopathologies. They feel they are victims of entity persecution, but most desperately want to be free from these. Their prognosis can be excellent.

This is a description of a six-hour session with a very serious case of "possession". This patient was a fifty-year-old woman, a self-employed commercial artist with a large clientele. Her possession had occurred nineteen years earlier. Since then she had had numerous unsuccessful psychotherapeutic procedures and was institutionalized after she stabbed herself at the command of her "entity." Other than during her hospital stay, she had not taken drugs. She had heard of my work with the "possessed" and had obtained my telephone number two years prior to our work. When we met, she vociferously expounded about her persecutions and all the books she had read to convince her of her suffering. She rambled on about her childhood, her failed marriage, and her current material problems. I cut short her patter because I know that this life is not the source of the problem, and I had enough information about how the "entity" operated. What she wanted was for me to see her and take "it" away—then she felt she would be able to live. She interrupted many times until I asked her to be still and listen. I told her that I knew the way, but that she must follow me and that would mean giving up some of her deep convictions about this "entity" that had not worked. She told me that I didn't understand because she had experienced the possession, I hadn't. I suggested that she think for a few days about whether she was ready to follow me; if so, we would work. If not,

I wished her well, but I could not help.

She came to her first appointment early and was very tense. "They" had put her through hell all night because she was coming to see me. She rattled on dramatically at length about being a victim. Every statement announced her weakness, her passivity, and the inevitability of her suffering. She had much more detail to fill me in on when I stopped her monologue. This was her way of releasing pent-up energy and feeding her psychic split.

Our work started quietly, she lying down and I sitting close beside her. I screened her electromagnetic field and taught her breathing exercises to ground and stabilize her field. The only normal parts of her field were the root chakra or life force, the third eye or spiritual center, and the crown chakra or higher consciousness area. All other chakras and joints showed strong anti-coherent magnetic fields of stress.

When she first saw the "possession" it was a huge black man, although later she reported many other "entities" because of her many possessions. I suggested we go ask him what he wanted from her. (Here I literally joined her imagery so I could lead her to confront it.) She was so frightened, she said she hid behind me as we approached him. Of course, as I described approaching him with her behind me, he disappeared. She said he was afraid of me. I asked her to command that he come back. He did, finally, only this time he wasn't very large and was not black. We played this game for several hours, until she was able to stand beside me, not behind me, when we confronted him. Now when the entity appeared, we used our growing strength to disarm him, not to physically kill him with our rage, but to render him powerless with our minds and watch him become small and weak. This was the beginning; she was gaining the strength of mind to know that she did not have to be a victim. "Perhaps I can rule him," she once said.

Next came the howling, shrieking noises from her mouth. "He" was screaming through her and over which she had no control. I was literally deafened. I told her my ears were so affected that she should ask him to cut the noise in half. To her surprise, it worked, and she was able to lower the sound to a mild whine. I reminded her that if "they" created these noises when she was alone, she should get angry and command them to cut it down. To practice her new-found skill, we brought "them" back screaming while she lowered their voices.

Next, "they" started doing horrible, immoral things, using vile language that she screamed could not be her—it was "them." She could never do what "they" did nor think what "they" thought. This belies the dynamics of "possession." Her anger and rage were so intense and her imagery so grotesque, her moral mind could not accept that these came from her, nor could she stop them. Her way out was to give these thoughts and violence to "them," to create entities out there, and to run away and be persecuted by them. As she continues to gain strength to command the entities, they will be gone and she will realize that her mind created these and has also eliminated them. Even then, she is not cured until she reaches the source. We have already found her deep needs to contact God, which she believes had been held back by "them." If she does, she will find great frustration and anger at God. And if she isn't able to take the next steps, she will at least profit from the control she has over victimship.

Some people, when they do this kind of work, wrap themselves in white light as a sort of protection. These ideas about "black" and "white" energy need to be clarified. Actually, energy is energy. We, on the other hand, judge the information by our worth and standards, so that the blackness and whiteness is our judgment; it has nothing to do with energy *per se*. For these reasons, I do not wrap myself in white light when I work. I am protected by the strength, clarity and spiritual vibrations of my field. I am therefore free to interact with whatever I choose and to radiate my coherent energy to the world and to all people. They in turn will resonate with me, and feed me, if there is compatibility in our fields.

What can we do personally to hasten our spiritual development? There are two musts. First, we must choose more carefully where and on what we spend our free time, and we must get more spiritual exercise. I don't think religious institutions are adequate. True, liturgy, ritual, song, group prayer and religious education are steps in the right direction, but there is no assurance that from these one will find his spiritual nature and grow. For one thing, the short length of time most spend in religious places is inadequate to offset the low vibrations and shady judgment of everyday life. One needs to schedule and practice regular meditation and contemplation in and out of religious places.

Secondly, religious leaders and counselors sometimes perpetuate the faith rather than serve as spiritual models. All spiritual leaders should personally hold spiritual vibrations that will set the tone for worship and all group endeavors—parishioners need an opportunity to resonate in a divine field. Perhaps we should even demand that our clergy carry abiding spiritual vibrations before they are ordained.

People needing divine motivation often say they don't get much out of today's churches. Can this account for the split-off, mystically-oriented churches that are attracting so many? While I don't condone many of the practices of charismatic churches, I do understand their appeal because I understand the mystical element of the deep spiritual experiences they promote. Spirituality is not rational or logical—those words best describe religion.

While we all acknowledge the wisdom of separation of church and state, we have confused religion with spirituality. Spiritual beliefs weave the fabric of our moral code and our successful life together. I believe that religious institutions should continue their educational programs, but if spiritual knowing is derived only from experience, then the community and the school should be involved as well as the church and home. A spiritual tenor should exist wherever words or deeds allow subtle information to be available for human consumption. This implies that we need spiritual models in every profession and in every workplace.

One of the primary concerns of all religious institutions today should be to provide opportunities for people to get in touch with their divine nature. The act of participation, singing and intoning in a group, for example, is probably much better at creating a vibrational state than just listening or watching. Unfortunately, larger churches hurry religious services to finish on time or to clear the church so that the next service can start. Without pauses for contemplation, the parishioner cannot absorb higher vibrations that enable him to be elevated to a spiritual state. Current scheduling practices need to be re-evaluated.

When we criticize some of the pitfalls of modern religious institutions, we must look to insights from other religions. Although the public forms of religions differ widely, the esoteric or inner circle, the spiritual core of all the great religions share much in common. This is the perennial wisdom Aldous Huxley spoke about in the religions around the world. All religions "recognize a Divine Reality substantial to the world of things, and lives, and minds. . . find in the soul something similar to, or even identical with Divine Reality. . . place man's final end in the knowledge of the imminent and transcendent God of all Beings."

Communication on any level, animal to man, man to man, or man to God, requires the mutual exchange of information by symbols and signs. For spiritual communication with a divine being, the human can initiate it with spiritual thoughts, ideas or actual questions, or God may provide signs as He did when the light blinded Saul (later Paul) on the road to Damascus. These signs must be received and decoded or interpreted, and then must be acknowledged and responded to with additional signs. Communication with God breaks down primarily at two places in the process—in the failure of the human to receive the message, and in the failure to recognize or decode its meaning and then to acknowledge it. I believe that God is always expressing, loving, and sending information that humans don't receive or interact with. The failure is primarily because humans have not reached the spiritual vibrational level that is necessary to receive the message. Divine vibrations are available constantly, at all times, and they contain all information. Human perception is the weak link. Yet how easy it is to become angry or disappointed with God when we think He does not hear or care—when the truth is that we are not aware of the messages. I have found that when a person clearly requests, and is high in vibrations and consciousness, the answers are immediate, clear, and often overwhelming, even if not exactly what was wished for or expected.

So that you can personalize the ideas presented in this chapter, read the following questions and quietly await your answer. If imagery and thoughts come, contemplate these to uncover your past spiritual experiences.

1. Have you ever been troubled and turned to the divine for help but there seemed to be a vacuum with no answer and no deep feeling? Why were you not answered?

2. Have you ever seen a magnificent sunset in a new way which seemed to envelop and enrapture you? Why is one sunset, lasting only a few moments, so different from others?

3. Have you ever knelt at an altar to receive a sacrament and experienced the Glory of God and the Holy Spirit round about you? Why is this not every time—only sometimes?

4. Have you ever watched a person come to the end of his life on Earth and realized the peaceful and glorious transition of a human? Why is it that we fear death?

5. Have you ever experienced lovingness so profoundly that all in its radiance were changed and healed? Why can't you willfully create such lovingness?

6. Have you ever seen a work of art glowing with a universal halo? If you haven't, why not?

7. Have you ever heard the perfect chorus as angels announced the resurrection from the world's trauma? Can you grasp and hold it?

The answers are clear and bold. What makes the difference? Consciousness. Conscious awareness is not off and on; it is always, though not always the same. We live in everyday reality of coping, solving problems, thinking and phatic communication. We forget super-consciousness, the place of spiritual awakening. And yet sometimes it breaks loose and we know its awesome power. The Haitians say that the Christians go to church to talk about God. They dance to become God. When they look into the sky, there may be only a few stars, and when the clouds come, even fewer. But behind their stars they see God. Behind our stars we see more stars. The difference is a matter of consciousness.

Man in his universe is endowed with God-given capacities which each of us glimpses occasionally. That is so seldom for some of us that we pass these off as strange, incomprehensible or coincidental, because we do not understand them. Spiritual development is difficult because, unlike perfecting physical or intellectual talents requiring the development of skills, spiritual development demands freedom to know one's role in the divine plan.

How can we grow to acknowledge our divine nature? First, we must quiet ourselves from the fury of living and doing, to the silence of being and feeling. We must recognize that we can't make it happen, but we can negotiate its occasion. Secondly, we must carefully survey the quality of human awareness around us, in our friends, acquaintances and work associates. Do these nourish our higher nature, drag us down, or provide nothing? You will notice that as you enliven spiritually, those of your friends who do not will fade from your orbit.

We modern humans announce that we are no longer content with vicarious religious experiences. We want our lives touched spiritually and deeply. A personal God who is accessible must be part of a new world model. We want to feel the hand of God touch us. Through that hand we will move others to higher levels, to heal and know beyond what we have learned. At these times we become human interveners. We sense the source of that power, but we are not merely channels. We are God manifest on this earth.

At first we will find it earth-shattering to comprehend humanness on the divine plane. Only by observing it in others and by comprehending its glory do we learn that it is our evolutionary work to bring such insights and experiences to this earth. For such knowledge we will give profound thanks.

Evolution does not occur by happenstance. Its goal is to bridge the levels of consciousness so that we live on all levels with all capacities simultaneously. It takes place in the mind with what that mind selects as worthy of its dedication. What has your mind selected from your experiences? Mind mastery is the soul's unavoidable journey.

When God is experienced, this event is as real as any sensory perception of one's own self. In those instances, we have victory over death and pain. We are in touch with the ongoingness of the soul. We understand the divine plan and our role in it. We come closer to perfection, and we are worthy being called God's co-creator. Science and spirituality started together and then diverged for many centuries. Now they are coming back together. Two of the greatest forces in human thoughts are science and spirituality. Lederman, one of our eminent particle physicists, said, "I think we're on the threshold of finding God—or at least higher glory. We haven't found it yet, but even science is looking in the right direction." Science has given us new insight that as our field grows in vibrational complexity, as we maintain its dynamic position on the ridge of chaos, our God-like nature will dominate our consciousness and our life.

I don't think you know yourself at the soul level until you come to a very divine spiritual experience in some physical life, at some actual time, and you recognize that it came from the heights and depths of you. I don't believe you can know your greatness as an individual until you have had and have acknowledged a profound spiritual experience, and realized that it is not outside of you—it is not God in heaven, it is you, experiencing divine vibrations in yourself. The most you can give to anyone is this level of what you are, a human manifesting the glory of God.

EXHIBITS

EXHIBIT 1

TELEMETRY ENERGY FIELD
SENSING INSTRUMENT

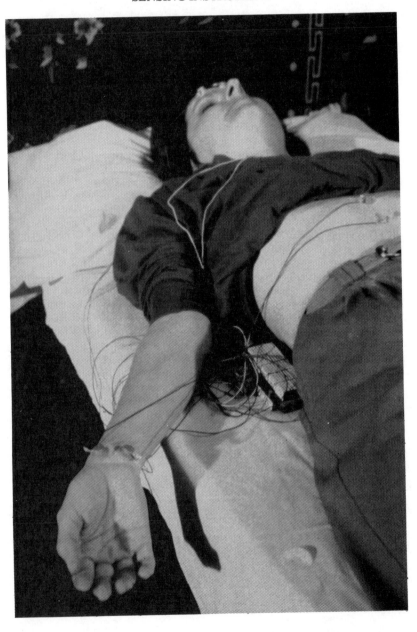

The small equipment shown beside the person is a miniaturized, modular sensing instrument, which is like a battery-powered telemetry EMG. Actually, it is a small FM broadcasting system with an amplifier and transmitter for each channel. Note the 12 modular plug-in, white boxes comprise six IRIG channels -- with an amplifier and transmitter for each channel. The IRIG channels that we used were numbered 11, 12, 13, and 14 to indicate the recording capacity of each channel. The highest channel that we used was IRIG 14, with a sensing capacity up to 20 thousand Hz.

We had discovered that the regular, hard-wire instruments (operated by electricity) used for EMG, ECG and EEG did not pick up the entire millivoltage signal of the energy field. Hard-wire equipment we designed later allowed us to capture up to 200 thousand cycles per second from the energy field. When the two instruments, telemetry and hard-wire simultaneously recorded the energy field, the telemetry information was a perfect harmonic of the hard-wire instrument, yet of lower frequencies.

In Exhibit 1, the bipolar (2) surface sensors of silver, silver chloride are affixed to the solar plexus or "emotional body" areas. The ground, or neutral reference electrode, is on the wrist.

Continuous energy field signals were beamed via the FM transmitter to receiving instrument panels. These data were observed from oscilloscopes, and a print-out, and by further amplifying the sound. At the same time, the energy field data were recorded on a magnetic tape.

EXHIBIT 2
MUSCLE WAVE SHAPE - EMG
(4 channel recording)

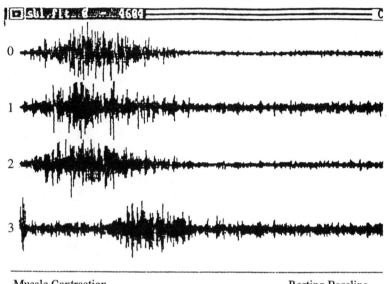

Muscle Contraction   Resting Baseline

EXHIBIT 3
FOURIER FREQUENCY ANALYSIS
(Muscle Contraction and Base Line - ENERGY FIELD)

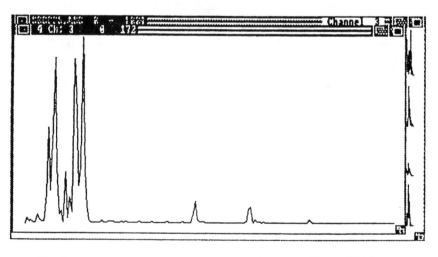

Muscle   Energy Field

0-150 Hz   495 Hz   525 Hz

The left of Exhibit 2 shows the normal myogram of four breathing muscles. On the right is the muscular relaxation following breaths. This is the energy we found to be the higher frequency of the energy field shown in Exhibit 3, the Fourier Frequency Analysis Chart.

EXHIBIT 4

SPECTROGRAM

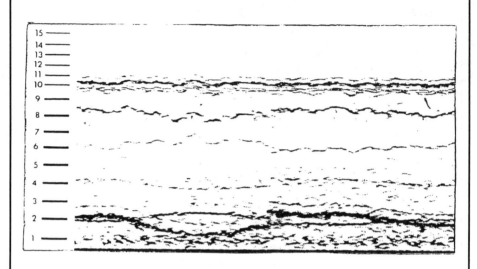

NORMAL FIELD

(Vertical - Each number equals 100 Hz)

We found that the color patterns of individuals' fields were shifted slightly upwards or downward. The more expansive fields were skewed upward and the more confined ones downward. Yet the colors remained in the same sequence with each analytic technique and each person.

SUMMARY OF AURIC COLOR FREQUENCIES

Color	Approximate Central Frequency
Low blue (muscle)	2 or 200 Hz
Green	3 or 300 Hz
Yellow	4 or 400 Hz
Red	5 or 500 Hz
Orange	6 or 600 Hz
High blue	7 or 700 Hz
Violet	8 or 800 Hz
Cream	10 or 1,000 Hz
White	11 or 1,100 Hz up

CONTINUED ON NEXT PAGE

EXHIBIT 5A
CROSS PLOT ANALYSIS
(Two simultaneous samples from different body locations)

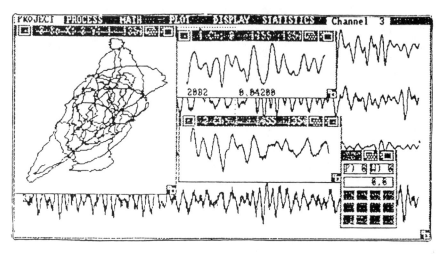

ANTI-COHERENT FIELD

EXHIBIT 5-B
CROSS PLOT ANALYSIS

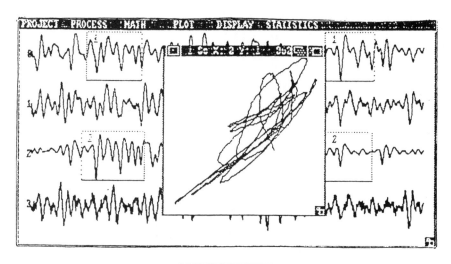

COHERENT FIELD

Exhibits 5A and 5B display a Cross Plot Analysis of two simultaneous data signals from different body parts. To the extreme right of Exhibit 5 are four simultaneous energy signals from different parts of the body. In the middle of that display is an enlargement of the two separate recordings that were compared. To the extreme left of the first display and the middle of the second one, is a graphic representation of this comparison. We found that when two energy field recordings were out of phase in frequency and different in strength, as shown in 5A, there was an anti-coherent random pattern resembling a tangled ball of string. The second picture or 5B shows a coherent field, the pattern being more organized in flow and direction.

The first cross plot picture (5A), showing anti-coherency of two locations, was similar to the cross plot picture derived by other researchers using two ECG recordings from different heart locations taken during cardiac dysrhythmia. The second (5B) or coherent field was likewise similar to the coherent pattern of recordings found in a normal cardiogram.

EXHIBIT 6

ENERGY FIELD SPECTROGRAMS
(Vertical 100-1500 Hz frequencies)

POWER DENSITY SPECTRUM
FOURIER ANALYSIS
Horizontal 100-1,000 Hz (freq.)
Vertical 10-30 decibels (power)

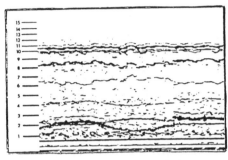

Blue A (Average Resting)

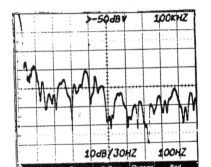

Blue A

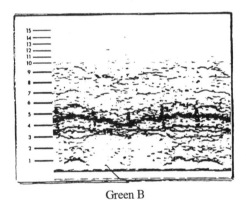

Green B

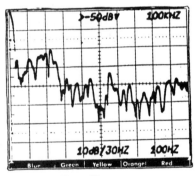

Green B

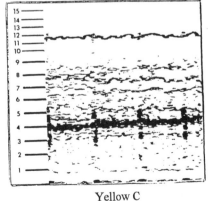

Yellow C

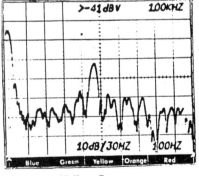

Yellow C

EXHIBIT 6 (continued)

ENERGY FIELD SPECTROGRAMS
(Vertical 100-1500 Hz frequencies)

POWER DENSITY SPECTRUM
FOURIER ANALYSIS
Horizontal 100-1000 Hz
Vertical 10-30 decibels (power)

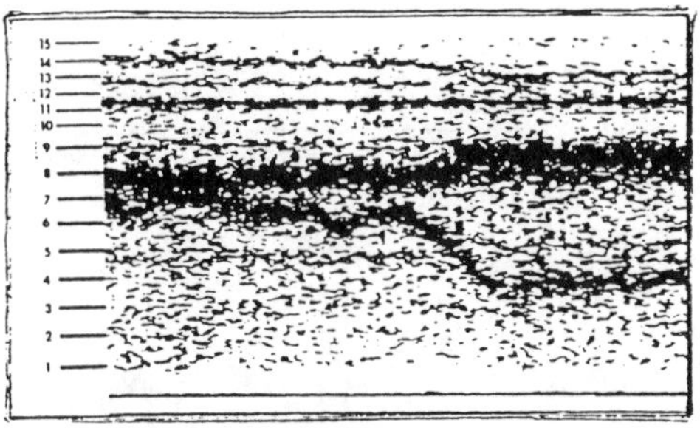

Red-Orange D

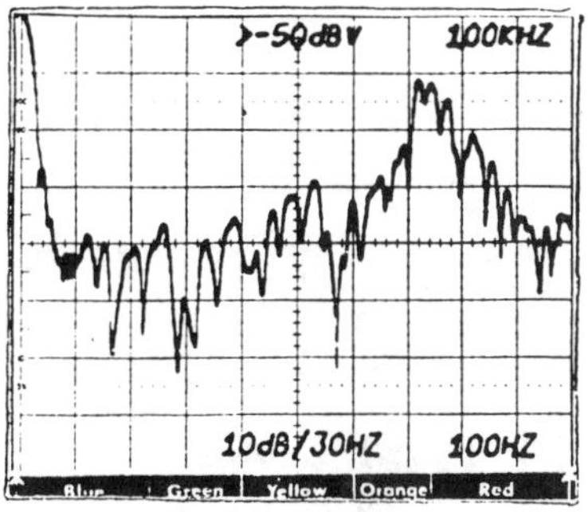

Red-Orange

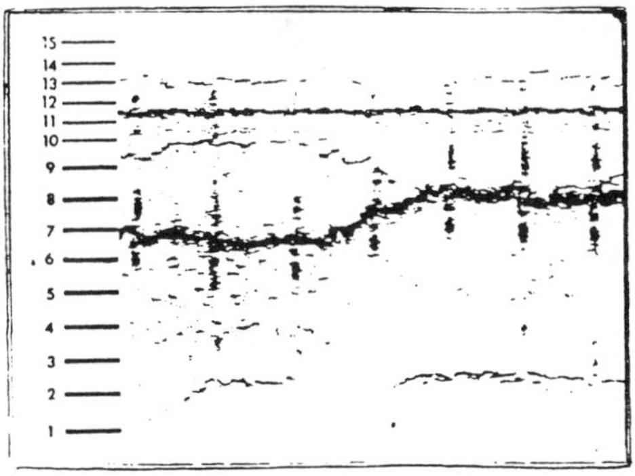

Red E - Pain

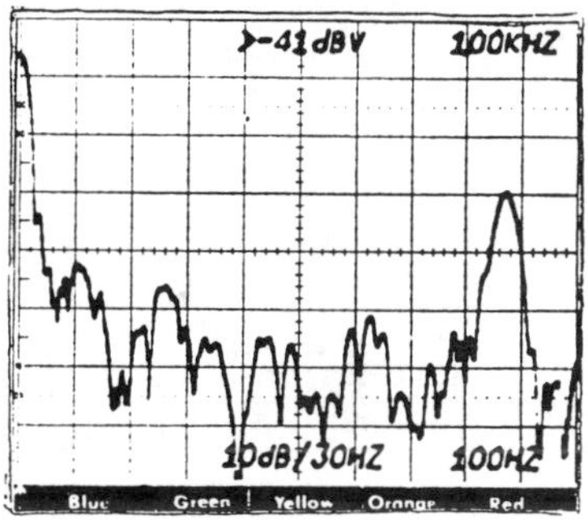

Red-Violet - Pain

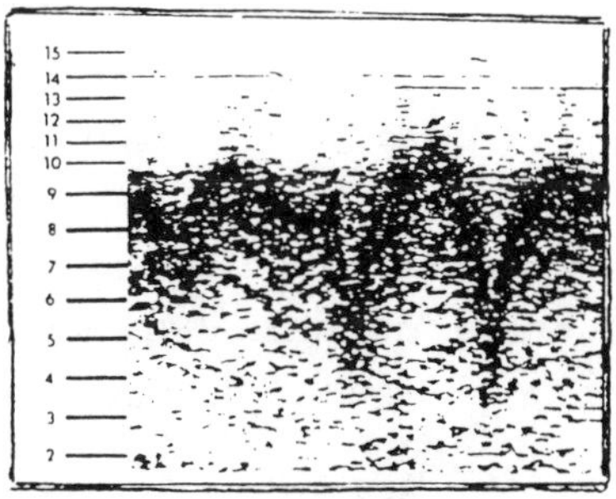

Violet F - Imaging

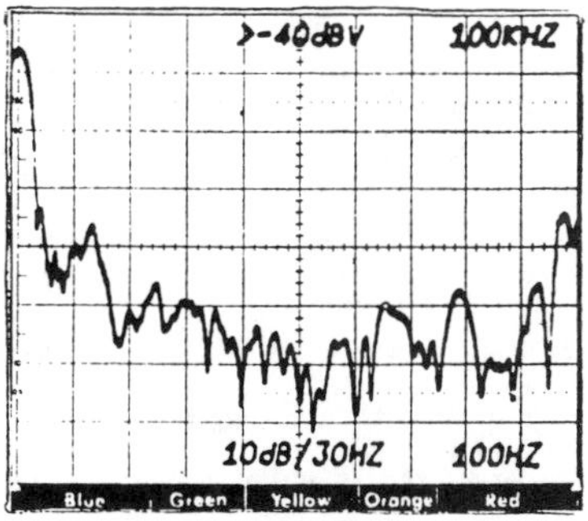

Violet

EXHIBIT 6 (continued)

ENRGY FIELD SPECTROGRAMS
(Vertical 200-1500 Hz frequencies)

POWER DENSITY SPECTRUM
FOURIER ANALYSIS
Horizontal 1-1000 Hz
Vertical 10-30 decibels (power)

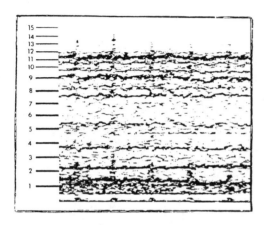

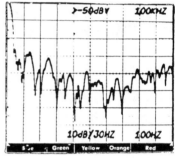

White - All Colors - G

In the Exhibit 6A Spectrogram, Column 1 shows the presence of all colors with a slightly greater intensity of 200 Hz, or blue. This is the low blue frequency connected with muscle contraction and is not part of the energy field. Aura readers describe this as a normal resting aura.

The 6B green spectrogram shows a predominant 300 Hz frequency with some blue frequencies at 200 and stronger yellow ones at 400 Hz.

The 6C spectrogram, yellow, at 400 Hz is accompanied by a strong white signal at 11 or 1100 Hz. The bold upright energy riding on the yellow band is the heartbeat. This recording was taken from the chest or heart chakra. The fainter lines between yellow and white are orange, red, violet and high blue, which make up the rainbow spectrum of white light.

At the left part of 6D, the red-orange spectrogram, the

strongest colors are orange at 700 and red at 800 Hz. This field was created by a healer when she was asked to change her red field to orange. At first, she created both colors, but to the right of the spectrogram she stated that she would bring in yellow or 400 Hz to create orange; it was much easier. Here, what the aura reader saw was a blend of red and yellow. The data showed it was created by red and yellow vibrations.

Exhibit 6E shows red accompanied by a strong white band. This is a classic field pattern that occurs during pain. It was taken from an athlete who was exhausted after running a long distance event. The white band at 11+ shows that his consciousness was high -- an altered state or runner's high.

See the dramatic wide band of the violet recording 6F, as it spreads from 9+ to 6+ with unexplained dips much lower. This is an example of what happens in the field when a person sees images. Violet, blue, and red are the dominant colors.

In the last "all color" spectrogram (6G), the aura reader described the energy field as white, containing all colors.

The same raw data used for the Spectrograms (Exhibit 6, Column I) was processed by Power Density Spectrum, a Fourier Analysis procedure (Exhibit 6, Column II). Note that both the Power Density Spectrum and the Energy Field Spectrogram (Exhibit 6) are in lower frequencies than the accepted light frequencies of colors. Remember the description of color that we used was determined by aura readers. These lower frequency recordings are subharmonics of light, color frequencies. Note also that all auric colors did not fall in the same positions as reported in color charts from red to indigo. The sequence of colors was rearranged like what happens when light falls through certain prisms. Notice the many dynamic lines in the spectrogram at numerous frequencies show that there may be several colors present even when one color predominates.

Since these early recordings using telemetry, we have redesigned the older hard-wire EMG and ECG equipment to bring in the same signal, but with much higher frequency recordings that are not possible with the limitations of the telemetry carrier bands.

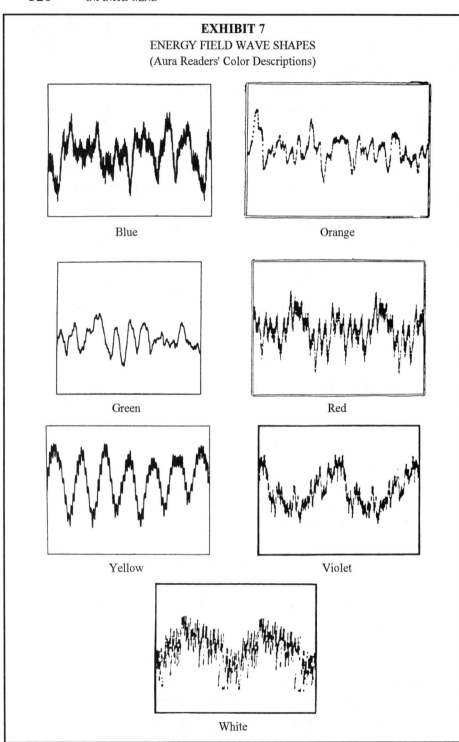

EXHIBIT 7
ENERGY FIELD WAVE SHAPES
(Aura Readers' Color Descriptions)

Blue

Orange

Green

Red

Yellow

Violet

White

In Exhibit 7, distinct wave shape patterns were obtained when aura readers described the primary and secondary colors of the auric field. Note the distinct differences: the blue spiking we describe as "saw tooth on the mountain", with slower sweeps of positive and negative deflection, but with faster deflexions riding on these "mountains." I believe this occurs because there is a low blue vibration (actually in the 80 to 100 Hz band) connected with muscle contraction, and a higher energy field blue, as described by aura readers to be at approximately 800+ Hz.

The yellow wave pattern always showed a more regular sine wave with small higher frequencies riding on the sine wave.

Red shows sharper, more spike-like positive and negative deflexions with clumps or plateaus of faster signals.

Observe that green does show characteristics of blue and yellow. Orange has more of the yellow sine wave with the plateaus of red. Violet does resemble a faster version of blue and red. White contains the wave shapes of all the color frequencies.

EXHIBIT 8

ENERGY FIELD SPECTROGRAM

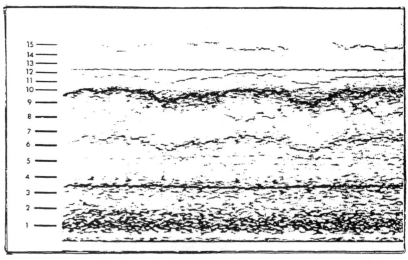

PAIN HEALER
(Violet-White)

Note in the Energy Field Spectrogram Exhibit 8 - Pain Healer (Violet-White), there are four primary bands of energy: 1 to 2 is blue, always present with muscle contraction; a narrow band at 3+ is green; a slight band at 6+ is orange, and the primary band at 9+ is violet. White is shown at 12 to 15. The green, blue and orange are unique frequencies of this healer and are not related to the violet-white characteristic of all pain healing vibrations. Healers who remove pain always display an intense blue-violet-white field which eliminates the patient's red pain vibration.

CONTINUED ON NEXT PAGE

EXHIBIT 9

ENERGY FIELD SPECTROGRAM

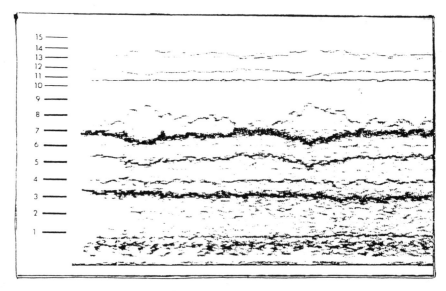

VITALITY HEALER
(Full Color Spectrum)

Exhibit 9 is a normal resting full color spectrum of an outstanding healer. Note blue or muscle vibration at 1 or 100 Hz, green at 3 or 300 Hz, yellow at 4 or 400 Hz, orange at 5 or 500 Hz, red at 7 or 700 Hz, violet at 10 or 1000 Hz, cream color at 12 or 1200 Hz, and white at 14 or 1400 Hz. Individual spectrograms show slight variations in numbers but the same relative positions of colors.

This healer shows a nearly complete color frequency field that is particularly effective after illness or surgery, to increase vitality, to eliminate asthenia and the fatigue accompanying emotional disturbances. The higher consciousness mind vibrations are present, but appear weak when compared to the strength of the red, orange, yellow, and green vibrations that we have found are more related to the health of the body.

EXHIBIT 10

ENERGY FIELD SPECTROGRAMS

REGENERATION HEALER
(Red-Double Helix)

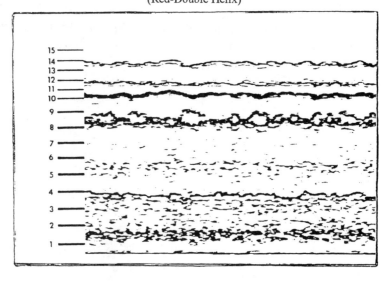

HEALEE

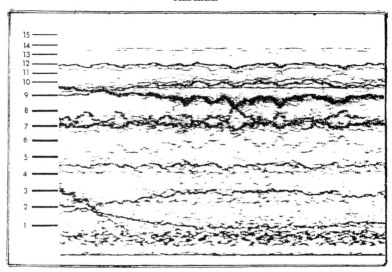

(Recordings taken simultaneously at end of healing.)

The most disclosing characteristics of the energy field of the regeneration healer lie in the less defined 1 to 5 spectrum of blue, green, yellow, and orange, and the increased strength and coherency in the upper energy bands from 7 to 14. The strong blue at 10, violet at 11+, and white at 14 all indicate a powerful elevated consciousness characteristic of many recordings. But the double helix of the red is unique to this healer, and maybe to all regenerative healers.

Note that the fields of the healer and healee, which were taken simultaneously by two separate instruments, are identical in pattern. They differ only in that the healee's frequencies are slightly lower.

These spectrograms were made when the healer sensed that their fields were identical, and therefore she stopped the healing procedures.

EXHIBIT 11

SPECTROGRAM (MU ROOM)

EXHAUSTED - ANTI-COHERENT FIELD

(Vertical - 100 to 1500 Hz frequencies)

Exhibit 11 of the auric fields of two subjects were recorded at the end of a 10-hour recording session in the Mu Room, where instruments operated by physicists altered the electrical and magnetic atmosphere. The human fields became so anti-coherent that all resemblance of a human energy field pattern was gone. The subjects complained of both utter fatigue and incoherent thought.

We believe these findings give clear indication of the tremendous importance of the human and environmental field transactions. When the atmospheric fields are deficient or anti-coherent, there is a corresponding confusion and inefficiency of physiological and mental functioning.

EXHIBIT 12

ENERGY FIELD WAVE SHAPE
(3 Seconds Energy Field Data)

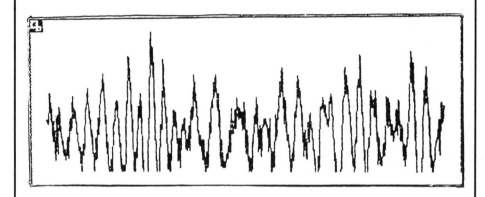

EXHIBIT 13
HUNT CHAOS ATTRACTOR GRAPH

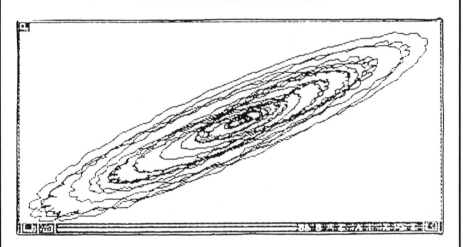

(Using Chaos Mathematical Formula -
Data Offset 1/10,000 sec.)

When three seconds' worth of human energy field data (Exhibit 12) was compared to itself, an identical sample but with one ten-thousandth of a second delay time, i.e., where two identical data samples were compared one ten-thousandth of a second out of sync (Exhibit 13), the Hunt Chaos Attractor Graph was obtained. Note that the spiral characteristics of this chaos pattern showed gaps in between lines, characteristic of all chaos attractors. The squiggly, uneven nature of the lines probably indicates the extreme dynamic nature of these biological data. With totally random data or white noise, all gaps would be filled in, losing the unique gap-pattern occurring when each part of a series of information is slightly different from every other part.

EXHIBIT 14

EXHIBIT 14
RÖSSLER CHAOS ATTRACTOR GRAPH
(Mathematical Model)

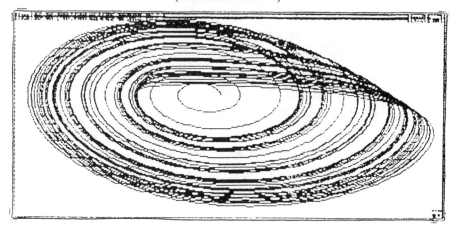

EXHIBIT 15
LORENZ CHAOS ATTRACTOR
(Weather Data)

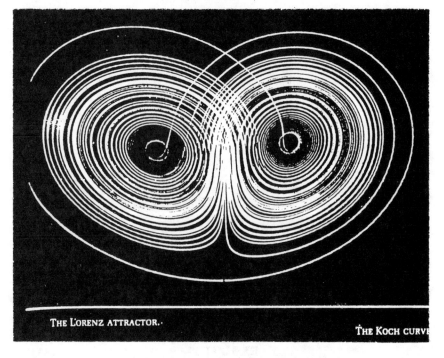

THE LORENZ ATTRACTOR.

THE KOCH CURVE

Note the dynamic wiggly nature of data lines in the Hunt Chaos Graph (Exhibit 13) from living high frequency data. Compare this with the Rössler Attractor (Exhibit 14), a mathematical model, and the Lorenz Chaos Attractor (Exhibit 15), from low frequency weather data. All three graphs are generated from non-linear data, but the Hunt pattern is the most dynamic and variable. Also, it occurred in the human field in three seconds' worth of time.

EXHIBIT 16

MUSCLE WAVE SHAPE - EMG

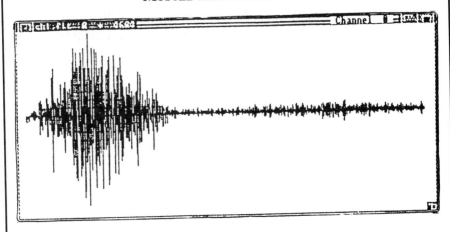

EXHIBIT 17

MUSCLE GRAPH

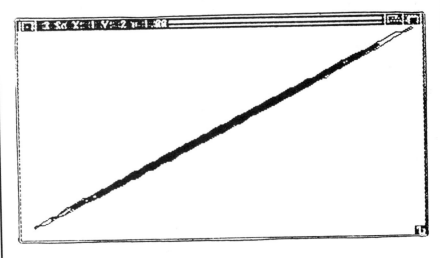

(Using Chaos Mathematical Formula
Data Offset 1/10,000 Sec.)

EXHIBIT 18

HEART WAVE SHAPE - ECG

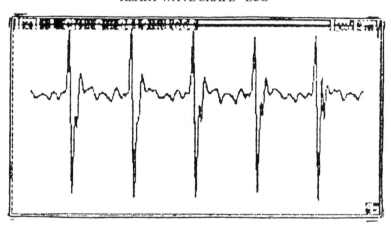

EXHIBIT 19

HEART GRAPH

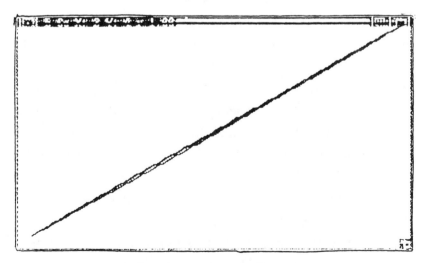

(Using Chaos Mathematical Formula
Data Offset 1/10,000 Sec.)

We wondered why an energy field chaos attractor had not been discovered in other global biological signals. To find out, we submitted three seconds' worth each of the brain, muscle, and heart recordings to the same offset procedure.

Exhibit 16 shows an EMG recording of a muscle contraction to the left of the picture and the baseline resting energy field electricity to the right. Note in Exhibit 17, the straight line that occurred when we compared three seconds' worth of the muscle activity with itself at one-ten-thousandth second offset.

Exhibits 18 and 19, using the same procedure with a heart (EKG) recording of a dog, again show the self similarity of a straight line. To reiterate, our biological data were sufficiently complex to carry the chaos dynamics in brief samplings, whereas three seconds of data from the heart and muscle recordings didn't demonstrate a chaos attractor.

In each instance, rather than obtaining the flowing vortex pattern of chaos, these data created a straight line. Apparently, small samples of brain and heart recordings are so periodic and symmetrical that when compared to itself revealed a non-dynamic, steady, predictable state. In other words, these vibrational dimensions of the heart, brain and muscle were too limited and too periodic or too linear. Recently, other researchers have found chaos attractors from heart and brain wave data, but only after crunching many hours and days of continuous data, not like the three seconds' worth of energy field recordings.

Apparently, if data are very complex, as ours was, or if the data are simple yet massive in quantity, such as hours, days or years of EEG, ECG data or weather recordings, a chaos pattern can be found showing a level of dynamic predictability. If, however, the data are simple and periodic or if there are small samples, a straight line appears in the graph (Exhibits 16 and 17, 18, and 19). They are said to be self similar.

EXHIBIT 20
CONSCIOUSNESS SPECTRUM SCHEMA
ORDINARY REALITY

O-Hz   200 KHz
(ELF ------ ➔ ------------------------------------➔ ---------------------------- ➔(EHF)

P
O
W
E
R

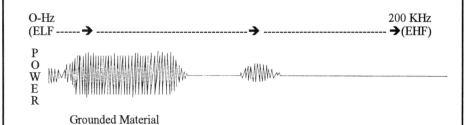

Grounded Material
Consciousness States

ALTERED REALITY

Metaphysical - Psychic
Hypnotic - Channeling States

TRANCE REALITY

Trance State

MYSTICAL REALITY

ALTERED   TRANCE   COSMIC

LEGEND
Horizontal: Frequency Pattern of Reality)-Hz (extremely low frequency)
to 200 Hz (extremely high frequency)
Vertical: Quantity or Power of Energy

At any moment in time, a person's state of consciousness and his level of awareness is predictable from his mind-field frequency pattern (Exhibit 20).

During the state of ordinary reality, focus is on the material world. The energies are confined to the lower frequencies up to 250 Hz, coming from nerve and brain activity.

In altered states,, with a psychic, hypnotic or metaphysical reality, the frequencies are extended above 400 Hz. These are the beginning frequencies of the mind-field. These people, who "channel" information about current life and who make predictions about future material happenings, have powerful energies in this lower mind-field spectrum. Some of these psychics display unusual skills to obtain hidden information.

Persons in trance states show small ranges of even higher vibrations that seem to stand alone, unconnected with other levels of reality or material thought. Here they obtain unbelievable information about distant happenings as they give predictions about distant events. This skill could be likened to the penetrating depth captured by a telephoto camera lens. However, in this state, trance mediums do not remember their channeled predictions because they have excluded the material reality stemming from the five senses.

There is another group of persons we describe as mystics, who display the broadest awareness with a complete range of uninterrupted frequencies. Mystics have available at all times the capacities of the psychics and the trance mediums, but they additionally tap into lofty spiritual knowings. Their predictions are universal and transcending and full of wisdom. We recorded their field frequencies to 200 KHz, as high as our instruments could record. In their presence one sees or senses powerful white light.

EXHIBIT 21

ENERGY FIELD SPECTROGRAM

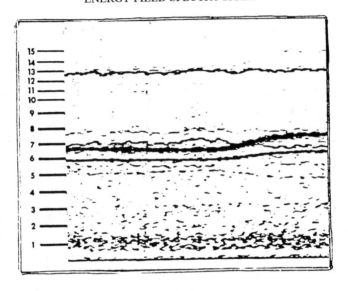

Here is an Energy Field Spectrogram of a man who felt pain from an acute muscle spasm while being Rolfed. Note the heavy black horizontal line at number 7 or 700 Hz represents the red energy of pain. But he processed and expressed his agony with emotional outbursts of displeasure, even anger. This is represented by orange, with the dark line at 6 or 600 cycles per second. The line at 13 is white, stemming from the presence of all color vibrations in small quantities. This is an altered state of consciousness when there are no strong intervening color frequencies.

EXHIBIT 22

ENERGY FIELD SPECTROGRAM

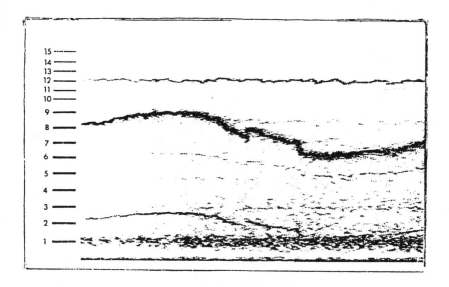

INTENSE PAIN - MUSCLE SPASM (RED)

Exhibit 22, intense emotional pain shows the strong coherent and irregular red vibrations from 8 to 7 to 6+. The vibration at 12, white, represents an altered state which frequently occurs with pain.

EXHIBIT 23

SPECTROGRAM

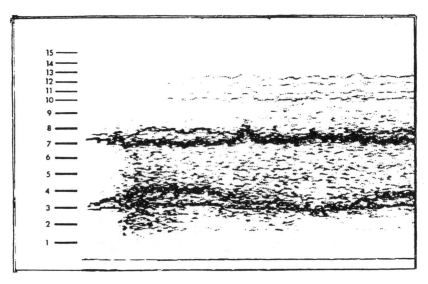

PAINFUL DIARRHEA (Red-Green)

Exhibit 23 is the energy field of a person with painful diarrhea. Here the red from 7 to 8 has a broader, less defined path with slightly lower red vibrations than in muscle spasm (Exhibit 22). Note that the wide green banding at 3 to 4 has spread into the yellow frequencies to give a muddy yellow-green color. Aura readers believe green represents a transition state which can also be applied to diarrhea.

REFERENCES

CHAPTER II

PAGE

9   Szent-Györgyi, Albert. Quoted in Robert O. Becker, *The Body Electric: Electromagnetism and the Foundation of Life*. N.Y.: Wm. Morrow and Co., 1985.

10   Mead, Margaret. "Inaugural Address," *Association for the Advancement of Science*, 1969.

12   Conrad, Emilie. *Continuum*. Santa Monica, CA.

12   Hunt, Valerie V., *et al*. "A Study of Structural Integration from Neuromuscular, Energy Field and Emotional Approaches, *Project Report, Rolf Institute*, Boulder, Co.: 1972.

14   Bruyere, Rosalyn. *Healing Light Center*, Sierra Madre, CA.

23   Hunt, Valerie V., *Project Report, Rolf Institute*, 1972

36   Garfinkle, Alan, "A Mathematics for Physiology," *American Journal of Physiology*. 245: R455-R466 (1983).

CHAPTER III

38   Kuhn, Thomas. *The Structure of Scientific Revolution*. Foundation of Unity of Science Service, Chicago: 1970.

38   Einstein, Albert. *The Evolution of Physics*. N.Y.: Simon & Schuster, 1961.

41   Maharishi University, Fairfield, Iowa.

43   Prigogine, Ira, and I. Stengers. *Order Out of Chaos: Man's New Dialogue with Nature*. N.Y.: Bantam Books, 1984.

43   Jahn, Robert G. and B.J. Dunne. *Margins of Reality: The Role of Consciousness in the Physical World*. San Diego: Harcourt Brace, 1987.

44   Jahn, p. 281.

46   Hawking, Steven. *A Brief History of Time: From the Big Bang to Black Holes*. N.Y.: Bantam Books, 1988, p. 18.

47   Jeans, James. *Physics and Philosophy*. Cambridge: The University Press, 1943.

48   Sheldrake, Rupert. *A New Science of Life: The Hypothesis of Formative Causation*. Los Angeles: Tarcher, 1981.

49   Jeans, *Physics and Philosophy*.

49   Wolf, Fred Alan. *Taking the Quantum Leap*. San Francisco: Harper & Row, 1981.

50   Lewin, Roger. *Complexity: Life at the Edge of Chaos*. N.Y.: Macmillan Pub. Co., 1992, p. 133.

50   Jahn and Dunne, *Margins of Reality*, p. 61.

50   Santa Fe Group, reported in Lewin, *Complexity*, 1992.

51   Bohm, David. *Wholeness and the Implicate Order*. London: Routledge and Kegan, 1980.

51   Lewin, *Complexity*, p. 32.

52   Gleick, James. *Chaos: Making a New Science.* N.Y.:
       Viking Penguin, Inc., 1987.

52   Gleick, *Chaos*, p. 23.

52   Lewin, *Complexity*

53   Mandelbrot, Benoit B., *The Fractal Geometry of Nature.*
       N.Y.: W.H. Freeman & Co., 1983.

53   Rössler and Lorenz, "Strange Attractors," in Gleich,
       Chaos, 1987.

56   Institute of Noetic Sciences, *Scientific Positivism: The
       New Dualism*, Palo Alto, CA.

57   Jahn and Dunne, *Margins of Reality*, p. 204.

57   Lewin, *Complexity*.

58   Lewin, *Complexity*, p. 136.

CHAPTER IV

62   Gabor, Dennis. Lensless photography, 1947.

63   Pribram, Karl H., "Holonomy and Structure in the
       Organization of Perception." Mimeographed.
       Department of Psychology, Stanford University,
       Stanford, CA, n.d..

63   Bohm, David. *Wholeness and the Implicate Order*. London: Routledge & Kegan, 1980.

63   Beck, Robert. Private conversation, 1976.

68   Prigogine, I., and I. Stengers. *Order Out of Chaos: Man's New Dialogue with Nature*. N.Y.: Bantam Books, 1984.

72   Harvard Medical School, Public Health. *Study of Environmental Contamination*, with U.S. Public Health.

73   Adey, W. Ross. "Cancer Linked with Electromagnetic Exposure," *P.T. Review*, (March 21, 1987).

78   Wilson, Robert A. *Cosmic Trigger*. New Falcon Publications, 1985.

CHAPTER V

83   Sherrington, Carl. *Man on His Nature*. London: Cambridge University Press, 1940.

83   Pribram, Karl. "Behaviorism Phrenomenology and Holism in Psychology: A Scientific Analysis," *Journal of Social and Biological Structures*, 2:65-72, 1979.

83   Penfield, Wilder. *The Mystery of the Mind*, Princeton, N.J.: Princeton University Press, 1975.

84   Eccles, John and D.N. Robinson. *The Wonder of Being Human: Our Brain and Our Mind.* Boston: Shambhala, 1985.

87   Hooper, Judith, and D. Teresi. *The Three Pound Universe.* N.Y.: Dell Pub. Co., 1986, p. 15.

89   Bateson, Gregory. *Steps to an Ecology of Mind.* N.Y.: Ballantine, 1975.

90   Eccles, John C. "Cerebral Activity and Consciousness," in *Studies of the Philosophy of Biology: Reduction and Related Problems.* Edited by F.J. Ayala and T. Dobzhansky. Berkeley, CA: Berkeley University Press, 1974.

90   Sperry, Roger W. "The Eye and the Brain." *Scientific American*, May, 1956.

90   Bogen, Joseph E. "The Other Side of the Brain: An Appositional Mind," *Bulletin of the Los Angeles Neurological Societies.* 34 (3): 135-162, (July 1969).

93   Pert, Candace, and S.H. Snyder. "Opiate Receptor: Demonstration in Nervous Tissue," *Science* 179: 1011-1014, (March 9, 1973).

99   Sheldrake, R. *A New Science of Life.* Los Angeles: J.P. Tarcher, 1981.

99   Bateson, Gregory, *Steps to an Ecology of Mind.*

103   *Bhagavad Gita.* Trans. Sargeant Winthrop, State U. of N.Y., Albany, N.Y.: 1984

CHAPTER VI

104   Buddha, Shakyamuni. *The Dhammapada.* Dharma Pub., Berkeley, CA, 1985.

105   Freud, Sigmund. *The Future of an Illusion.* N.Y.: Norton and Co., 1971.

109   Lewin, *Complexity*, p. 16.

109   Lewin, *Complexity*, p. 127.

114   Frank, Walter. Private conversation, 1989.

CHAPTER VII

147   Targ, Russell, and K. Haray. *The Mind Race.* N.Y.: Villard Books, 1984.

148   Dunne, B.J. and J.P. Bisaka. "Precognitive Remote Perception: A Critical Overview of the Experimental Program," in W.G. Roll (ed) *Research in Parapsychology.* Metuchen, N.J.: Scarecrow, 1980.

149   Verny, Thomas, and J. Kelly. *Secret Life of the Unborn Child.* N.Y.: Summit Books, 1981.

154   Bronowski, Jacob. *The Ascent of Man.* Boston: Little, Brown, 1973.

154   DeBono, Edward. *Lateral Thinking.* Int. Ctr. Creative Thinking, 1990.

157 Lewin, *Complexity*, p. 18.

158 Lewin, *Complexity*, pp. 51-52.

159 Green, Elmer. *ISSSEEM Annual Conference Proceedings.* Monterey, CA: 1993.

CHAPTER VIII

162 Einstein, Albert. In L. Barnett, *The Universe of Dr. Einstein.* Rev. ed. N.Y.: Wm. Morrow, Bantam Books, 1979, p. 108.

163 James, William. *The Principles of Psychology.* N.Y.: Dover, 1950.

165 Sorokin. *Harvard University Research Center for Creative Altruism.*

172 Reich, Wilhelm. *Character Analysis.* Trans. from German by Vincent R. Carfagno, 1980.

183 Noetic Sciences Review, *Emotion.*

183 Gibran, Kahlil. *Secrets of the Heart.* Trans., Citadel, N.Y.: Carol Pub. Group, 1978.

185 Gibran, *Secrets of the Heart.*

193 Pir Vilayat, Khan. *Introducing Sprituality Into Counseling and Therapy.* N.Y.: Omega Pubs., 1982.

CHAPTER IX

206   Tart, Charles. *Waking Up: Overcoming the Obstacles to Human Potential.* Boston: Shambhala, 1986.

211   Verny, Thomas, and J. Kelly. *The Secret Life of the Unborn Child.* N.Y.: Summit Books, 1981.

214   Wilbur, Ken. *Quantum Questions: Mystical Writings of the World's Great Physicists.* Boston: Shambhala, 1984.

215   Blavatsky, H.P.. An abridgement of *The Secret Doctrine.* Eds., E. Preston and Humphreys. London: Theosophical Pub. House, 1966.

222   Meek, George W. *After We Die What Then? Life's Energy Fields.* Ser. Vol. 3, Ariel, GA: Metascience, 1980.

223   Stevenson, Ian. *Omni*, January, 1988.

225   Weiss, Brian. *Omni*, March, 1994.

225   Wambach, Helen. *Life Before Life.* N.Y.: Bantam, 1984.

231   Tolstoy, Leo. *A Confession and Other Religious Writings.* N.Y.: Viking-Penguin, 1988.

CHAPTER X

237   Adey, W.R. "Whispering Between Cells: Electromagnetic
       Fields and Regulatory Mechanisms in Tissue."
       Frontier Perspectives. Temple Univ. Center for
       Frontier Sciences, vol 3, no. 2, Fall, 1993.

237   Truelinger, S.E. "Where Do We Go From Here," in
       Solutions, Condensed Matter Physics. Edited by
       A.R. Bishop and T.Schneider. Berlin: Springer
       Verlag, pp. 338-340.

237   Adey, W. Ross. *Brain/Mind Bulletin*. Vol. 14, no. 1,
       October, 1988.

238   Byrd, Randy. San Francisco General Hospital "Doctors
       Pray for Patients," *Brain-Mind Bulletin*, vol. 11,
       no. 7. March 24, 1986.

242   Lewin, *Complexity*, p. 51.

245   Burr, Harold Saxton. *Blueprint for Immortality*. London:
       Neville Spearman, 1972.
245   Lewin, *Complexity*, p. 186.

240   Becker, Robert O. and Gary Selden. *The Body Electric*.
       NY: William Morrow and Co., 1985.

251   Rossi, Ernest. *Psychobiology of Mind/Body Healing*.
       N.Y.: W. W. Norton, 1988.

252   Selye, Hans. *The Stress of Life*. NY: McGraw-Hill,
       1956.

252   O'Regan, Brendon. *Noetic Sciences Review.* Autumn, 1987.

254   Adey, W. Ross. *Medical Hypothesis.* 24: pp. 291-292.

254   Delgado, J.M.R., *et al.* "Reports on developmental defects in chick embryos exposed to various ELF frequencies." *Journal of Anatomy.* 134: 533 (1982).

263   Green, Elmer. *Subtle Energies*, 2: 69-94, ISSSSEEM Annual Conference, Monterey, CA, 1993.

266   Pert, Candace. *Science*, 179: pp. 1011-1014, March 9, 1973.

266   McClelland, David. "Sister Theresa", *Documentary, British Broadcasting Corp.*, 1993.

267   Brennan, Barbara Ann. *Hands of Light: A Guide to Healing Through the Human Energy Field.* N.Y.: Pleiades Books, 1987.

267   Bruyere, Rosalyn. *Wheels of Light: A Study of the Chakras.* Vol. 1. Sierra Madre, CA: Bon Productions, 1989.

270   Smith, Lendon H. *Feed Your Body Right.* N.Y.: M. Evans & Co., 1994.

CHAPTER XI

276   Jastrow, Robert. "The Post Human World," *Science Digest.* Jan-Feb., 1981.

286　Wilbur, Ken. *Eye to Eye: The Quest for the New Paradigm*. N.Y.: Anchor Press, 1983.

288　Slawinski, Janusz. *Brain-Mind Bulletin*, vol. 10, no. 9, May 6, 1985.

302　DiMele, Armand. *Psychotherapist*, N.Y.: New York.

308　Huxley, Aldous. *The Perennial Philosophy*. N.Y.: Harper, 1994.

311　Lederman, Leon, and D. Schramm. *From Quarks to Cosmos: Tools of Discovery*. N.Y.: W.H. Freeman, 1989.

BOOKS, VIDEOS, MUSIC, LECTURES
By Dr. Valerie V. Hunt

BOOK

INFINITE MIND $27.50

SCIENCE OF THE HUMAN VIBRATIONS OF CONSCIOUSNESS

For centuries man has experienced, but could not explain consciousness. *INFINITE MIND* presents a vibrational "Rosetta Stone" for understanding all acceptable theories of healing, psychic phenomena and consciousness. Presented is a new vision, a fresh perspective of human energy field interaction. This inclusive model will unify the fragmented knowledges of sound, rituals, movement and thought.

With each consecutive chapter, you are introduced to Dr. Hunt's research which shows the vibrational differences in energy field disturbances and their results in illness, diminished capacity and emotional stress. These energy field findings, combined with fascinating human interest stories, lead to stunning new insights concerning the mind and body, emotions and creativity, extrasensory human capacities in higher consciousness and the mystical connections of spirit.

BOOK

MIND MASTERY MEDITATIONS $16.95

A WORKBOOK FOR INFINITE MIND

Ask yourself, "Who should I be?", "What should I do?". Do you find clear answers, or are you confused? When you are in control, you have the correct answers to your questions from your own highest source. You will have the ability to carry out these answers in your life.

The meditations in this book are designed to give you mastery of your mind — your mind has all the answers as to why you are the way you are, your soul's needs, your unique capabilities, and your self-designed destiny.

You will learn to relax, balance and activate your energy systems, hasten healing with specific tools, discover and enhance your own spirituality, open your emotions, and uncover present and past lifehoods.

Mind Mastery Meditations can empower you to live your life with greater ease and success.

BOOK

NAIBHU $17.95

A lost child ... An isolated adolescent A tormented adult ... An enlightened sage.

Amidst a background of bustling camel caravans and towering Himalayas, Naibhu's story of personal evolution unfolds.

As a lost child, Naibhu was mystically guided to live with goat herds in the Himalayan foothills, learning the primitive lessons of survival. With age, he longed for the social warmth of human bonding, but had forgotten his language and possessed no social skills. As an adult he sought unique encounters to learn cultural lessons and gain social acceptance.

The mystical knowing that had saved and developed Naibhu's life resurfaced, displaying profound healing capabilities and extraordinary spiritual episodes. He became a self-ordained priest, successfully serving others while struggling with powerful emotional insecurities of his combined limited mortal identity and his glorious divine spirit.

Read and contemplate the lessons of Naibhu, because his evolutionary struggles are universal, transcending time.

THE MUSIC OF LIGHT
5 tapes – Not sold separately $130
2 CD's - $65.00

Feeling tired? Stressed out? Intellectually drained?

Imagine playing a cassette and experiencing feelings of increased vitality, heightened creativity, or improved physical performance. Surrounding yourself with the Music of Light can result in enhanced physical and emotional well-being.

This album contains five tapes, each with a different auric sound harmonically correlated with contemporary, classical, or new age music. For example, the red auric sound mixed with contemporary African music revitalizes the body. The blue auric sound, combined with Mozart, Brahms, and Beethoven's music, relaxes and calms the field. Playing the yellow auric sound with vibrant waltzes fills the room and brings coherent flow of energy to the body.

Dr. Hunt is the first person to record the human auric field. Over a period of 15 years she has researched and discovered the effects these sounds have on human performance and consciousness. These tapes have brought together for the first time the inner living sounds, the perfect rhythms, the complex wave forms, and resonances of a human interacting with his world.

Red - Orange - Amber
Vibrant, stimulating sounds revitalize the
physical body and activate spontaneous emotions.

Yellow - Green - Gold
Fine tuning of sensation and perception, improves nervous
system efficiency and creatively activates the mind.

Blue - Violet - Mauve
Soothing, relaxing spectrum encourages a quiet,
contemplative state of peaceful, higher consciousness.

White - Blue - Gold
Etheric spiritual tones elevate thoughts and imagery to
a broader world, richer beauty, and deeper wisdom.

Rainbow
Progressing in frequency, 13 rich, nourishing and
coherent color blends stabilize the field and
encourage broad awareness.

LECTURE TAPE 1

(45 minutes) $15.00
MIND MASTERY MEDITATIONS
Side A ACTIVATING THE PHYSICAL FIELD

Meditation exercises will activate smooth flow and coherency of the electromagnetic field. These provide skills required for healing disease and dysfunction, essential for all higher meditative experiences.

Side B OPENING THE MIND-FIELD AND EMOTIONS

Meditative exercises will open closets of our minds where past and present life experiences are stored. By subliminally tapping into super and subconscious states, you safely learn to measure your stream of emotions, to know your deep sources of motivation and to change.

LECTURE TAPE 2

(45 minutes) $15.00

Side A TELEPATHIC KNOWING: THE TRANSFER OF THOUGHT

Meditation experiences will get in touch with and monitor the mind. You can learn to tap into and decode constantly the telepathic messages available. You can improve communication skills by projecting your thoughts powerfully over distances.

Side B UNCOVERING PAST LIVES

Meditative experiences will allow you to recall and integrate present and past life experiences. You can learn to be in touch with all motivations operating in your life today so you can relieve stress, and have available the power of your emotions.

LECTURE TAPE A

INTERNATIONAL HEALING
ENERGY MEDICINE CONFERENCE $45.00

Regent's College, England - October, 1992

Dr. Valerie V. Hunt, Principal Lecturer

(3 lectures, as follows: 4 tapes, 60 min. each.)

I. BIOLOGICAL ENERGY FIELD AND ENERGY MEDICINE/ INTUITIVE DIAGNOSIS

New concepts of the electromagnetic source of life and disease elucidate the current major medical problems: diabetes, heart, sclerosis, fatigue symptoms, viruses and Alzheimer's disease. All point to new diagnoses and treatment modes with close cooperation of physicians, psychics and healers.

II. MIND, THE SOURCE OF PHYSICAL AND EMOTIONAL DISEASES

Major gaps in brain neurophysiology and emphasis on chemistry with shots and pills to cure all health problems have treated symptoms with limited success and growing danger. Redirected basic research, however, discovers that the mind is a field of information, the true source of all health problems. Energy medicine is the visionary medicine of the future.

III. FUTURE HEALING: ENERGY FIELD TRANSACTIONS AND CHANGE

Understanding the subtle energy systems that flow through body meridians, connective tissues and by neuropeptide transmission, along with discovery of the elegant chaos pattern in the human field, make understandable why a gentle energy nudge can snatch order out of the random chaos of extensive dysfunction and bring about miraculous healing and regeneration.

LECTURE TAPE B

(90 minutes) $18.00
COLOR PREFERENCES,
COLOR NEEDS, COLOR EFFECTS

Color preferences, effects and needs reflect our deepest responses to color. The color vibrations of our own "aura" constitute a color screen which alters and accentuates our visual color perception.

Objects do not possess a fixed color of their own; they only have changing vibrations which result in light reflections from the pigment these contain. It is the reflected light filtered through a person's aura from which he makes judgments which creates his physical and emotional experience with color.

Electronic research is discussed as applied to the effects of color upon vitality and strength, relaxation and calmness and extended sensory awareness.

LECTURE TAPE C

(90 minutes $18.00)
MIND FIELD MODEL:
BIOSPHERE, COSMOSPHERE CONNECTION

Research with brain waves, holograms, and energy fields is broadly publicized in popular magazines so that many people embrace the philosophical beliefs of the oneness of man and the universe. But we have not known how these two separate material entities actually interact as one on another level or the practical application to our lives. For the first time, pioneering research with high frequency electronics captured and elucidated the human energy field and observed field transactions; people with people, with atmosphere, with Earth vibrations, and with thought waves. From these studies a new model emerged of the macrocosmic links of humans and cosmos, and how the mind-field creates illness and health, underlies all communication and creativity and makes telepathy and clairvoyance rational.

VIDEO TAPE

THE HUMAN ENERGY FIELD AND HEALTH
(1 video – VHS or PAL) $45.00

The aura, that intangible and elusive human energy field, now can finally be seen and understood by all. Its colors are vibrant and its interactions are unique. For 60 minutes you will have numerous revelations and ultimately gain a clear understanding of the human energy field.

The video shows graphics, pictures, sounds, and slides of the actual data of Dr. Hunt's amazing energy field research (aura) during health, disease, pain, emotion, imagery, and consciousness states.
You will see dramatic graphics of the first chaos patterns ever discovered in the human body and the anticoherency scheme of aging and illness.

The complex human energy field is presented in this video with such clarity and depth that all viewers can recognize the profound effects of energy field changes upon their lives. Meditation teachers, body workers, and alternative medical professionals report its profound impact with their clients.

For Tape and Book Orders:
Malibu Publishing Co.
P.O. Box 4234
Malibu, California 90264
(310) 457-4694
FAX (310) 457-2717
www.malibupublishing.com